SAS® Programming by Example

Ron Cody and Ray Pass

Ssas. | SAS Publishing

Comments or Questions?

The authors assume complete responsibility for the technical accuracy of the content of this book. If you have any questions about the material in this book, please write to the authors at this address:

> SAS Institute Inc.
> Books by Users
> Attn: *Ron Cody and Ray Pass*
> SAS Campus Drive
> Cary, NC 27513

If you prefer, you can send e-mail to sasbbu@sas.com with "comments for Ron Cody and Ray Pass" as the subject line, or you can fax the Books by Users program at (919) 677-4444.

The correct bibliographic citation for this manual is as follows: Cody, Ronald P., and Pass, Raymond, *SAS® Programming by Example*, Cary, NC: SAS Institute Inc., 1995. 337 pp.

SAS® Programming by Example

Copyright © 1995 by SAS Institute Inc., Cary, NC, USA.

ISBN 1-55544-681-7

SAS Institute Inc., SAS Campus Drive, Cary, North Carolina 27513.

1st printing, March 1995

2nd printing, June 1997

3rd printing, August 1998

4th printing, October 1999

5th printing, September 2000

Note that text corrections may have been made at each printing.

Contents

Preface

With all the SAS System manuals already available, why would we think to write yet one more book? Good question.

Having taught SAS System programming for many years to ourselves and to others in both formal classroom settings and informally, we have come to the conclusion that many people learn how to program by examining specific concrete examples in manuals, forming their own generalizations of how the program statements work, and then applying these generalizations to their own individual tasks. Through a process of repeated trial and error, tasks are performed and learning is accomplished. At that point, a return visit to the more general descriptions given in the reference manuals is usually more productive than an initial attack would have been. When you want to see how a particular statement works, you probably look for a programming example in one of your manuals first and then read the more general description.

This book is a collection of SAS System programming examples accompanied by detailed annotations of each program. Each chapter begins with an **Introduction** followed by the **Examples**, which contain sample programs, explanations, and output. Many of the examples begin with a simple idea and build on that idea step by step. Hopefully, this approach will teach you one or more new skills with each example.

One of the main strengths of SAS software is that it can process data in almost any format. Although the SAS System can deal directly with many types of proprietary data formats by using various engines, this book limits its scope to processing SAS data sets only.

Each chapter ends with a series of **Problems**. Your learning will be enhanced if you work out these problems yourself without first peeking at the **Solutions**. Also, don't always expect your solutions and those in the book to be the same. There are many different, and correct, ways to solve these problems.

Putting this collection of annotated examples together has been laborious and grueling at times, but it has also been rewarding and, dare we say it? Fun. As you read through the chapters and work through the examples, there will be times when you too will experience some of the frustration. There will also be times when the lightbulb suddenly comes on for you. You can't escape the work involved in learning — don't try. You can, however, miss out on the joy — don't let that happen. Have fun!

Ron Cody and Ray Pass

Acknowledgments

Putting together a project like this always requires more than the sole efforts of the authors. They must be joined in the undertaking by a team of editors, reviewers, and other production specialists. There are, however, varying levels of ease with which this process can unfold. It has been our pleasure to have worked on this book with the productive, patient, good-natured, supportive, and all-around top-level staff members of the SAS Institute Books By Users program. We wish to thank as a group the entire staff that was involved with this effort and to single out a few key individuals.

David Baggett initially coaxed us into taking on this project, and his gentle and patient leadership and support has helped us carry it to fruition. **Jennifer Ginn** added sage advice throughout and, at times, helped to free us of inter-author entanglements that may not have been so easily resolved without her intervention. **Hanna Schoenrock**, in calmly putting up with the obsessive nitpicking ruminations of one of the authors, provided a model of lasting and moderate temperament through many editing, re-editing, and re-re-editing cycles. The entire team of Institute reviewers, and in particular, **Carol Linden** and **Tom Hahl**, gave us just the right amount of technical and editorial advice to keep us on the right path. **Candy Farrell, Blanche Phillips,** and **John West** provided outstanding production and proofreading services. We wish to extend our sincerest appreciation to all the members of this highly professional team.

The other teams that deserve special recognition are our families. Their continued and loving support throughout the process of putting this book together made our efforts all that much more worthwhile and meaningful. It is with gratitude, affection, and appreciation that this book is dedicated to **Jan**, **Russell**, and **Preston Cody**, and to **Wendy**, **Erica**, and **Dory Pass**.

Ron Cody and Ray Pass

Manipulating Data

CHAPTERS

Chapter 1

INPUT and INFILE

Building a SAS Data Set from Raw Data

EXAMPLES

Introduction

SAS System procedures can operate only on SAS data sets. Quite often, however, the data that you need to process are in a raw form. The first step is, therefore, to transform the raw data into a SAS data set. The work of manufacturing this is done in a SAS DATA step through the use of a DATA statement. This statement names the SAS data set you are creating. The raw data are then read into the data set via an INPUT statement. The seemingly simple INPUT statement is really a SAS System powerhouse in that it can create a SAS data set from raw data existing in a wide variety of formats. The raw data may exist in a file external to the environment in which the SAS code is being prepared (in which case they are usually referred to by an INFILE statement), or they can be entered instream along with the SAS code by means of a DATALINES statement. SAS software will also recognize the older CARDS statement as the beginning of raw data input. In this first chapter, you will see the power, ease of use, and flexibility of this key DATA statement.

Example 1

Reading Raw Data Separated by Spaces

FEATURES: **DATA, INPUT, and DATALINES Statements, List Input, Missing Data**

There are a variety of different styles of INPUT code that can be used to read raw data. List input reads data into a SAS data set using a "space delimited" form of data entry. This method can be used when each raw data value is separated from the next one by one or more spaces. This form of data entry has its limitations to be sure, but let us first lay it out via an example before we pick it apart.

Suppose you have the following raw data values and you want to create a SAS data set from them:

ID	HEIGHT	WEIGHT	GENDER	AGE
1	68	144	M	23
2	78	202	M	34
3	62	99	F	37
4	61	101	F	45

This can be done using list input as follows:

Example 1

```
DATA LISTINP;
   INPUT ID HEIGHT WEIGHT GENDER $ AGE;
DATALINES;
1 68 144 M 23
2 78 202 M 34
3 62 99 F 37
4 61 101 F 45
;

PROC PRINT DATA=LISTINP;
   TITLE 'Example 1';
RUN;
```

See Chapter 9, "PROC PRINT," Example 2, for an explanation of TITLE statements. Now, on to the program.

The previous code produces the following output:

Output from Example 1 - Reading Raw Data Separated by Spaces

```
                         Example 1

       OBS   ID   HEIGHT   WEIGHT    GENDER   AGE

        1    1      68       144       M       23
        2    2      78       202       M       34
        3    3      62        99       F       37
        4    4      61       101       F       45
```

There are several important points to notice about this basic example. Raw data lines are read beginning with the line immediately following the DATALINES statement. You signify the end of your data input with a lone semicolon (called a NULL statement) on the line following your last line of data. Some programmers prefer a RUN statement followed by a semicolon instead. Take your choice.

Next, the INPUT statement lists the variables you wish to create in the same order as the corresponding data values listed below the DATALINES statement. You cannot skip over any data values with this simple form of list input. Later in this chapter we'll demonstrate how to jump around the raw data line when reading in the data.

The SAS System reads data as either character or numeric, and then stores them as such. Numeric data can contain numbers or numeric missing values (see below), while character data can contain numbers, letters, character missing values, and any special characters (e.g. _, #, &). In this example, GENDER is a character variable because it contains the alphanumeric characters, M or F. We indicate that GENDER is a character variable by following it with a dollar sign ($) in the INPUT statement. Without the dollar sign, the program would be expecting numerical values for GENDER (and would get really upset when it encountered M's and F's).

Another point to notice is that the data values have to be separated by at least one blank space as they all are in the previous example. Data values can be separated by more than one space (possibly to improve readability). The lines of data in the following code could be substituted for the original four lines of data with no change in the resulting data set:

```
DATALINES;
1    68 144    M 23
  2     78    202 M    34
    3    62  99 F   37
4    61 101 F 45
```

Messy isn't it? It will, however, work just fine.

The PRINT procedure statements are included in this program so that you can see that the DATA step reads the data as expected. For now, all you need to know about PROC PRINT is that it is a procedure that will print the contents of a SAS data set. Chapter 9, "PROC PRINT," contains more information on PROC PRINT.

Handling Missing Values

Now suppose you have a missing value of HEIGHT for observation 2, and enter your data as follows:

```
DATALINES;
1 68 144 M 23
2    202 M 34
3 62 99 F 37
4 61 101 F 45
```

The data item is missing so why not just leave it out? Although it looks right, this will get you into big trouble with list input. If you leave the value blank, the program will just look for the next value it finds, after at least one space and read it as the data for the second variable.

In this case, after reading in a value of 2 for ID, the SAS System looks for a value for HEIGHT. It finds 202 and accepts it as a value for HEIGHT. It then attempts to read M as the value for WEIGHT. WEIGHT is a numeric variable and cannot have a non-number as a value. The result will be an error message in the log and a missing value for WEIGHT.

Next, 34 is read as the value for GENDER. This is legal because GENDER is a character variable and can have any alphanumeric content. The program is still looking for a value for AGE, so it goes to the next line to read the first data value on that line, 3, as AGE. Since the value for AGE is the last value the INPUT statement looks for, the program completes building the current observation, brings in the next input line, and starts building the next observation. It's really amazing how wrong things can get when you make one simple innocent mistake.

So how do you solve this problem when reading in list input data? Use a period (.), separated by one or more blanks from surrounding data to indicate that a data value is missing. The period acts as a place holder. It tells the INPUT statement that there is no value to be read here, and to get on about its business. In our example, the correct way to indicate a missing value for HEIGHT for observation 2 is as follows:

```
DATALINES;
1 68 144 M 23
2 . 202 M 34
3 62 99 F 37
4 61 101 F 45
```

Example 2

> ## Reading Data Values Separated by Commas or Other Delimiters
>
> *FEATURES:* **INFILE DATALINES options DLM= and DSD, Comma-Delimited List Input**

A fairly common practice is to separate adjacent data values with a comma (,). These comma-delimited data can be easily read by a SAS program as long as you tell the program what to expect. In this case you do so through the use of an INFILE statement as follows (output would be identical to the previous output, with the exception of the title):

Example 2.1

```
DATA COMMAS;
   INFILE DATALINES DLM=',';
   INPUT ID HEIGHT WEIGHT GENDER $ AGE;
DATALINES;
1,68,144,M,23
2,78,202,M,34
3,62,99,F,37
4,61,101,F,45
;


PROC PRINT DATA=COMMAS;
   TITLE 'Example 2.1';
RUN;
```

As you will see later in this chapter, an INFILE statement is usually used to indicate that the raw data are stored in, and are being read from, an external file. The location, or source, or file specification of the external data is named in the INFILE statement, and a number of options that control how the data are read can also be included. By using the reserved filename DATALINES, you can apply some of these options to instream data. (Note: the older term CARDS still works even if you use a DATALINES statement to begin your data.) In the present example, the option DLM=',' tells the program to use commas rather than spaces as data delimiters. You may choose any data delimiter you wish with this option. You can even choose multiple characters such as DLM='XX' for your delimiter.

An improvement to the DLM= option was made available in Release 6.07 of the SAS System. A new option, DSD, allows you to treat two consecutive delimiters as containing a missing value. In addition, you can read a text string that contains the delimiter if it is contained in quotes. Further, quoted text strings can also be read. In both cases, the quotes surrounding the text string are not included in the stored value. If the DSD option is used without the DLM= option, the SAS System assumes that you are using commas as your delimiter.

The following program demonstrates the use of the DSD option:

Example 2.2

```
DATA COMMAS;
   INFILE DATALINES DSD;
   INPUT X Y TEXT $;
DATALINES;
1,2,XYZ
3,,STRING
4,5,"TESTING"
6,,"ABC,XYZ"
;

PROC PRINT DATA=COMMAS;
   TITLE 'Example 2.2';
RUN;
```

The output from Example 2.2 is as follows:

Output from Example 2.2 - Reading Data Values Separated by Commas or Other Delimiters

```
                        Example 2.2

             OBS    X    Y    TEXT

              1     1    2    XYZ
              2     3    .    STRING
              3     4    5    TESTING
              4     6    .    ABC,XYZ
```

Notice that the SAS System treats the consecutive commas as containing a missing value, omits the quotes from the data values, and allows you to include a comma in a text string. The DSD option is probably most useful in reading files produced by spreadsheet and database programs that produce DIF (data interchange format) files.

Example 3

Applying an INFORMAT Statement to List Input

FEATURES: INFORMAT Statement, : Format Modifier

When you use a simple list INPUT statement such as the one in Example 1, the default length for character variables is 8. This means that all character variables are created and stored with a length of 8 bytes. This creates two potential problems. First, if you are reading small length values as you did for GENDER (1 byte), you are wasting storage space using 8 bytes when 1 will suffice. Second, if you read character values longer than 8 bytes, the stored value will be truncated to 8. Another shortcoming of default list input is that data cannot be read that occur in standard configurations, such as dates in MM/DD/YY format. In this example, you can modify your list input by including an INFORMAT statement to define certain patterns or informats in which the raw data occur. Let's read two additional variables, LASTNAME and DOB, which needs special attention (and you can save some storage space as well). Here is the example:

Example 3.1

```
DATA INFORMS;
    INFORMAT LASTNAME $20. DOB MMDDYY8. GENDER $1.;
    INPUT ID LASTNAME DOB HEIGHT WEIGHT GENDER AGE;
    FORMAT DOB MMDDYY8.;
DATALINES;
1 SMITH 1/23/66 68 144 M 26
2 JONES 3/14/60 78 202 M 32
3 DOE 11/26/47 62 99 F 45
4 WASHINGTON 8/1/70 66 101 F 22
;

PROC PRINT DATA=INFORMS;
    TITLE 'Example 3.1';
RUN;
```

This code produces the following output:

Output from Example 3.1 - Applying an INFORMAT Statement to List Input

			Example 3.1				
OBS	LASTNAME	DOB	GENDER	ID	HEIGHT	WEIGHT	AGE
1	SMITH	01/23/66	M	1	68	144	26
2	JONES	03/14/60	M	2	78	202	32
3	DOE	11/26/47	F	3	62	99	45
4	WASHINGTON	08/01/70	F	4	66	101	22

Note that the order of the variables in the output is not the same as the order in the INPUT statement. When the SAS System builds a data set, it stores its variables in the order in which they are encountered in the DATA step. Since the first three variables encountered in the DATA step are LASTNAME, DOB, and GENDER (in the INFORMAT statement), they are the first three variables stored in the SAS data set. The other variables, ID, HEIGHT, WEIGHT, and AGE follow the order in the INPUT statement.

Here the INFORMAT statement gives the following information about the patterns in which some of the raw data elements are found:

- the length of LASTNAME can be up to 20 characters
- the data for DOB are found in MM/DD/YY form
- GENDER is only one character long.

The MMDDYY8. specification after DOB instructs the program to recognize these raw data in MM/DD/YY form and to translate and store them as SAS date values. You also use a FORMAT statement to associate an output pattern, or format with DOB. If you didn't do this, the program would have printed the DOB variable in a SAS date value format. The DOB for SMITH, for example, would have printed as 2214. We cover the fascinating and mysterious world of SAS date values in depth in Chapter 6, "SAS Dates." (Bet you just can't wait!)

You could have accomplished the same goal as above by supplying your informats directly in the INPUT statement. This is called modified list input. You simply follow any variable name you wish to modify by a colon (:) and an informat. The colon tells the program to read the next non-blank value it finds with the specified informat. The previous program could have been written as follows, yielding the same output as the previous example (except for the title and the order of the variables):

Example 3.2

```
DATA COLONS;
    INPUT ID LASTNAME : $20. DOB : MMDDYY8.
    HEIGHT WEIGHT GENDER : $1. AGE;
FORMAT DOB MMDDYY8.;
DATALINES;
1 SMITH 01/23/66 68 144 M 26
2 JONES 3/14/60 78 202 M 32
3 DOE 11/26/47 62 99 F 45
4 WASHINGTON 8/1/70 66 101 F 22
;

PROC PRINT DATA=COLONS;
    TITLE 'Example 3.2';
RUN;
```

In this example, the SAS System

- reads the second non-blank value it finds as the value for LASTNAME, but it allows up to 20 characters for the value instead of only the default eight characters.
- reads the next non-blank value as DOB, but it realizes that the data being read is a date that occurs in MM/DD/YY form.
- knows that the data for GENDER always occurs as a 1-byte value, and therefore does not use up an extra 7 bytes to save it.

In Chapter 11, "PROC FORMAT," we show you how to modify data values as they are read in. Stay tuned.

Example 4

Reading Character Values That Contain Blanks

FEATURE: & Format Modifier

The key property of list input is that at least one blank space separates each data value from the next. But what if the data value contains blanks, like a first and last name combination, or a multi-word city name like New York? All is not lost. With a little help, a SAS INPUT statement can read data values that contain one or more single blanks. You do this by following the variable name that contains the blank spaces with the ampersand (&) format modifier. You can then also use an informat if you wish, as you did with the colon modifier. The rule now is that there must be at least two consecutive blank spaces separating data values. So, in order to read data containing a 25-byte character variable NAME, which could be made up of multiple words, use the following code:

Example 4

```
DATA AMPERS;
   INPUT NAME & $25. AGE GENDER : $1.;
DATALINES;
RASPUTIN    45 M
BETSY ROSS  62 F
ROBERT LOUIS STEVENSON  75 M
;

PROC PRINT DATA=AMPERS;
   TITLE 'Example 4';
RUN;
```

Notice that there are at least two spaces after each complete name. In fact, there are four spaces after RASPUTIN. The output for this example follows:

Output from Example 4 - Reading Character Values That Contain Blanks

```
                        Example 4

          NAME                      AGE     GENDER

          RASPUTIN                   45        M
          BETSY ROSS                 62        F
          ROBERT LOUIS STEVENSON     75        M
```

Example 5

Reading Data Arranged in Columns

FEATURE: **INPUT Column Specification**

In addition to being able to read raw data values that are separated from each other by one or more spaces, the SAS System provides two methods of reading data values that are uniformly aligned in columns: column input and formatted input. Both provide the ability to read data from fixed locations in the input record, and both therefore expect to find the data in those locations. Formatted input provides the additional feature of allowing you to read data that occur in other than standard numeric or character formats, but this is one of those "beyond the scope of this book" topics. Column input and formatted input, as well as list input, can be freely intermixed within the same INPUT statement, as you will see in later examples in this chapter.

A column INPUT statement can be used to read lines of data that are aligned in uniform columns. With this method, the name of the variable being read is followed by the column, or column range (starting and ending columns), containing the data for that variable. If you are defining a character variable, the identifying "$" comes before the column numbers. Here is an example.

Example 5.1

```
DATA COLINPUT;
    INPUT ID 1 HEIGHT 2-3 WEIGHT 4-6 GENDER $ 7 AGE 8-9;
DATALINES;
168144M23
278202M34
362 99F37
461101F45
;

PROC PRINT DATA=COLINPUT;
    TITLE 'Example 5.1';
RUN;
```

This code produces the following output, Example 5.1 (identical to that displayed in Example 1 except for the title.)

Output from Example 5.1 - Reading Data Arranged in Columns

```
                    Example 5.1

    OBS  ID  HEIGHT  WEIGHT   GENDER  AGE

     1   1     68     144       M      23
     2   2     78     202       M      34
     3   3     62      99       F      37
     4   4     61     101       F      45
```

In this example, you do not leave any spaces between data values. You can if you wish, but unlike list input, it is not necessary to delimit the data values in any way. The column specifications in the INPUT statement provide instructions as to where to find the data values. Also, notice that we placed the value 99 (for the variable WEIGHT for observation 3) in columns 5-6 rather than in columns 4-5 as we did in previous examples. Numbers placed right-most in a field are called right adjusted; this is the standard convention for numbers in most computer systems. You could have placed the 99 in columns 4-5 here as well because your instructions were to read the value for AGE anywhere in columns 4-6. The SAS System correctly reads the value even if it is not right adjusted, but it is a good habit to right adjust numbers in general since other computer programs aren't quite as smart as SAS software.

Making Your Program More Readable

Speaking of good habits, let's adopt another one. (If these habits truly yield more productive programming, then they will be easy to make and hard to break.) When using column and formatted input, it's worth the extra effort to code the variables in the INPUT statement in a uniform columnar fashion. It makes for easier code proofreading and maintainability. Here is another version of the previous program that will yield exactly the same output (except for the title):

Example 5.2

```
DATA COLINPUT;
    INPUT ID          1
          HEIGHT     2-3
          WEIGHT     4-6
          GENDER $    7
          AGE        8-9;
DATALINES;
168144M23
278202M34
362 99F37
461101F45
;

PROC PRINT DATA=COLINPUT;
    TITLE 'Example 5.2';
RUN;
```

Notice that each variable name in the INPUT statement is on a separate line and that the column specifications all line up. This makes for a neater, easier to read, program.

Reading Selected Variables from Your Data

When you read data in columns, you indicate missing values by leaving the columns blank. You also have the freedom to skip any columns you wish and read only those variables of interest to you. If, for example, you only wanted to read ID and AGE from the previous data, you could use the following code:

Example 5.3

```
DATA COLINPUT;
    INPUT  ID  1
           AGE 8-9;
DATALINES;
168144M23
278202M34
362 99F37
461101F45
;

PROC PRINT DATA=COLINPUT;
    TITLE 'Example 5.3';
RUN;
```

This code produces the following output:

Output from Example 5.3 - Reading Selected Variables from Your Data

```
                        Example 5.3

                    OBS   ID   AGE

                     1    1    23
                     2    2    34
                     3    3    37
                     4    4    45
```

Reading Values in Different Order

In this example you did not eliminate any data from the lines of data, but you chose to read only part of each line, specifically columns 1 (ID) and 8-9 (AGE). When using column or formatted input, you can read data fields in any order you want to. You do not have to read them in order, from left to right, in ascending column order. You can also read column ranges more than once, or read parts of previously read ranges, or even read overlapping column ranges as different variables. The next set of code shows an example of reading the same data that you have been working with, but by jumping around the input record.

Example 5.4

```
DATA COLINPUT;
   INPUT   AGE      8-9
           ID       1
           WEIGHT   4-6
           HEIGHT   2-3
           GENDER $ 7;
DATALINES;
168144M23
278202M34
362 99F37
461101F45
;

PROC PRINT DATA=COLINPUT;
   TITLE 'Example 5.4';
RUN;
```

This code produces the following output:

Output from Example 5.4 - Reading Values in Different Order

			Example 5.4		
OBS	AGE	ID	WEIGHT	HEIGHT	GENDER
1	23	1	144	68	M
2	34	2	202	78	M
3	37	3	99	62	F
4	45	4	101	61	F

Notice that the variables exist in the data set COLINPUT, and are therefore displayed in the output, in the same order in which they are read via the INPUT statement.

Example 6

> ## Reading Column Data That Require Informats
>
> *FEATURES:* @ Column Pointer, SAS Informats

Instead of using starting and ending column numbers to describe the location of the data, you can use the starting column number, the length of the data value (number of columns it occupies), and a SAS informat. A typical data description containing information about the previous collection of data might look like the following:

Variable Name	Starting Column	Length	Format	Description
ID	1	3	Numeric	Subject ID
GENDER	4	1	Char	M=Male, F=Female
AGE	9	2	Numeric	Age of subject
HEIGHT	11	2	Numeric	Height in inches
DOB	13	6	MMDDYY6	Date of birth

The following code uses pointers and informats to read instream data that occur in the pattern described above.

Example 6

```
DATA POINTER;
   INPUT @1  ID       3.
         @5  GENDER   $1.
         @7  AGE      2.
         @10 HEIGHT   2.
         @13 DOB      MMDDYY6.;
FORMAT DOB MMDDYY8.;
DATALINES;
101 M 26 68 012366
102 M 32 78 031460
103 F 45 62 112647
104 F 22 66 080170
;

PROC PRINT DATA=POINTER;
   TITLE 'Example 6';
RUN;
```

The @ characters (at signs) are called column pointers; they indicate the starting column for an action. When they appear before a variable name in an INPUT statement, they tell the SAS System to go to a certain column. Following the name of the variable, you can use an informat to tell the program how to read the data.

There are many types of SAS informats, but we only use a few common ones here. Numeric variables use an informat of the form *w.d,* where *w* is the width of the field (number of columns) containing the data, and *d* is the number of places to the right of the decimal point in the value. When *d* is omitted, it is assumed to be 0. If the data values actually contain decimal points, the *d* part of the specification is ignored. A minus sign (–) may be included in a negative value, but it must immediately precede the value with no intervening space. The width, *w*, must be large enough to include any decimal points or minus signs found in the data. Character informats are of the form $w., where *w* is the width of the field (number of columns) containing the data.

There are a large number of date informats in the SAS System. The one used here, MMDDYY6., instructs the software to read a data value from six columns, the first two being the month, the next two the day of the month, and the last two being the year. If the values contain special characters (typically slashes or dashes) separating the three parts of the date, you can use MMDDYY8. instead.

All SAS informats contain a period (.), either as the last character in the format or immediately preceding the number of decimal places contained in a data value. Omitting this period, like omitting the "sacred semicolon," can, under the right circumstances, cause countless hours of head-scratching while trying to discover why the obtained results are so wrong! It is quite possible to omit a period or semicolon and still have "syntactically correct" code. Of course the results may be pure garbage. Two words to the wise are all that we can offer. BE CAREFUL!!

Output from the previous code in Example 6 is as follows:

Output from Example 6 - Reading Column Data That Require Informats

```
                            Example 6

     OBS     ID    GENDER    AGE    HEIGHT      DOB

      1      101      M       26      68      01/23/66
      2      102      M       32      78      03/14/60
      3      103      F       45      62      11/26/47
      4      104      F       22      66      08/01/70
```

Notice that the values for DOB are printed in MM/DD/YY format. This is accomplished with the line of code, FORMAT DOB MMDDYY8. (See the writeup accompanying Example 3.1 for an explanation).

Reading Multiple Lines of Data per Observation

Example 7

Reading Two Lines (Records) per Observation

FEATURES: #, / Line Pointers

You now know how to specify column ranges of raw data when reading values into SAS variables, and you can even jump around within a line of data. But what if a set of data for an observation spans multiple lines (records) on the raw data input file? You can easily tell the SAS System which line contains the next data value to read by using a line pointer (# or /). We will only cover the basic situation here where each observation contains the same number of lines; however, real life situations can get much more complicated where there can be different numbers of records for different observations. We leave this and other advanced tasks as lookup assignments for you, to be completed when the need arises.

Suppose we extend the last example by adding a second line of data per observation. The new data description is as follows:

Variable Name	Starting Column	Length	Format	Description
Record 1				
ID	1	3	Numeric	Subject ID
GENDER	4	1	Char	M=Male, F=Female
AGE	9	2	Numeric	Age of subject
HEIGHT	11	2	Numeric	Height in inches
DOB	13	6	MMDDYY6	Date of birth
Record 2				
ID	1	3	Numeric	Subject ID
SBP	5	3	Numeric	Systolic blood pressure
DBP	9	3	Numeric	Diastolic blood pressure
HP	13	3	Numeric	Heart rate

Notice that both lines of raw data contain the subject ID number. This is a good policy in general and will aid in data integrity and validity checking. Although you could read the ID number from both records for each subject (with a different variable name for each), and then check one against the other for validity before proceeding to the next observation, you do not do so here. The following code reads the data, two records per observation.

Example 7.1

```
DATA POINTER;
    INPUT #1 @1  ID       3.
             @5  GENDER   $1.
             @7  AGE      2.
             @10 HEIGHT   2.
             @13 DOB      MMDDYY6.
         #2 @5  SBP      3.
             @9  DBP      3.
             @13 HR       3.;
FORMAT DOB MMDDYY8.;
DATALINES;
101 M 26 68 012366
101 120   80 68
102 M 32 78 031460
102 162   92 74
103 F 45 62 112647
103 134   86 74
104 F 22 66 080170
104 116   72 67
;

PROC PRINT DATA=POINTER;
    TITLE 'Example 7.1';
RUN;
```

The #'s in the INPUT statement tell the SAS System which raw data lines to access when reading in values. In this case, the instructions are to obtain values for ID, GENDER, AGE, HEIGHT and DOB from line 1 (#1) for each observation, and to obtain values for SBP, DBP and HR from line 2 (#2) of each observation. Although values for the ID number are present on both records for each observation, you only read them from line 1 in this example.

Output for this code is as follows:

Output from Example 7.1 - Reading Two Lines (Records) per Observation

```
                          Example 7.1

    OBS   ID    GENDER   AGE   HEIGHT     DOB      SBP   DBP  HR

     1    101     M       26     68     01/23/66   120   80   68
     2    102     M       32     78     03/14/60   162   92   74
     3    103     F       45     62     11/26/47   134   86   74
     4    104     F       22     66     08/01/70   116   72   67
```

If the raw data consist of the same number of records per observation, and if all records are to be read for each observation, as is the case in the current example, then instead of explicitly denoting which numbered record to go to for each subset of variables, you can just tell the system to go to the next line after reading the final value from the current line. This is accomplished by using the relative line pointer (/) indicator. The following INPUT statement could be used instead of the previous one, and the output would be identical:

```
INPUT     @1   ID        3.
          @5   GENDER    $1.
          @7   AGE       2.
          @10  HEIGHT    2.
          @13  DOB       MMDDYY6.
       /  @5   SBP       3.
          @9   DBP       3.
          @13  HR        3.;
```

In this case, the SAS System begins to read data from the first raw data input record. After reading values for ID through DOB, it moves to the next raw data record for three more variables (SBP, DBP, HR). These variables are all part of the same observation being built in the SAS data set. When the system finishes building the current observation, it advances to the next raw data record and starts to build the next one.

Using the absolute line pointer specifications in Example 7.1 is preferable to using the relative control shown above. Absolute line pointer control allows you to go forward or backward, makes it less likely to miscount the number of slashes, and makes for code that is easier to read. We show you the relative line pointer method since you may encounter programs that use it.

Skipping Selected Input Records

And now, one last wrinkle before we abandon the topic of multiple raw data input records per observation. Suppose there are many (or even two) lines of raw data, and you only wish to read from a few lines (or even one) per observation. You might wonder why you should type in extra lines to begin with. One answer is that you may be wrapping SAS code around an existing file of raw data that contains more than you need for the current application, but there are compelling reasons not to reshape the data (extra effort involved, chance of mutilating perfectly good valid data, etc.). How can you not read certain lines? There are two methods. Either use multiple slashes (////) to skip unwanted lines, or explicitly direct the INPUT statement to only the desired lines by using numbered #'s. In either case, if there are unwanted records at the end of each set of raw data lines, they must be accounted for.

Suppose you have a file of raw data consisting of four records per observation, and you only want to read two variables from the second record of the four. The following code accomplishes this.

Example 7.2

```
DATA SKIPSOME;
   INPUT #2 @1  ID    3.
             @12 SEX $6.
         #4;
DATALINES;
101 256 RED    9870980
101 898245 FEMALE 7987644
101 BIG    9887987
101 CAT 397  BOAT 68
102 809 BLUE   7918787
102 732866 MALE    6856976
102 SMALL 3884987
102 DOG 111   CAR   14
;

PROC PRINT DATA=SKIPSOME;
   TITLE 'Example 7.2';
RUN;
```

The previous INPUT statement instructs the system to go directly to the second available line of input data (#2), read data for two variables from that line (ID, SEX), and then go directly to the fourth line of input (#4). It is essential to include the #4 pointer even though you are not reading any data from line 4. It is needed so that the correct number of lines are skipped, and the program reads the correct line of data for the beginning of each observation. On each iteration of the DATA step, line 2 is read and the pointer then moves to the fourth line.

The previous code yields the following output:

Output from Example 7.2 - Skipping Selected Input Records

```
                    Example 7.2

               OBS   ID     SEX

                1   101     FEMALE
                2   102     MALE
```

As expected, the only data that are read and converted into data set variables, and subsequently printed out, are those for ID and SEX.

Example 8

Reading Parts of Your Data More Than Once

FEATURES: @ Pointer Control

There are often times when it is useful to read the same raw data columns more than once to create different SAS data set variables. You can read the exact same range of columns multiple times and create variables of different types (e.g. numeric, character, date, etc.), or read a subset of a previously read column range into a new variable, or even read overlapping ranges into different variables.

Suppose you are dealing with inventory data where it is important to know in which state a part was manufactured, the weight of the part, and the year in which it was made. Each part has a 14-character part ID made up of four components: a two-character state code, a three-digit part number, a three-digit part weight, and a six-digit manufacture date in MMDDYY format. Each part also has a description and a quantity-on-hand value.

You have to build a SAS data set that includes the following independent variables: PARTID (part ID), ST (state of manufacture), WT (part weight), YR (year of manufacture), PARTDESC (part description), and QUANT (quantity on hand.) PARTID must be read as a character variable because it contains alphanumeric characters (the state abbreviations). You also want ST read separately. WT must be read as a numeric variable because you have to do arithmetic calculations with it (e.g. total weight for all pieces in the warehouse). You only need the year at present for YR, so you don't read the entire date.

Once again, there are many ways to accomplish your task. The following code represents one method:

Example 8

```
DATA PARTS;
    INPUT @1    PARTID     $14.
          @1    ST         $2.
          @6    WT         3.
          @13   YR         2.
          @16   PARTDESC   $24.
          @41   QUANT      4.;
DATALINES;
NY101110060172 LEFT-HANDED WHIZZER       233
MA102085112885 FULL-NOSE BLINK TRAP     1423
CA112216111291 DOUBLE TONE SAND BIT       45
NC222845071970 REVERSE SPIRAL RIPSHANK   876
;

PROC PRINT DATA=PARTS;
    TITLE 'Example 8';
RUN;
```

PARTID is first read as a 14-byte character variable starting in column 1. By re-reading columns 1 and 2, you obtain a value for the 2-byte character variable, ST. You then read data from within the same column range that you read as character for PARTID and obtain two numeric variables: WT from columns 6-8 and YR from columns 13-14. The INPUT statement completes the process by reading in a 24-byte character variable PARTDESC starting in column 16 and a 4-byte numeric variable QUANT starting in column 41.

The previous code yields the following output:

Output from Example 8 - Reading Parts of Your Data More Than Once

```
                              Example 8

 OBS     PARTID           ST   WT   YR    PARTDESC                QUANT

  1    NY101110060172    NY   110   72    LEFT-HANDED WHIZZER       233
  2    MA102085112885    MA    85   85    FULL-NOSE BLINK TRAP    1,423
  3    CA112216111291    CA   216   91    DOUBLE TONE SAND BIT       45
  4    NC222845071970    NC   845   90    REVERSE SPIRAL RIPSHANK   876
```

There are actually other ways to accomplish these goals (but there aren't better ways to get basic concepts across.) You could use character substring functions and date functions and PUT and INPUT functions, etc., but let's wait until Chapter 5, "SAS Functions," to meet these powerful tools.

Example 9

> ## Using Informat Lists and Relative Pointer Controls
>
> **FEATURES:** Informat Lists, **+***n* Relative Pointer Controls

Repetition, repetition, repetition. Repetitious isn't it? It definitely has its place in certain areas, such as teaching if it's done right, but the whole basis of "computing" in general is to let the machine do the repetitive work, right? Take a look at the following code (typical for a beginning SAS System programmer):

Example 9.1

```
DATA LONGWAY;
    INPUT ID      1-3
          Q1      4
          Q2      5
          Q3      6
          Q4      7
          Q5      8
          Q6      9-10
          Q7      11-12
          Q8      13-14
          Q9      15-16
          Q10     17-18
          HEIGHT  19-20
          AGE     21-22;
DATALINES;
101113241016141515 56823
102143321212141316 7221
103233421414121210 6628
104155321616131412 6622
;

PROC PRINT DATA=LONGWAY;
    TITLE 'Example 9.1';
RUN;
```

The objective here is obviously to read data consisting of an ID number, answers to ten questions, and height and age for each subject. There is a better way. The SAS System provides the ability to read a repetitive series of data items by using a variable list and an informat list.

The variable list contains the variables to be read; the informat list contains the informat(s) for these variables. The previous code can be rewritten, using a variable list and an informat list, as follows:

Example 9.2

```
DATA SHORTWAY;
   INPUT ID 1-3
        @4 (Q1-Q5)(1.)
        @9 (Q6-Q10 HEIGHT AGE)(2.);
DATALINES;
1011132410161415156823
1021433212121413167221
1032334214141212106628
1041553216161314126622
;

PROC PRINT DATA=SHORTWAY;
   TITLE 'Example 9.2';
RUN;
```

The INPUT statement here works as follows: after reading in a value for ID, five values are read for variables Q1, Q2, Q3, Q4, and Q5. They are all read with a 1. informat, and they are all contiguous in the raw data. (A small digression is in order. A list of variables, all having the same base and each one having a sequential numeric suffix, can be abbreviated as BASE#-BASE#. In this case, Q1, Q2, Q3, Q4, and Q5, can be written as Q1-Q5. End of small digression.) After the last variable in the list, Q5, is read, a new list is initiated. This one consists of variables Q6-Q10, HEIGHT and AGE. This time they are all read with a 2. informat.

An alternate coding for the previous INPUT statement is:

```
INPUT @1 (ID Q1-Q10 HEIGHT AGE)(3. 5*1. 7*2.);
```

In this case there is only one variable list and one informat list, but the instructions are identical to the last example. The $n*$ denotes how many times a particular informat is to be used; 5*1. means, "use the 1. informat five times, i.e. for the next five variables."

Aside from the title, either of the previous two sets of code produces the following output.

Output from Example 9.2 - Using Informat Lists and Relative Pointer Controls

```
                                Example 9.2

    OBS   ID   Q1  Q2  Q3  Q4  Q5  Q6  Q7  Q8  Q9  Q10  HEIGHT  AGE

     1   101   1   1   3   2   4   10  16  14  15   15     68    23
     2   102   1   4   3   3   2   12  12  14  13   16     72    21
     3   103   2   3   3   4   2   14  14  12  12   10     66    28
     4   104   1   5   5   3   2   16  16  13  14   12     66    22
```

When using informat lists, the raw data do not have to be all contiguous and of the same type, as they are in the last example. Any informats can be used and intermixed, and blank spaces can be skipped with the relative +*n* pointer controls. These pointer controls can be used anywhere in an INPUT statement and merely move the column pointer forward or backward +(-*n*) the designated (*n*) number of spaces. Since there is no negative pointer control available, in order to go backwards, you actually have to advance a negative amount. Silly looking at first, but it is logical.

Suppose your 10 questions occur in five pairs, each pair consisting of a numerically answered question and then a characterly answered question (not really sure about "characterly", but you get the point.) Suppose further that all pairs are separated from other pairs, and from other variables, by two spaces. The following code handles this situation:

Example 9.3

```
DATA PAIRS;
   INPUT @1 ID 3.                  ❶
      @6  (QN1-QN5)(1. +3)         ❷
      @7  (QC1-QC5)($1. +3)        ❸
      @26 (HEIGHT AGE)(2. +1 2.);  ❹
DATALINES;
101  1A  3A  4B  4A  6A  68 26
102  1A  3B  2B  2A  2B  78 32
103  2B  3D  2C  4C  4B  62 45
104  1C  5C  2D  6A  6A  66 22
;

PROC PRINT DATA=PAIRS;
   TITLE 'Example 9.3';
RUN;
```

OK, what's happening here? It's really pretty straightforward. The INPUT statement performs the following tasks:

❶ Start at column 1 and read a 3-byte numeric field into variable ID.

❷ Go to column 6 and repeat the following five times: read a 1-byte numeric field into a variable and then move forward 3 columns from the current position to get ready for the next variable in the list. Name the variables QN1-QN5.

❸ Go back to column 7 and repeat the following 5 times: read a 1-byte character field into a variable and then move forward 3 columns to get ready for the next variable in the list. Name the variables QC1-QC5.

❹ Go to column 26 and read a 2-byte field into the numeric variable HEIGHT. Advance the column pointer 1 column, and read another 2-byte field into the numeric variable AGE.

That's it. Powerful and efficient. The resulting output is as follows:

Output from Example 9.3 - Using Informat Lists and Relative Pointer Controls

<table>
<tr><td colspan="15" align="center">Example 9.3</td></tr>
<tr><td>OBS</td><td>ID</td><td>QN1</td><td>QN2</td><td>QN3</td><td>QN4</td><td>QN5</td><td>QC1</td><td>QC2</td><td>QC3</td><td>QC4</td><td>QC5</td><td>HEIGHT</td><td>AGE</td></tr>
<tr><td>1</td><td>101</td><td>1</td><td>3</td><td>4</td><td>4</td><td>6</td><td>A</td><td>A</td><td>B</td><td>A</td><td>A</td><td>68</td><td>26</td></tr>
<tr><td>2</td><td>102</td><td>1</td><td>3</td><td>2</td><td>2</td><td>2</td><td>A</td><td>B</td><td>B</td><td>A</td><td>B</td><td>78</td><td>32</td></tr>
<tr><td>3</td><td>103</td><td>2</td><td>3</td><td>2</td><td>4</td><td>4</td><td>B</td><td>D</td><td>C</td><td>C</td><td>B</td><td>62</td><td>45</td></tr>
<tr><td>4</td><td>104</td><td>1</td><td>5</td><td>2</td><td>6</td><td>6</td><td>C</td><td>C</td><td>D</td><td>A</td><td>A</td><td>66</td><td>22</td></tr>
</table>

The key to using variable and informat lists is patterns. If you can arrange your data in repeating patterns, then these repetitions can be put to your advantage. Look for them.

Example 10

Reading a Mixture of Record Types in One DATA Step

FEATURES: Reading Data Conditionally, @ (Single Trailing At Sign)

Consider the following situation: you've been given a set of raw data which are a combination of data lines from different sources. They all contain the same data fields, but they are in different positions in each raw data line depending on the source of the data. There is an identifying value in each observation that denotes the source of the data and, therefore, the format of the data values for that observation.

This is not at all an unusual situation, and it is one that the SAS System can handle readily. By using a trailing @, the INPUT statement gives you the ability to read a part of your raw data line, test it, and then decide how to read additional data from the same record.

Background: How a DATA Step Builds an Observation

Before you proceed further, you have to know a little about how a DATA step builds an observation in a SAS data set and how an INPUT statement operates with multiple lines of raw data. A DATA step begins when the DATA keyword is encountered, and ends when a DATALINES statement, a RUN statement, another DATA keyword, or a PROC keyword is encountered. In all the examples so far, each time an INPUT statement executed, a pointer moved to a new record. If, however, you include a single @ at the end of the INPUT statement (before the semicolon), the next INPUT statement in the same DATA step does not bring a new record into the input buffer but continues reading from the same raw data line as the preceding one. At the end of the DATA step an observation is written to the SAS data set (unless you explicitly use an OUTPUT statement somewhere in the DATA step—see Example 15.2 in this chapter and Example 6.1 in Chapter 3). On the next iteration of the DATA step, the pointer moves to the next record and the INPUT statement begins processing again.

Back to Our Reading Mixed Records Example

Now back to our example with mixed records. A 1 in column 20 specifies that your data contain values for ID in columns 1-3, AGE in columns 4-5, and WEIGHT in columns 6-8; a 2 in column 20 specifies that the value for ID is in columns 1-3, AGE is in columns 10-11, and WEIGHT is in columns 15-17. The following code correctly reads the data:

Example 10

```
DATA MIXED;
   INPUT @20 TYPE $1. @;   ❶
   IF TYPE = '1' THEN      ❷
      INPUT ID     1-3
            AGE    4-5
            WEIGHT 6-8;
   ELSE IF TYPE = '2' THEN   ❸
      INPUT ID     1-3
            AGE    10-11
            WEIGHT 15-17;
DATALINES;
00134168           1
00245155           1
003     23    220  2
00467180           1
005     35    190  2
;

PROC PRINT DATA=MIXED;
   TITLE 'Example 10';
RUN;
```

The program works as follows:

❶ After reading a value for TYPE in the first INPUT statement, the single trailing @ says, "hold the line," that is, do not go to a new data line if you encounter another INPUT statement.

❷ The IF-THEN/ELSE code tests the current value of TYPE and proceeds accordingly. If the value of TYPE is 1, then the program uses the next INPUT statement to read ID, AGE, and WEIGHT.

❸ If TYPE = 2, then an alternate INPUT statement is used.

When a second INPUT statement (one without a trailing @) is encountered, the data line is released and you are ready for the next iteration of the DATA step.

The code produces the following output:

Output from Example 10 - Reading a Mixture of Record Types in One DATA Step

```
                        Example 10

        OBS     TYPE   ID   AGE   WEIGHT

         1       1      1   34     168
         2       1      2    45     155
         3       2      3   23     220
         4       1      4   67     180
         5       2      5   35     190
```

As you can see, all values are assigned to their proper data set variables, regardless of which columns they are read from. Now if you think that a single trailing @ was neat stuff, just wait till the next example.

Example 11

Holding the Data Line through Multiple Iterations of the DATA Step

FEATURE: **@@ (Double Trailing At Sign)**

If a single trailing @ tells the system to "hold the line", what do you suppose a double trailing @ would instruct it to do? Why, "hold the line more strongly", of course! What does this translate into? Remember that under normal conditions, a complete iteration of the DATA step constructs one observation in a SAS data set from one raw data line. The DATA step then repeats this process, again and again, until there are no raw data lines left to read. Each time an INPUT statement ending with a semicolon (and no trailing @) is executed, the pointer moves to the next record. By using a double trailing @ (@@), you can instruct the SAS System to use multiple iterations of the DATA step to build multiple observations from each record of raw data.

An INPUT statement ending with @@ instructs the program to release the current raw data line only when there are no data values left to be read from that line. The @@, therefore, holds an input record *even across multiple iterations of the DATA step*. This is different from the single trailing @, which holds the line for the next INPUT statement but releases it when an INPUT statement is executed in the next iteration of the DATA step.

The next two programs both accomplish the same result; they build identical SAS data sets. Notice that you are using list input in these examples. You can use @@ in other kinds of INPUT code, but it makes the most sense with list input. As a matter of fact, we're hard pressed to think of a non-esoteric situation in which you would want to use @@ with column input. The first following program does not use @@ so that you can see the comparison:

Example 11.1

```
DATA LONGWAY;
    INPUT X Y;
DATALINES;
1 2
3 4
5 6
6 9
10 12
13 14
;

PROC PRINT DATA=LONGWAY;
    TITLE 'Example 11.1';
RUN;
```

Now here is the short way, using @@, with considerably fewer data lines:

Example 11.2

```
DATA SHORTWAY;
    INPUT X Y @@;
DATALINES;
1 2 3 4 5 6
6 9 10 12 13 14
;

PROC PRINT DATA=SHORTWAY;
    TITLE 'Example 11.2';
RUN;
```

Here's how it works. Data values are read in pairs. Three pairs are read from the first data line, and then the INPUT statement goes to the next data line for more data. The important thing to realize is that, although there are only two raw data lines, the DATA step actually iterates six times, one for each set of variables (X and Y) named on the INPUT statement. The @@ stops the system from going to a new raw data line each time the INPUT statement executes. In effect, all the data values can be thought of as strung out in one continuous line of data. Using @@ causes the DATA step to keep reading from a data line until there are no more data values to read from that record (reaches an end-of-record marker), or until a subsequent INPUT statement (that does not have a single trailing @) executes. Here is the output.

Output from Example 11.2 - Holding the Data Line through Multiple Executions of the DATA Step

```
                        Example 11.2

                    OBS    X     Y

                     1     1     2
                     2     3     4
                     3     5     6
                     4     6     9
                     5    10    12
                     6    13    14
```

Extra Caution with Missing Values and @@

Remember what happened way back at the beginning of this monumental chapter when you were missing input data for a single variable and didn't use a period to represent the missing value? Two raw input data lines were incorrectly merged into one very wrong data set observation. Only a small amount of data was affected because each new execution of the DATA step started with a new data line. The system "caught up" with itself and then got back on track. If the same missing data situation were present when using @@, all succeeding values in all succeeding observations would be in error. (This is not to say that one incorrect data value is better than many!)

To illustrate what we mean about compounding errors, suppose you inadvertently omitted the second X value 3 in the previous code and entered the first line of data as 1 2 4 5 6. From that point on, the program would be "out of whack" and would be reading Y values for X's, and vice versa, until it reached the end of the raw data where it would look in vain for that last Y value.

The output would be as follows:

Output from Example 11.2 - When a Data Value is Left Out

```
                        Example 11.2

                      OBS   X    Y

                       1    1    2
                       2    4    5
                       3    6    6
                       4    9   10
                       5   12   13
```

Read the SAS Log!

If you just skim the output, everything might look right. Don't stop there! All SAS System jobs are accompanied by a SAS log that documents the processing of the SAS statements and the manipulation of SAS data sets, and presents notification that various procedures were executed. The SAS log accompanying the previous SAS program looks (in part) something like this:

```
1      DATA SHORTWAY;
2          INPUT X Y @@;
3      DATALINES;

NOTE: LOST CARD.
RULE: ----+----1----+----2----+----3----+----4----+---5----+
6      ;
X=14 Y=. _ERROR_=1 _N_=6
NOTE: SAS went to a new line when INPUT statement reached
      past the end of a line.
NOTE: The data set WORK.SHORTWAY has 5 observations and 2
      variables.
NOTE: The DATA statement used 0.06 CPU seconds and 2389K.
```

The LOST CARD note in the SAS log is the system's way of telling you that a problem has occurred. In this case, it should lead to an examination of the raw data input values where the problem could be easily found and corrected. Of course this is a simple illustrative example, and real life situations are not this easy to deal with. The moral is abundantly clear. When you see messages like this in the SAS log, *do not ignore them*. The system is trying to tell you something.

By the way, if you had been unlucky enough to omit two values somewhere in the data stream above, the system would never figure it out. Although the two omissions would seem to cancel each other out, all intervening data values in the SAS data set would be wrong. As is true with most SAS System tools, double trailing @'s are very powerful. But you must use them with care.

Example 12

> ### Suppressing Error Messages
>
> *FEATURES:* ? and ?? (Single and Double Question Marks)

There may be situations when your numeric data will intentionally contain character values, such as the characters NA, meaning "Not Applicable", or other meaningful abbreviations. Although this will have meaning to you, the SAS System will complain about seeing these "invalid" character strings when it is expecting only pure numeric data. When this happens, the SAS log will ordinarily notify you that it has encountered invalid data. If this occurs often enough as a SAS data set is being built, the system log will eventually stop issuing the error messages and notify you that it has stopped, its error message limit having been exceeded. Here is a short program with some invalid data and the accompanying SAS log:

Example 12.1

```
DATA ERRORS;
    INPUT X 1-2
          Y 4-5;
DATALINES;
11 23
23 NA
NA 47
55 66
;
```

Here is the SAS log:

```
1    DATA ERRORS;
2    INPUT X 1-2
3          Y 4-5;
4    DATALINES;

NOTE: Invalid data for Y in line 5 4-5.
RULE: ----+----1----+----2----+----3----+----4----+----5----
5      23 NA
X=23 Y=. _ERROR_=1 _N_=2
NOTE: Invalid data for X in line 7 1-2.
7      NA 47
X=. Y=47 _ERROR_=1 _N_=3
```

```
NOTE: The data set WORK.ERRORS has 4 observations and 2
      variables.
NOTE: The DATA statement used 0.06 CPU seconds and 2385K.

9    ;
```

When the system encounters an invalid value for a variable, it does a number of things: first, it informs you of its discovery and displays the offensive value. Next it assigns a missing value, . , to the offending variable for the current observation. If you know beforehand that your raw data contain values that the system will consider invalid, such as NA for a numeric variable, you may want to avoid the possibly numerous pages of SAS System error messages. You have two choices:

1. You can save paper by placing a single question mark (?) following a variable name to instruct the system to suppress this type of error message while continuing to print the offending line of data to the log.
2. You can save even more paper by using a double question mark (??) to suppress the printing of all error messages as well as the offending data lines. Here is the example with double ??'s being used, along with the resulting SAS log.

The program:

Example 12.2

```
DATA ERRORS;
    INPUT X ?? 1-2
          Y ?? 4-5;
DATALINES;
11 23
23 NA
NA 47
55 66
;
```

And the SAS log:

```
1    DATA ERRORS;
2        INPUT X ?? 1-2
3              Y ?? 4-5;
4    DATALINES;

NOTE: The data set WORK.ERRORS has 4 observations and 2
      variables.
NOTE: The DATA statement used 0.05 CPU seconds and 2361K.

9    ;
```

It goes without saying (but as is our wont, we'll say it anyway), that the single and double question marks should be used with caution.

Example 13

> ### Reading Data from External Files
>
> *FEATURES:* **INFILE and FILENAME Statements**

All of the examples so far have had the raw data included along with the SAS code. You therefore used the DATALINES statement to signal the start of the data. Much of the time your raw data values are stored in a separate file, external to the code. The only changes you need to make to your SAS program are to include an INFILE statement that identifies the location (file specification) where the data values are stored, and omit the DATALINES statement (obviously the data lines themselves are also omitted).

The file specification can take one of two forms when the data reside external to the file containing the SAS code.

Method 1 - Identifying the Filename Directly with the INFILE Statement

With this method, you identify the external data source directly in the INFILE statement by simply enclosing its name in single quotation marks. Suppose the data for Example 13.1 is stored in a file called 'C:\MYDATA\HTWT'. You indicate this in the INFILE statement as follows:

Example 13.1

```
DATA EXTERNAL;
    INFILE  'C:\MYDATA\HTWT';
    INPUT    ID HEIGHT WEIGHT GENDER $ AGE;
RUN;
```

The SAS System then reads the data from the C:\MYDATA\HTWT file, one data line at a time, and applies the INPUT statement to each record as if it had been read instream.

Method 2 - Using a Separate FILENAME Statement to Identify an External File

The other method of identifying the location of the raw data lines is to create a fileref (file reference) by means of a FILENAME statement and then to refer to this fileref in the INFILE statement. Filerefs are not enclosed in quotation marks as are external filenames. Some platforms supply alternate methods for specifying filerefs, such as DD cards in MVS or filedefs in CMS. Suppose, for example, you set up a fileref called OSCAR to refer to the file called

C:\MYDATA\HTWT. The previous code could be rewritten as follows, making use of the fileref OSCAR:

Example 13.2

```
FILENAME OSCAR 'C:\MYDATA\HTWT';

DATA EXTERNAL;
   INFILE   OSCAR;
   INPUT    ID HEIGHT WEIGHT GENDER $ AGE;
RUN;
```

Why Filerefs are Useful

Older versions of the SAS System required the use of a fileref; external files could not be directly referenced in the INFILE statement. Although this is not the case with Version 6 of the SAS System, there are times when the use of filerefs can greatly enhance your programming in terms of convenience, efficiency, and power. Long filenames (fully qualified mainframe data set names can get quite lengthy) can be abbreviated with short descriptive "handles." There are also techniques that can be used to access different data sources dynamically without the need for manual recoding (see Example 15.2 in this chapter for an example).

Using an INFILE Statement with Instream Data to Specify Options

As you will recall in Example 2 (if you don't, go take a look -- it's been a while), you used the special DATALINES file specification in the INFILE statement to tell the SAS System that the data lines were included instream with the code. This was only necessary because you wanted to use the DLM= and DSD options of the INFILE statement on your instream data. In order to use an INFILE statement option, you must have an INFILE statement, and every INFILE statement must have a file specification. We now show some examples of other options that give you control over reading data from external files.

Example 14

> ## Reading in Parts of Raw Data Files
>
> *FEATURES:* **INFILE and OPTIONS Statements, (OBS=, FIRSTOBS=, PAD, and MISSOVER options)**

Up till now you have always read the entire raw data file as input to your program. That is usually what is desired, but there are cases in which only part of the raw data file needs to be read. You can read a specified number of records from the beginning of the file, from the end of the file, or from the middle of the file. When developing a program, it is always a good idea to work with a small subset of the data until the code is working exactly as desired. The easiest thing to do in the developmental stage is to read only the first *n* records of a file by using the OBS=*n* option in the INFILE statement. The value of *n* is actually the record number of the last record to be read, but if you are starting from the beginning of the file, then *n* will also give you *n* records.

Reading the First 100 Records

Suppose you want to read only the first 100 records of a file called BIGDATA. The following INFILE statement accomplishes this handily:

```
INFILE 'BIGDATA' OBS=100;
```

This could also have been accomplished globally by using an OPTIONS statement of the form:

```
OPTIONS OBS=100;
```

However, the use of an OBS= option in an INFILE statement allows you to control how many records should be processed from individual raw data files if more than one is being read (we'll get to how to read multiple data files in the next example). There are many processing options that can be set via the OPTIONS statement; we touch upon only some of them throughout this book. The OPTIONS statement can appear before or after any DATA step or procedure. The included options take effect from that point onward and remain in effect until they are changed by subsequent OPTIONS statements or you exit out of the SAS System. Be forewarned, don't forget to turn off the OBS= option when you no longer want or need it. To set the observation limit back to the default value, use:

```
OPTIONS OBS=MAX;
```

Skipping the First *n* Records of a File

The INPUT statement begins reading from the first data line encountered in the raw data file by default. This does not have to be the case. You can instruct the SAS System which record to read first by use of the FIRSTOBS= option in the INFILE statement. From that point on, records are read sequentially. Suppose your file were constructed in such a way that the first 100 records were preliminary and not part of the real data set. After using these first 100 records for development as above, you could then start your real analysis with the next record as follows:

```
INFILE 'BIGFILE' FIRSTOBS=101;
```

Reading a Subset from the Middle of a File

You can also deal with subsets of records from the middle of a raw data file. If, for example, your data set was constructed in such a fashion that you wanted to analyze subsets of 100 records sequentially, you could accomplish this by picking out 100 records to deal with at a time. The FIRSTOBS= option denotes the first record to read, and the OBS= option denotes the last record to read. The thing to remember is that OBS= does not refer to the *number* of records to read, but rather it refers to the *last* record to read. So, to read the second 100 records in the raw data file, code the INFILE statement as follows:

```
INFILE 'BIGFILE' FIRSTOBS=101 OBS=200;
```

A Special Caution with Short Records in an External File

If you have missing values at the end of a record of an external file, you have to be very careful. Suppose you have a raw data file called HT_WT that contains values for an ID number, HEIGHT, and WEIGHT. Suppose further, that you are missing either weights, or both heights and weights, for some of the subjects. A typical file might look something like this:

```
File HT_WT

001 68 155
002 64
003
004 72 220
```

Notice that you are missing a value for WEIGHT for observation 2 and both a HEIGHT and WEIGHT for observation 3. If these lines do not contain blanks to indicate that you are missing values for these observations, you need to use an option to indicate this. By the way, just looking at the file on your computer screen may not tell you that there are blanks in these missing positions. You need an editor that shows you where the records end to see if there are blanks or not. To be on the safe side, you should use the PAD or MISSING option in the INFILE statement to be sure that external files with short records are read correctly. The MISSOVER option is used with list input. It instructs the program not to go to a new record if all the variables have not been assigned values when the end of the current record is reached. Instead, variables that have not received values are set to missing. The PAD option is used with fixed record layouts and pads all short records to the length specified by the logical record length (see Example 16).

For example, to read data from the HT_WT file, you use the following INFILE and INPUT statements:

```
INFILE 'HT_WT' PAD;
INPUT ID 1-3 HEIGHT 5-6 WEIGHT 8-10;
```

or, using list input:

```
INFILE 'HT_WT' MISSOVER;
INPUT  ID HEIGHT WEIGHT;
```

Example 15

Reading Data from Multiple External Files

FEATURES: **INFILE, DO UNTIL and DO WHILE Statements, END= and FILEVAR= Options**

Suppose you have two separate files, FILE1 and FILE2, each containing raw data for the same set of variables. You want to read all the data from both files and create a SAS data set from the aggregate. Here is one way to code it.

Example 15.1

```
DATA TWOFILES;
   IF NOT LASTREC1 THEN INFILE 'FILE1' END=LASTREC1;
                   ELSE INFILE 'FILE2';
   INPUT ID AGE WEIGHT;
RUN;
```

The key to this program is the END= option in the first INFILE statement. It works like this: a temporary variable defined by the user is created and given the name specified after the = sign, in this case, LASTREC1. This variable is given a value of 0 each time a record is read from FILE1 except when the last record is read; it is then set to 1. Each time the DATA step iterates, it checks the value of LASTREC1. The phrase IF NOT LASTREC1 is equivalent to IF LASTREC1 NE 1. When this is true, (this will be true after each record is read from FILE1 except the last one), the first INFILE statement is executed. After the last record from FILE1 is read, LASTREC1 is set to 1. From then on, IF NOT LASTREC1 is false, and the second INFILE statement is executed (the ELSE condition).

A More Flexible Approach: Using a Variable to Indicate the External Filename

The previous approach works fine, but there is another way—a little complicated, but pretty neat. You can include the names of the external files you wish to read as values in instream data lines. You accomplish this by using a FILEVAR= option in the INFILE statement. Here is the previous code rewritten using this alternate method:

Example 15.2

```
DATA TWOFILES;
    INPUT EXTNAME $; ❶
    INFILE DUMMY FILEVAR=EXTNAME END=LASTREC; ❷
    DO UNTIL (LASTREC=1);   ❸
        INPUT ID AGE WEIGHT;
        OUTPUT; ❹
    END;
DATALINES;
FILE1
FILE2
;
```

Here's how this program works. The first INPUT statement ❶ reads a value for the variable EXTNAME from the data line following the DATALINES statement. The first value read is FILE1. This is fed to the INFILE statement ❷ via the FILEVAR= option. The system now knows to read data from FILE1. The DO loop ❸ then processes each data line from the current source, FILE1. When the last record is read, the value of LASTREC is set to 1. The DO loop then stops processing, and the DATA step starts over again, reading a new value (FILE2) in to EXTNAME. LASTREC is reinitialized to 0, and the DO loop starts up again, this time reading from FILE2. When LASTREC is once again set to 1, the loop stops. Since there are no more raw data lines instream to read, the DATA step ends.

Now, what about that DUMMY file specification and the OUTPUT statement? ❷ The DUMMY is just that. The source of raw data for the INFILE statement is actually the value of the FILEVAR variable (EXTNAME in this example.) Since an INFILE statement needs a file specification, we supply a dummy, and call it DUMMY. Pretty clever, huh?

The OUTPUT statement ❹ is necessary because data are only written to the SAS data set being built at the end of each iteration of a DATA step unless an OUTPUT statement is encountered. You need the OUTPUT statement here because this DATA step iterates only twice -- after the last record is read from each raw data file. Without the OUTPUT statement, this DATA step would only write two records to the data set you are building.

Here is the general syntax for the DO UNTIL statement:

```
DO UNTIL (condition);

    SAS statements

END;
```

The SAS statements in the DO UNTIL block are repeatedly executed until the condition (always placed in parentheses) is true. The DO UNTIL loop always executes at least once, regardless of the logical value of the condition.

Another useful looping structure is DO WHILE. The syntax is identical to DO UNTIL. The statements in the DO UNTIL loop only execute when the condition is true. If the condition is false, the DO WHILE loop does not execute at all.

An easy way to remember the difference between these two looping statements is that the DO UNTIL statement tests the condition at the bottom of the loop while the DO WHILE statement tests at the top.

Example 16

Reading Long Records from an External File

FEATURE: INFILE Option LRECL

When reading in external raw data files, you can, for the most part, rely on default values for describing architectural features of the files. You can override defaults when necessary, to describe such features as the record format, block size, or logical record length of the file. These features are described by the INFILE statement options RECFM=, BLKSIZE=, and LRECL= respectively. We only concern ourselves here with the last one, LRECL=. (By the way, this option is named after that famous Spanish bullfighter, "El Rec-el.") You use this option to indicate the maximum record length of the input file and only need it when the record length exceeds your system dependent default. Suppose you have a file, LONGFILE, with 256-byte records and a system default logical record length of 80. You can account for the long record length by coding the INFILE statement as follows:

```
INFILE 'LONGFILE' LRECL=256;
```

You can also use the LRECL= option when you want to read only part of very long records. You may code an LRECL= value larger or smaller than the actual record length in your input file and it will work just fine.

Conclusion

Well, we've finally come to the end of this seemingly endless chapter. From here on in, it's relatively easy going, at least in terms of chapter lengths.

You have seen how to read a variety of data arrangements from both instream data lines and external files. You can read data values separated by delimiters such as blanks or commas or data arranged in columns. You can read data from external files and can control which values are to be read and how to use an informat to read data values such as dates. You can read multiple records to create one observation or create multiple observations from one record. Using INFILE options, you can read selected portions of an external file.

As long as we are at the end of the chapter, why not try a few simple exercises to test what you've learned? "Exercise" sounds a bit like work, and that's no fun, so let's call them problems. Actually, that's not much better, but problems usually have solutions, and that's not necessarily so with exercises. Remember, there are no absolutely "correct" solutions, but we do give you some that will work. If yours are different, test them. They may be just fine. Our solutions to all problems in this book will be found in the Appendix, "Problem Solutions." Here goes.

Problems

1-1. Write a program to read the raw data stored in an external file called VITAL (shown below), and create a SAS System data set called VSIGNS. VITAL contains the following variables, in the order listed: ID, HR (heart rate), SBP (systolic blood pressure), and DBP (diastolic blood pressure).

```
external file VITAL

A1 68 130 80
B3 101 148 86
C2 . . 72
D1 72 140 88
```

1-2. Redo problem 1-1 to read the comma-delimited raw data file VITALC shown below:

```
external file VITALC

A1,68,130,80
B3,101, 148,86
C2,.,.,72
D1, 72, 140 , 88
```

1-3. Given the raw data lines below, write a program to read these data and create a SAS data set called COLLEGE. The values are separated by one or more spaces, and they represent NAME, TITLE, TENURE (Y or N), and NUMBER (number of classes taught). Notice that some of the names are more than eight characters long.

```
Sample data for Problem 1-3

Stevenson Ph.D. Y 2
Smith Ph.D. N 3
Goldstein M.D. Y 1
```

1-4. This example is similar to Problem 1-3 except the values for NAME may include a single blank. The name is separated from the other values by at least two blanks. Modify the program to take this into account. Some sample data are shown below:

```
Sample data for Problem 1-4

George Stevenson Ph.D. Y 2
Fred Smith Ph.D. N 3
Alissa Goldstein M.D. Y 1
```

1-5. Given the raw data file description below, write a program to read this data file. Use starting and ending columns. Create a SAS data set called RESPOND. Use an INFORMAT statement if needed. A sample set of data is shown for you to use to test your program.

File FIRE

Variable Name	Starting Column	Ending Column	Format	Description
CALL_NO	1	3	Numeric	Call number
DATE	5	12	MM/DD/YY	Date of service
TRUCKS	14	15	Numeric	Number of trucks
ALARM	17	17	Numeric	Number of alarms

Sample data (in file FIRE)

```
001 10/21/94 03 2
002 10/23/94 01 1
003 11/01/94 11 3
```

1-6. Given the raw data file description below and the same sample data as in Problem 1-5, write a SAS System DATA step to read this data file, and create a SAS data set called RESPOND. Use formatted input; do not use ending columns.

File FIRE

Variable Name	Starting Column	Length	Format	Description
CALL_NO	1	3	Numeric	Call number
DATE	5	8	MM/DD/YY	Date of service
TRUCKS	14	2	Numeric	Number of trucks
ALARM	17	1	Numeric	Number of alarms

1-7. A data file contains a seven-character ID, a quantity, and a price. The first two
characters of the ID represent a factory number, and the last two characters represent
state abbreviations. The column specifications and some sample data values are
shown. Write a program to read these data instream and produce a SAS data set
called FACTORY.

File Inventory

Variable Name	Starting Column	Length	Format
ID	1	7	Character
QUANTITY	8	2	Numeric
PRICE	10	7	Numeric (contains dollar sign and comma)

```
13AB2NY44   $123
22XXXCT88 $1,033
37123TX11$22,999
```

Hint: Use the DOLLAR7. informat to read PRICE.

1-8. You have a Social Security number in columns 1-11 of a file, followed by one space,
followed by ten 3-digit scores. Using a variable list and an informat list, write a SAS
program to read the sample data below, and create a SAS data set called SCORES.
Name the 10 scores SCORE1 to SCORE10.

Sample data for Problem 1-8

```
123-45-6789 100 98 96 95 92 88 95 98100 90
344-56-7234  69 79 82 65 88 78 78 92 66 77
898-23-1234  80 80 82 86 92 78 88 84 85 83
```

1-9. You have collected four systolic and four diastolic blood pressure readings (the higher and lower numbers in a reading such as 120/80, respectively) over a period of four months. They are recorded as follows:

Variable Name	Start-End Column
SBP1	1-3
DBP1	4-6
SBP2	7-9
DBP2	10-12
SBP3	13-15
DBP3	16-18
SBP4	19-21
DBP4	22-24

Write a program that uses absolute and relative pointers to read the sample data below. Create a SAS data set called PRESSURE.
Hint: Read all the SBP's first, then go back and read the DBP's.

```
Sample data for Problem 1-9

120 80122 84128 90130 92
140102138 96136 92128 84
122 80122 80124 82122 78
```

1-10. You are given a raw data file called MIXED_UP that contains two types of records. If column 12 is a 1, the record layout is:

```
            File MIXED_UP
(Record Layout Where Column 12 = 1)
```

Variable Name	Start-End Column
EMP_ID	1-3
HEIGHT	4-5
WEIGHT	6-8

If column 12 is a 2, the record layout is:

```
              File MIXED_UP
   (Record Layout Where Column 12 = 2)

        Variable        Start-End
          Name            Column
   -------------------------------------
         EMP_ID            1-3
         HEIGHT            5-6
         WEIGHT            8-10
```

Write a SAS program to create a SAS data set called HTWT. Use column input and do not include the data instream.

```
Sample data (in file MIXED_UP)

00168155   1
002 70 200 2
00362102   1
004 74 180 2
```

1-11. Write a program to read in pairs of values from the sample data below, representing make of car and gas mileage. Have the program create a SAS data set called CARS. Notice that there are several pairs of values per line. Note also that the names of some makes of cars are more than eight characters long.

```
Sample Data

Ford 20 Honda 29 Oldsmobile 20 Cadillac 17
Toyota 24 Chevrolet 17
```

1-12. You have names and test scores in two files, FILE_ONE and FILE_TWO. NAME is in columns 1-10 and SCORE is in columns 11-13. Write a SAS program to read data from both files and create a SAS data set called SCORES. Some sample data are shown below:

```
          FILE_ONE
   ----------------
      CODY       100
      PASS        98
      BAGGETT     96
      JOYNER      45


          FILE_TWO
   ----------------
      FRANKS      66
      BEANS       68
```

.

Chapter 2

Data Recoding

Grouping Data Values

Introduction

When dealing with data, there are often times when you would like to have the collected values recoded as other values in a uniform manner. This could be for analytic reasons or for cosmetic purposes. Typically, the need is to condense, or collapse, ranges of values into a smaller set of "grouped" values. A simple, and fairly common, example of this type of process would be to recode collected subject age values into categories, such as 0-20, 21-40, 41-60, and greater than 60.

There are several ways to carry out this data recoding process using SAS software. We show the straightforward "brute-force" way to accomplish this goal, as well as a few refined methods which are actually easier (fewer lines) to code and more efficient!

Sample Data

All the examples in this chapter deal with a SAS data set called GRADES which contains two variables, ID and SCORE (test score). Data set GRADES has the following contents:

```
Data set GRADES

   ID  SCORE
    1    55
    2    65
    3    74
    4    76
    5    88
    6    92
    7    94
    8    96
    9    98
```

Example 1

Using IF-THEN/ELSE Statements to Recode a Variable

FEATURE: **IF-THEN/ELSE Recoding**

In this first example, you create a new variable, GRADE, by recoding the values of the variable SCORE into groups using IF-THEN/ELSE statements in the DATA step. The ranges of the values for SCORE for each of the five GRADE levels are:

```
SCORE Range                GRADE
------------------------------
<65                        0
>=65 and <70               1
>=70 and <80               2
>=80 and <90               3
>=90                       4
```

The following simple program accomplishes the desired transformation in a straightforward manner. It certainly gets the job done, and it serves to illustrate a number of good coding features.

Example 1

```
DATA RECODE;
   SET GRADES;
   IF       0 LE SCORE LT 65 THEN GRADE=0;
   ELSE IF 65 LE SCORE LT 70 THEN GRADE=1;
   ELSE IF 70 LE SCORE LT 80 THEN GRADE=2;
   ELSE IF 80 LE SCORE LT 90 THEN GRADE=3;
   ELSE IF       SCORE GE 90 THEN GRADE=4;
RUN;

PROC PRINT DATA=RECODE;
   TITLE 'Example 1';
RUN;
```

Output from this program is as follows:

Output from Example 1 - Using IF-THEN/ELSE Statements to Recode a Variable

```
                         Example 1

            OBS    ID    SCORE    GRADE

             1      1      55       0
             2      2      65       1
             3      3      74       2
             4      4      76       2
             5      5      88       3
             6      6      92       4
             7      7      94       4
             8      8      96       4
             9      9      98       4
```

This simple example serves to illustrate three points about coding:

- a style issue
- an efficiency tip
- a danger zone to avoid.

Style Issues

There is more than one equivalent way to write these IF statements. The previous program uses the form:

```
IF value_1 LE SCORE LT value_2 THEN GRADE=assigned value;
```

An alternative syntax (which requires a bit more typing) is:

```
IF value_1 LE SCORE AND SCORE LT value_2 THEN GRADE=assigned value;
```

A further alternative is:

```
IF SCORE GE value_1 AND SCORE LT value_2 THEN GRADE=assigned value;
```

They are all equivalent. Take your pick. Some people find it easier to understand the recoding process at a glance when the statements are expanded; some find it easier to use the condensed, almost graphical, version. Do what's best for you.

A Note on Efficiency

A point to observe here is the use of ELSE wherever appropriate. The code could have been written without the ELSE statements, and the results would have been the same, but the program would have taken longer to run. In this simple case, the increase in CPU time would be negligible, but with long complex programs with many observations and tight resources, the savings can be substantial, if not critical. Practicing good habits is never wasteful. Without the ELSE statements, the program would execute each IF statement on each observation, regardless of the value of SCORE. All IF tests would be conducted, even after an assignment was made for GRADE. With the ELSE statements in the program, the system stops testing an observation as soon as a "hit" is made. For the first observation, since the value of SCORE is between 0 and 65, the value of GRADE is set equal to 0, and the last three IF tests are not performed. (You may want to examine Chapter 14, "Example 8," for more information.)

A Common Error

And now for the danger zone. A common error is to code the first IF statement as follows:

```
IF SCORE LT 65 THEN GRADE=0;  *** WRONG WAY!  ;
```

instead of the following:

```
IF 0 LE SCORE LT 65 THEN GRADE=0;  *** CORRECT WAY  ;
```

At first glance it seems like these two statements are equivalent. The difference here is a bit subtle, but it belies a common trap, and is one that even the most experienced programmers have fallen into. The first statement above assigns a value of 0 to the variable GRADE for any observation that is missing a value for SCORE. The reason for this is the way in which the SAS System stores missing values. Suffice it to say that they are smaller than any negative number, and therefore if the value for SCORE is missing, GRADE receives a value of 0. So, writing the IF statement the wrong way causes all the students with missing values for SCORE to be grouped with the failing students. This may be what some evil teacher wished, but the important point to remember is that if the code is written one way, missing values are included in a category; if it is written the other way, they are not. Always watch out for this when writing statements containing tests based on inequality operators.

A short comment about comments is needed here. Any section of a SAS program that begins with an asterisk (*) and ends with a semicolon (;) is interpreted as a comment by the SAS System and is not executed as are other programming lines.

Example 2

> ## Using a SELECT Statement to Recode a Variable
>
> *FEATURE:* SELECT Statement

An alternative to IF-THEN/ELSE coding is to use the SELECT statement. It is usually more efficient than IF-THEN/ELSE, especially if you are recoding a variable into a large number of categories. There are various forms of the SELECT statement, but the one that does the trick here looks like the following:

Example 2

```
DATA RECODE;
   SET GRADES;
   SELECT;
       WHEN (0 LE SCORE LT 65)  GRADE=0;
       WHEN (65 LE SCORE LT 70) GRADE=1;
       WHEN (70 LE SCORE LT 80) GRADE=2;
       WHEN (80 LE SCORE LT 90) GRADE=3;
       WHEN (SCORE GE 90)       GRADE=4;
   END;
RUN;

PROC PRINT DATA=RECODE;
   TITLE 'Example 2';
RUN;
```

As you can see in this example, one or more WHEN statements can be placed between the SELECT and END statements. The statement following the true WHEN condition is executed. Another useful feature of the SELECT statement is to follow your last WHEN statement with an OTHERWISE statement which is executed if none of the WHEN conditions is true. There are other, more advanced, features of the SELECT statement which we do not cover here. The code above yields the same output (except for the title) as Example 1.

Example 3

> ## Using Formats to Recode a Variable
>
> *FEATURE:* FORMAT Statements in PROC Steps

Now let's get just a little fancy with code that's a little more useful and only a little more difficult to understand. In this example, you do not use a DATA step to create a new grouped variable as you did in the last example; instead, you make use of a FORMAT statement in a PROC step to achieve the desired grouping. First the code, then the explanation.

Example 3

```
PROC FORMAT;
   VALUE SCOREFMT   0-64='Fail'
                    65-69='Low Pass'
                    70-79='Pass'
                    80-89='High Pass'
                    90-HIGH='Honors';
RUN;

PROC FREQ DATA=GRADES;
   TITLE 'Example 3';
   TABLES SCORE;
   FORMAT SCORE SCOREFMT.;
RUN;
```

You first need to set up a SAS output format by using the FORMAT procedure (this is covered in greater depth in Chapter 11, "PROC FORMAT.") Any value that falls in a range of values on the left of the = sign is assigned the format on the right. It's like setting up an output translation table. (In this example, you create a format called SCOREFMT.) You then use the FORMAT statement in the frequency distribution creating procedure, the FREQ procedure, to assign the output format SCOREFMT to the variable SCORE. Since the format you are using is a grouped format, the end result is the desired grouping, or collapsing, of the original data values into your desired groups. This works because PROC FREQ groups data values based on their formatted value (if there is one).

You can also place a FORMAT statement in the DATA step used to create a SAS data set. This permanently associates a particular format to a variable in the data set. In this example, you could have associated the format SCOREFMT to the variable SCORE in the DATA step code (which is not shown in this example). Of course, the format SCOREFMT would have to have been created in a FORMAT procedure previous to the DATA step. The format SCOREFMT would then automatically be associated with the variable SCORE in all procedures which operate on the data set GRADES; you would not need to include the FORMAT statement in the procedure code. In either case, the results from the PROC FREQ code are frequency counts on the age categories as shown below:

Output from Example 3 - Using Formats to Recode a Variable

```
                                Example 3

                                    Cumulative  Cumulative
           SCORE   Frequency   Percent  Frequency    Percent
        ------------------------------------------------------
        Fail           1        11.1        1         11.1
        Low Pass       1        11.1        2         22.2
        Pass           2        22.2        4         44.4
        High Pass      1        11.1        5         55.6
        Honors         4        44.4        9        100.0
```

This example also allows us to point out other danger zones to avoid, both having to do with setting up ranges by using the FORMAT statement. First of all, always make sure that the boundaries of the ranges you set up do not overlap. If they do, PROC FORMAT will let you know about it, but it's better to be careful in the first place. Also, make sure that there are no "cracks" into which a value can fall. In other words, make sure that the ranges are totally inclusive. In this example, SCORE is an integer, and the code covers all possible values. If, however, SCORE was a computed value which could have a non-integer value, you would have to modify the FORMAT statement to eliminate the "cracks." If the scores were not integers, you could rewrite the PROC FORMAT statements like this:

```
PROC FORMAT;
    VALUE SCOREFMT  0-<65='Fail'
                    65-<70='Low Pass'
                    70-<80='Pass'
                    80-<90='High Pass'
                    90-HIGH='Honors';
    RUN;
```

See Chapter 11, "PROC FORMAT," for more details on PROC FORMAT, including information on the special range values LOW and HIGH.

Example 4

> ## Using a PUT Function to Create a New Variable
>
> *FEATURE:* Recoding with the FORMAT Statement and the PUT Function

Although the previous method (using FORMAT in a PROC step) works for the purpose illustrated without having to create a new variable, you may indeed have the need to create a new variable whose values represent the recoded values. You can, of course, use the method noted in Example 1, or you can make a minor change to the program in Example 3 to create the new variable. To do this, you employ the powerful PUT function. This function takes the form:

char_var=PUT (*arg_var*, *any_fmt*.);

This statement creates a character variable *char_var* (note that the PUT function *always* creates a character variable regardless of the format specification) whose value is the formatted value (using *any_fmt*.) of the argument variable *arg_var*. For example, the expression

```
GRADE=PUT (SCORE,SCOREFMT.);
```

creates a character variable GRADE with values of `Fail`, `Low Pass`, etc. You can then use this variable in any subsequent procedure you like. For example:

Example 4

```
DATA NEW;
   SET GRADES;
   CATEGORY=PUT (SCORE,SCOREFMT.);
RUN;

PROC PRINT DATA=NEW;
   TITLE 'Example 4';
RUN;
```

The resulting output is as follows:

Output from Example 4 - Using a PUT Function to Create a New Variable

```
                          Example 4

           OBS    ID    SCORE    CATEGORY

            1     1      55      Fail
            2     2      65      Low Pass
            3     3      74      Pass
            4     4      76      Pass
            5     5      88      High Pass
            6     6      92      Honors
            7     7      94      Honors
            8     8      96      Honors
            9     9      98      Honors
```

Look for more examples of the PUT function in Chapter 5, "Example 6."

Conclusion

You will find many occasions in which you will need to group data values for analysis. By grouping values into broader categories, you can often see relationships that are not obvious in the individual data values.

This short chapter demonstrates several methods of recoding variables. Most new programmers gravitate to the IF-THEN/ELSE method (many get stuck at IF-THEN) and never get beyond that. We strongly encourage you to experiment with all methods. Certainly try creating your own formats (after reading Chapter 11, of course) to be used along with the PUT function. We think you will find it easier to code (less typing), and it will often be more efficient as well.

Problems

2-1.   You have a SAS data set called HTWT which contains variables ID, HEIGHT, and WEIGHT. You want a crosstabulation of HEIGHT by WEIGHT, where HEIGHT and WEIGHT are to be grouped as follows (heights and weights are all integers):

$$\text{HEIGHT groupings:} \quad \begin{array}{rcl} 0 \text{ to } 36 & = & 1 \\ 37 \text{ to } 48 & = & 2 \\ 49 \text{ to } 60 & = & 3 \\ > 60 & = & 4 \end{array}$$

WEIGHT groupings: 0 to 100 = 1
101 to 200 = 2
> 200 = 3

Use all four recoding methods described in this chapter to either create a new SAS data set HTWT_2 which contains grouping variables HT_GROUP and WT_GROUP, or to do the grouping in the PROC step. Then write the code to produce the crosstabulations.

Hint: The PROC FREQ code to perform a crosstabulation of VAR_X by VAR_Y is:

```
PROC FREQ;
   TABLES VAR_X*VAR_Y;
RUN;
```

Chapter 3   SET, MERGE, and UPDATE

Reading and Combining SAS Data Sets

EXAMPLES

Introduction

In this chapter we present examples which demonstrate how to create new SAS data sets from existing ones. Each newly created data set can be:

- a subset of an old one
- a combination of multiple existing SAS data sets
- a new version (update) of an existing data set.

Different methods and different SAS statements are used to accomplish these different tasks.

The introduction of SQL (Structured Query Language) into the SAS System (via the SQL procedure) provides a whole new methodology for combining data sets, but there are still many instances in which the old tools are not only easier to use, but are actually the preferred methods. The basic statements we cover here are SET, MERGE, and UPDATE, but we also present methods using subsetting IF, as well as WHERE, statements.

Example 1

Subsetting a SAS Data Set: Selecting Observations That Meet Certain Conditions

FEATURES: SET, IN, LIBNAME, subsetting IF, and WHERE Statements, DROP and KEEP Statements and Options

Suppose you have employee records in a SAS data set EMPLOY that contains the variables ID, GENDER (1=male, 2=female), DEPT (department code), SALARY (yearly salary), YEARS (number of years employed with the firm), and STATE (2 digit state of residence code). You want to create a new SAS data set, NJEMPLOY, which is a subset of EMPLOY made up of only those employees who live in New Jersey. You want NJEMPLOY to contain all the variables from the original EMPLOY file. There are several ways to accomplish this. Here's one:

Example 1.1

```
LIBNAME MARY 'C:\EMPLOYEE\JOBDATA';

DATA NJEMPLOY;
   SET MARY.EMPLOY;
   IF STATE EQ 'NJ';
RUN;
```

Reading Observations from an Existing SAS Data Set

Before we discuss the process of selecting a subset of data, we have to talk about how you access the existing SAS data set that you are going to subset. This process is handled by the SET statement. Think of the SET statement as being similar to an INPUT statement, with the difference being that a SET statement reads records from a SAS data set while an INPUT statement reads raw data from an external file (or instream data). In this case, the data being used to create the SAS data set NJEMPLOY are being read in from the existing SAS data set EMPLOY. But what about that LIBNAME statement?

In Chapter 1, "INPUT and INFILE," you used a FILENAME statement to create a fileref (file reference). This enabled you to access raw data stored external to the code you were writing. The LIBNAME statement is similar in that it creates a libref (library reference) to refer to an external SAS data library where you store SAS data sets (along with other SAS entities). Here, the LIBNAME statement creates the libref called MARY that refers to the SAS data library called C:\EMPLOYEE\JOBDATA which contains a SAS data set called EMPLOY, possibly among other things. If it all seems a little confusing, it's because it all is a little confusing. Don't worry though; it all does make sense and will become second nature to you.

Subsetting IF Statement

When an IF statement is used in this context, it is called a subsetting IF statement. It is shorthand for, IF NOT *condition* THEN DELETE; (i.e., if this condition is true, continue processing the remaining statements in the DATA step; if not, delete this observation and return to the top of the DATA step). In this case, it stands for IF NOT (STATE EQ 'NJ') THEN DELETE;. The resulting SAS data set NJEMPLOY contains only those observations from EMPLOY where STATE is equal to NJ.

Subsetting IF statements often do the job quite adequately, but there is an alternative method called a WHERE statement. (There is also a WHERE data set option available, but this time you use the statement version.)

WHERE Statement

Here is the code to accomplish the subsetting you want by using a WHERE statement:

Example 1.2

```
LIBNAME MARY 'C:\EMPLOYEE\JOBDATA';

DATA NJEMPLOY;
    SET MARY.EMPLOY;
    WHERE STATE EQ 'NJ';
RUN;
```

Differences between IF and WHERE Statements

This program is identical to the previous example except that the subsetting IF statement is replaced with a WHERE statement. Are there important differences? Both of these programs produce identical results, but there *are* differences between IF and WHERE statements. The WHERE statement may be more efficient then the subsetting IF (especially if you are taking a very small subset from a large file) because it checks on the validity of the condition before the observation is brought into a temporary holding area, whereas the subsetting IF statement brings in the entire observation and then checks the condition to see if the observation is to be kept or not. This temporary holding area is called the program data vector (PDV). A WHERE statement can only be used with variables in the existing data set, whereas a subsetting IF statement can be used with raw data as well.

Another difference between a subsetting IF statement and a WHERE statement may surface when you use the FIRST. and LAST. logical variables (discussed in Chapter 7, "Example 4"). When the WHERE condition is not true, the observation is not brought into the PDV, and therefore it does not affect the logical values of the FIRST. and LAST. variables.

Another *major* difference between IF and WHERE statements is that you may include WHERE statements in SAS procedures! For example, if you have a data set called ALL (containing the variables ID, SEX, and SALARY), and you want a listing only for MALES (M), you could code this as:

```
PROC PRINT DATA=ALL;
    WHERE SEX = 'M';
RUN;
```

This saves you the work of creating a new data set just to obtain your listing.

WHERE Statement Operators

Before we consider variations on this example, let's discuss some of the special WHERE statement operators. Suppose you want to select only people between the ages of 20 and 40 (inclusive). There are several ways to code this using the WHERE statement. You could write:

```
WHERE AGE GE 20 AND AGE LE 40;
```

or,

```
WHERE 20 LE AGE LE 40;
```

or you could use the BETWEEN-AND operator like this:

```
WHERE AGE BETWEEN 20 AND 40;
```

The BETWEEN values can be constants (numeric or character) or expressions.
Some useful WHERE operators and their actions are as follows:

Operator	Action
BETWEEN-AND	Selects observations which fall (inclusively) within a specified range.
	Example: `WHERE AGE BETWEEN 20 AND 40;`
	Selects ages between 20 and 40 (inclusive)
CONTAINS or ?	Used for character variables only, selects records that include or contain the specified string. **Note:** The CONTAINS or ? operator is case-sensitive.
	Example: `WHERE NAME CONTAINS 'Mc';` or `WHERE NAME ? 'Mc';`
	Selects all names that contain the string `Mc`. This would match on `McGregor` and `McFly` but not on `Tomcat` because the m in `Tomcat` is in lowercase.
IS MISSING or IS NULL	Selects observations for which the value of the variable is missing. This is particularly useful since it works with both numeric and character variables.
	Example: `WHERE AGE IS MISSING;`
	Selects observations where `AGE` is missing.
	Example: `WHERE NAME IS NULL;`
	Selects observations where `NAME` is missing.

(continued on next page)

Operator	Action
LIKE	Allows you to select observations based on patterns using the percent sign (%) and underscore (_) wildcard operators.

The percent sign (%) is a variable length wildcard (like * in DOS or UNIX.) It matches on any string (including a null string).

The underscore (_) wildcard operator is a pattern match for one character only.

You may use several underscore operators and combine them with the % operator. **Note:** The LIKE operator is only used with character variables and is case sensitive.

Example: `WHERE NAME LIKE 'BOY%';`

Selects observations that start with the letters BOY followed by anything. Examples of matches are: BOY, BOYCE, BOYXYZ.

Example: `WHERE NAME LIKE 'A___;`
(**Note:** There are three underscores following the A.)

Selects all names of length 4, beginning with A.

Example: `WHERE NAME LIKE 'A_%';`

You can use % and _ in the same statement. The above line selects all names that begin with A and are at least two characters in length.

=*	A phonetic match (called a SOUNDEX operator) used for matches that "sound like" the given expression. The =* operator attempts a phonetic match based on a Soundex algorithm. It is a very powerful operator and should be used with care. It is useful for "fuzzy matches" where you suspect a name might be misspelled or you are not sure of the correct spelling of a name. **Note:** The SOUNDEX operator is *not* case sensitive.

Example: `WHERE NAME =* 'CODY';`

Given the names: CODY, Codey, KODY, Coty, and COOKY, the above line of code selects: CODY, Codey, KODY and Coty, but not COOKY.

Example: `WHERE NAME =* 'MCHENRY';`

Given the names: MCHENRY, MACHENRY, MCHENRI, and MKHENRY, the above line of code selects all the names. This is obviously an operator to be used with considerable caution.

KEEP and DROP Statements

Now let's get back to the example at hand. Let's modify this program in several ways. First, suppose that you only require the variables ID and DEPT in the new data set. You can easily accomplish this with a KEEP statement or a KEEP= data set option. First, let's see how KEEP and DROP statements work.

When you create a new data set from an old one, you may want to keep only selected variables. You have several ways to do this. A KEEP statement placed anywhere in the DATA step causes only those variables listed to be written to the newly created SAS data set. For example, if you want to keep only ID and DEPT in the new data set (and also want to do the NJ subsetting), you can do it like this:

Example 1.3

```
LIBNAME MARY 'C:\EMPLOYEE\JOBDATA';

DATA NJEMPLOY;
   SET MARY.EMPLOY;
   WHERE STATE EQ 'NJ';
   KEEP ID DEPT;
RUN;
```

Data set NJEMPLOY contains only the variables ID and DEPT and only those observations for which the STATE code is equal to NJ.

If you want to keep most of the variables from the old data set in the one you are creating, you may choose to use a DROP statement to exclude the variables you *don't* want. There is absolutely no difference between keeping the variables you want or dropping the variables you don't want. The choice usually depends on which list is shorter to write. You can replace the previous KEEP statement with the equivalent DROP statement:

```
DROP GENDER SALARY YEARS STATE;
```

Since SAS programmers (actually, all programmers that we know) don't like to type any more than necessary, the KEEP statement is the preferred one to use here. When in doubt about which to use, give the edge to the KEEP statement since it is clearer to see which variables will be in the new data set.

KEEP= and DROP= Data Set Options

An alternative to a KEEP or DROP statement is a KEEP= or DROP= data set option. The variables to be kept or dropped are listed following the data set name, in parentheses. Following is a program that produces identical results to the previous one except that it uses a KEEP= data set option instead of a KEEP statement. In this case, the data set option is more efficient than the statement version. First we show the code and then the explanation.

Example 1.4

```
LIBNAME MARY 'C:\EMPLOYEE\JOBDATA';

DATA NJEMPLOY;
   SET MARY.EMPLOY (KEEP=ID DEPT STATE);
   WHERE STATE EQ 'NJ';
   DROP STATE;
RUN;
```

The KEEP= data set option instructs the DATA step to read only the variables ID, DEPT, and STATE into the PDV (remember this stands for the program data vector) for processing. Only those variables listed in the KEEP= option list are available in the DATA step, and only those same variables are written out to the SAS data set you are creating. Using the KEEP= data set option instead of the KEEP statement allows the software to deal with fewer variables in the PDV and is therefore more efficient. (See Chapter 14, "Example 5," for more on this topic.)

Now you understand the difference between the KEEP= data set option and the KEEP statement. But why include STATE in the KEEP= data set option if you only want to keep DEPT and ID in the new data set you are building? The answer lies in the WHERE statement.

In order to test the value of STATE, the SAS System has to have it included in the PDV. If you omit STATE from the KEEP= list, the WHERE statement will not work, and the log will show you the error of your ways. Since you do not want the variable STATE in your new data set, use a DROP statement to indicate that it is not to be written to the data set NJEMPLOY.

For the last subsetting example, suppose you want to choose records from the states of NY, NJ, FL, and CA. You can do this the long way as follows:

```
WHERE STATE EQ 'NJ' OR STATE EQ 'NY' OR
      STATE EQ 'FL' OR STATE EQ 'CA';
```

or you can do it the short way like this:

```
WHERE STATE IN ('NJ','NY','FL','CA');
```

The two expressions produce identical results. (See Chapter 14, "Example 10," for a comparison of these two statements.)

The IN operator also works with numeric variables. To select observations for ID values 3, 7, and 9, you would write:

```
WHERE ID IN (3,7,9);
```

or

```
WHERE ID IN (3 7 9);
```

You may use either commas or spaces to separate the numeric values.

Example 2

Combining SAS Data Sets by Adding Observations

FEATURE: SET Statement

In this example, we show you how to add observations from one SAS data set to another SAS data set. This is a frequently encountered need. For example, you may have a data set for each year of a study and you want to analyze all years together.

For this example, suppose you have two permanent SAS data sets, SURVEY1 and SURVEY2, both stored in a SAS data library in subdirectory C:\DATA\SURVEYS, and both containing the following variables: ID, GENDER, HEIGHT, WEIGHT, YEAR.

The contents of these two data sets are as follows:

Data set SURVEY1

ID	GENDER	HEIGHT	WEIGHT	YEAR
1	1	68	155	91
7	2	72	205	90
9	1	66	120	93

Data set SURVEY2

ID	GENDER	HEIGHT	WEIGHT	YEAR
5	2	63	102	92
8	1	70	250	91

You want a single data set SURV1_2 which contains all the observations from SURVEY1 and SURVEY2, and this time you want to store it in the SAS data library SURVEYS along with SURVEY1 and SURVEY2. Here is the code:

Example 2.1

```
LIBNAME GEORGE 'C:\DATA\SURVEYS';

DATA GEORGE.SURV1_2;
   SET GEORGE.SURVEY1 GEORGE.SURVEY2;
RUN;

PROC PRINT DATA=GEORGE.SURV1_2;
   TITLE 'Combined Data Sets 1 and 2';
RUN;
```

Note that the libref GEORGE is used to refer to all three permanent SAS data sets. Results of the PROC PRINT are as follows:

Output from Example 2.1 - Combining SAS Data Sets by Adding Observations

```
                 Combined Data Sets 1 and 2

            OBS ID GENDER WEIGHT HEIGHT YEAR

             1   1    1      68    155    91
             2   7    2      72    205    90
             3   9    1      66    120    93
             4   5    2      63    102    92
             5   8    1      70    250    91
```

As you can see, the effect of including multiple data sets in a SET statement is to combine the data sets in the order in which they are listed in the SET statement. In this case, the observations of SURVEY1 are followed by those of SURVEY2. You will find other, more efficient, methods of combining data sets in Chapter 14, "Example 15."

Now let's see what happens when the two data sets do not contain identical sets of variables. Suppose you have a third data set SURVEY3 which contains ID, GENDER, HEIGHT, YEAR, and IQ (WEIGHT is not included, but a new variable, IQ is in the data set). What happens when you SET this new data set with SURVEY1? First, here are the observations from SURVEY3:

```
    Data set SURVEY3

ID GENDER HEIGHT YEAR  IQ
 5    2      63    92  120
 8    1      70    91  110
```

The program to combine SURVEY1 and SURVEY3 is almost identical to the previous program, with minor changes:

Example 2.2

```
LIBNAME GEORGE 'C:\DATA\SURVEYS';

DATA GEORGE.SURV1_3;
   SET GEORGE.SURVEY1 GEORGE.SURVEY3;
RUN;

PROC PRINT DATA=GEORGE.SURV1_3;
   TITLE 'Combined Data Sets 1 and 3';
RUN;
```

Here is the output:

Output from Example 2.2 - Combining SAS Data Sets by Adding Observations

```
                    Combined Data Sets 1 and 3

            OBS ID GENDER HEIGHT WEIGHT YEAR  IQ

             1   1   1      68    155    91    .
             2   7   2      72    205    90    .
             3   9   1      66    120    93    .
             4   5   2      63     .     92   120
             5   8   1      70     .     91   110
```

The program performs exactly as you might have expected; it contains all the variables that are contained in SURVEY1 and SURVEY3, with missing values for IQ in the observations that come from SURVEY1 and missing values for WEIGHT in the observations that come from SURVEY3. If this is not what you expected, it's time to read this section again.

Example 3

Combining SAS Data Sets by Adding Variables

FEATURE: MERGE Statement

In the previous examples you combined two data sets by adding the observations of one to the observations of the other, typically with both data sets having the same set of variables to deal with, or at least partially the same. It's sort of like visually stacking one data set on top of another and lining up the columns.

Now let's change the scenario a bit. Let's combine two data sets by adding the variables of one to the variables of the other, typically with both data sets having the same set of observations, or once again, at least partially the same. This time it's like placing one data set next to the other. Think of it like adding the variables (columns) from one data set on to the variables of the other.

We start out with perhaps the simplest merge of all. You have two data sets LEFT and RIGHT. Data set LEFT contains variables ID, HEIGHT, and WEIGHT. Data set RIGHT contains variables GENDER and RACE. Both data sets contain three observations, as follows:

```
      Data set LEFT                Data set RIGHT

   ID   HEIGHT   WEIGHT         GENDER      RACE
    1     68      155              M          B
    2     62      102              F          H
    3     72      220              M          W
```

You can combine the variables from these two data sets into a single data set simply by using the MERGE statement as follows:

Example 3

```
DATA AMBIDEX;
   MERGE LEFT RIGHT;
RUN;

PROC PRINT DATA=AMBIDEX;
   TITLE 'Simple One-to-One Merge';
RUN;
```

This code merges the variables from data set LEFT with those from data set RIGHT, one observation at a time, in the order that the observations occur in the two data sets. The resultant data set, AMBIDEX, is a "one-to-one" merge of LEFT and RIGHT. The output, as you might have guessed, looks like this:

Output from Example 3 - Combining SAS Data Sets by Adding Variables

```
                  Simple One-to-One Merge

        OBS   ID HEIGHT WEIGHT GENDER RACE

         1    1    68     155     M     B
         2    2    62     102     F     H
         3    3    72     220     M     W
```

This type of merge (one-to-one) can get you into *big* trouble and is rarely used (notice we did not say "never" — one should never say never!) It is just too "dumb" to be of much use in most real world situations. The typical need when merging data sets together is to align or match the records or observations on a matching variable, such as ID number. The obvious problem with a one-to-one match is that the process will merge records side by side, regardless if they match up or not on any matching variable. If the two data sets do not have the exact same set of observations, in the exact same order, the final merged data set will contain mismatched observations. Of course, if the data sets are properly aligned, the final merged data set will be accurate. This may well be the case, but it's a bad habit to rely on it being that way. So what's the answer? Read on.

Example 4

> ## Adding Variables from One Data Set to Another Based on an Identifying Variable
>
> *FEATURES:* MERGE and BY Statements, SORT Procedure

Now that you understand the basics of merging, let's add a BY statement which allows you to correctly match up observations from two data sets based on a common variable.

For this example, consider two SAS data sets: data set DEMOG (demographic data) contains ID, GENDER, and STATE, and is sorted by GENDER; data set EMPLOYEE contains ID, DEPT, and SALARY, and is sorted by ID. You want a composite report which lists all the variables for each employee. To do this, you have to match the records in the DEMOG data set to the corresponding records in the EMPLOYEE data set (by ID) so you can list values for GENDER and STATE along with values for DEPT and SALARY for each employee. Here are the two data sets:

```
    Data set DEMOG           Data set EMPLOYEE

ID   GENDER  STATE        ID    DEPT   SALARY

 1     M      NY           1   PARTS   21,000
 5     M      NY           2   SALES   45,000
 2     F      NJ           3   PARTS   20,000
 3     F      NJ           5   SALES   35,000
```

Notice that, although both data sets contain ID, which is the "matching" variable, the observations in the DEMOG data set are not in order by ID. If you conducted a simple one-to-one merge, you would be combining the wrong observations. You have to make sure both data sets are sorted by ID and then match-merge them. Here is the code:

Example 4.1

```
PROC SORT DATA=DEMOG;
    BY ID;
RUN;

PROC SORT DATA=EMPLOYEE;
    BY ID;
RUN;

DATA COMBINED;
    MERGE DEMOG EMPLOYEE;
    BY ID;
RUN;

PROC PRINT DATA=COMBINED;
    TITLE 'DEMOG-EMPLOYEE Match-Merged Data';
RUN;
```

You use the SORT procedure to sort both data sets by ID. Actually, in this example, the second SORT procedure (for data set EMPLOYEE) does not take place because this data set is already in ID order. In SAS Releases 6.07 and higher, a sort flag is stored with each data set, indicating if it is sorted and how. If you include a SORT procedure to sort an already sorted data set again in the same way, the sort does not take place and a note is written to the SAS log informing you of this. You use the BY statement to instruct the system to match-merge records from both data sets on the matching variable (ID). The output of the previous code is as follows:

Output from Example 4.1 - Adding Variables from One Data Set to Another Based on an Identifying Variable

```
              DEMOG-EMPLOYEE Match-Merged Data

          OBS ID GENDER STATE  DEPT    SALARY

           1   1    M     NY    PARTS   21,000
           2   2    F     NJ    SALES   45,000
           3   3    F     NJ    PARTS   20,000
           4   5    M     NY    SALES   35,000
```

As you can see, the resulting data set contains all the variables from the two merged data sets, matched by ID and occurring in ID sorted order. But what if there were a different number of observations in one of the data sets? Suppose, for example, that DEMOG contains more records than EMPLOYEE (perhaps DEMOG contains all employees ever associated with the company and EMPLOYEE only contains active employees). Let's add a record (ID=4) to DEMOG (we'll call it DEMOG2) to see what happens when there is no corresponding record in EMPLOYEE. Here are the contents of data set DEMOG2, along with data set EMPLOYEE:

Data set DEMOG2		
ID	GENDER	STATE
1	M	NY
4	M	NY
5	M	NY
2	F	NJ
3	F	NJ

Data set EMPLOYEE		
ID	DEPT	SALARY
1	PARTS	21,000
2	SALES	45,000
3	PARTS	20,000
5	SALES	35,000

You need only change the code by substituting DEMOG2 for DEMOG and making a few cosmetic changes:

Example 4.2

```
PROC SORT DATA=DEMOG2;
   BY ID;
RUN;

PROC SORT DATA=EMPLOYEE;
   BY ID;
RUN;

DATA COMBINED;
   MERGE DEMOG2 EMPLOYEE;
   BY ID;
RUN;

PROC PRINT DATA=COMBINED;
   TITLE 'DEMOG2-EMPLOYEE Match-Merged Data';
RUN;
```

Here is the new combined data set:

Output from Example 4.2 - Adding Variables from One Data Set to Another Based on an Identifying Variable

```
            DEMOG2-EMPLOYEE Match-Merged Data

            OBS ID GENDER STATE DEPT   SALARY

             1   1   M     NY    PARTS  21,000
             2   2   F     NJ    SALES  45,000
             3   3   F     NJ    PARTS  20,000
             4   4   M     NY     .
             5   5   M     NY    SALES  35,000
```

As you might have expected, the combined data set contains the data for ID number 4 from the DEMOG2 data set and missing values for DEPT and SALARY (represented by a blank for the character variable DEPT and by a period for the numeric variable SALARY).

Example 5

Controlling Which Observations are Added to the Merged Data Set

FEATURES: MERGE, Subsetting IF, BY Statements, IN= Data Set Option

Situations like the previous one in Example 4.2 are commonplace wherein you have unequal sets of observations in multiple data sets to be merged into one. If your goal is for the merged data set to contain only those observations which exist in one of the data sets being merged, all is not lost. SAS software can easily handle that by making use of special IN= variables. Let's get to the example.

Using the two files DEMOG2 and EMPLOYEE, let's see how you can control which observations get included in the merged data set. Here are the two data sets after they have been sorted:

```
Data set DEMOG2                 Data set EMPLOYEE

ID  GENDER  STATE               ID  DEPT   SALARY

 1    M     NY                   1  PARTS  21,000
 2    F     NJ                   2  SALES  45,000
 3    F     NJ                   3  PARTS  20,000
 4    M     NY                   5  SALES  35,000
 5    M     NY
```

Employee 4, which exists in the DEMOG2 data set, does not exist in the EMPLOYEE data set. When you perform a match-merge using a BY variable, the SAS System can check if an observation is being contributed from each data set in the MERGE list. For example, for ID = 1, you have an observation from both data sets; for ID = 4 you only have a contribution from the DEMOG2 data set. You can test for this as follows: (Assume you have already sorted both data sets by ID.)

Example 5.1

```
DATA BOTH;
   MERGE DEMOG2  EMPLOYEE (IN=EMP);
   BY ID;
   IF EMP=1;
RUN;
```

The variable name following the IN= data set option, EMP in this case, refers to a logical variable which will be created with a value of true (1) or false (0). As each observation is built, if EMPLOYEE has data to contribute, EMP will equal 1; if not, EMP will equal 0. These IN= variables are temporary in that they exist only during the execution of the DATA step. They are not saved with the data set(s) upon completion. In this example, EMP is true for every value of ID except for ID = 4. You use a subsetting IF (remember that?) to include only observations where EMP is true. The resulting data set BOTH contains observations for ID's 1, 2, 3, and 5 only. If you wanted to be sure that you were selecting employees which were in *both* the DEMOG2 file *and* the EMPLOYEE file, you would include an IN= option on both data sets like this:

Example 5.2

```
DATA BOTH;
   MERGE DEMOG2 (IN=DEM)  EMPLOYEE (IN=EMP);
   BY ID;
   IF DEM=1 AND EMP=1;
RUN;
```

This would ensure that the values of ID added to the new data set BOTH existed in the DEMOG2 data set *and* the EMPLOYEE data set.

Example 6

> ## Creating More Than One Data Set at a Time
>
> *FEATURES:* **MERGE and OUTPUT Statements, IN=, DATA=, and RENAME=**
> **Data Set Options**

Now let's once again change the scenario a bit. Suppose the demographic data set, DEMOG2 contains data on all employees, both active and inactive, and the EMPLOYEE data set contains data on only the active employees. You want to see *all* the data for active employees in one listing, and only the demographic data for the inactive employees in another listing. By introducing a few more tools of the SAS System, you can accomplish your goals easily. As usual, first we show you the code and then the explanation.

Example 6.1

```
PROC SORT DATA=DEMOG2;
   BY ID;
RUN;

PROC SORT DATA=EMPLOYEE;
   BY ID;
RUN;

DATA ACTIVE INACTIVE (KEEP=ID GENDER STATE);
   MERGE DEMOG2 EMPLOYEE (IN=ACT);
   BY ID;
   IF ACT=1 THEN OUTPUT ACTIVE;
              ELSE OUTPUT INACTIVE;
RUN;

PROC PRINT DATA=ACTIVE;
   TITLE 'Active Employees';
RUN;

PROC PRINT DATA=INACTIVE;
   TITLE 'Inactive Employees';
RUN;
```

Now here's what's happening in the expanded DATA step. First of all, you are creating more than one SAS data set in the same DATA step. You do this by placing both data set names in the DATA statement. You control which variables get written to each data set with KEEP= or DROP= data set options and which observations get written to each one with OUTPUT statements later in the DATA step.

ACTIVE will contain all the variables that are in DEMOG2 and EMPLOYEE, whereas INACTIVE will only contain ID, GENDER, and STATE. The IN= data set option is associated with data set EMPLOYEE and will be true (equal to 1) if a contribution is being made from the EMPLOYEE data set for a given ID.

The next feature to explain is the OUTPUT statement. By default, the end of every DATA step has an implicit OUTPUT statement in it which adds each observation to the data set(s) being built. If an actual explicit OUTPUT statement is contained anywhere in the DATA step, then each observation is added to the data set(s) being built *only* as explicitly directed by an OUTPUT statement.

The IF ACT=1 part of the IF statement can also be written in a shorthand manner as: IF ACT (since ACT is a logical variable and if true (1), will satisfy the condition of the IF statement.) If the value of ACT is 1, the subsetting IF statement instructs the system to output (add) the observation being built to the ACTIVE data set only, not to the INACTIVE data set. This will only be the case when EMPLOYEE adds data to the observation. In other words, the ACTIVE data set will only contain observations for those records found in EMPLOYEE. If the condition is not true (no data came from EMPLOYEE, only from DEMOG2), then ACT will be false (equal to 0) and the observation being built will only be output to the INACTIVE data set.

There is also something of importance to note here in the PROC PRINT statements. You must explicitly tell the system which data set to print with the DATA= option. By default (no DATA= option), the PRINT procedure operates on the last data set created in the code. Since you are creating more than one data set, you have to be explicit. Here is the output:

Output from Example 6.1 - Creating More Than One Data Set at a Time

```
                       Active Employees


          OBS ID GENDER STATE DEPT     SALARY

           1    1    M      NY    PARTS    21,000
           2    2    F      NJ    SALES    45,000
           3    3    F      NJ    PARTS    20,000
           4    5    M      NY    SALES    35,000


                     Inactive Employees


                OBS ID GENDER STATE


                 1    4    M      NJ
```

What If the BY Variable Has a Different Name in Each Data Set?

Let's throw another monkey wrench into the mix. Suppose you have to merge two data sets on a common identifier, but this identifier has a different variable name in each of the two data sets. Let's say you have a variable called EMP_ID in data set ONE and a variable called EMP_NUM in data set TWO. They both represent employee identification numbers but have different variable names. Since you need to have the same variable name in both data sets to use as a BY variable, you have to change one of the names. Easy. Here's how: (let's assume that the two data sets are already sorted, ONE by EMP_ID and TWO by EMP_NUM.)

Example 6.2

```
DATA COMBINED;
   MERGE ONE TWO (RENAME=(EMP_NUM=EMP_ID));
   BY EMP_ID;
RUN;
```

As you can see, the solution is to use the RENAME=(*old_name=new_name*) data set option following the data set name containing the variable to be renamed. The renaming is temporary for data set TWO in this case since it is not being output; it is only serving as input to the merging process being used to build data set COMBINED. Data set COMBINED contains a variable called EMP_ID; it does not contain a variable called EMP_NUM. All of the data set options are placed in parentheses. In addition, some of the options such as RENAME= have the list of old and new variable names in their own set of parentheses. Be careful with the parentheses.

Chapter 4, "Table Lookup," contains examples of merging with more than one BY variable. You may also want to refer to *SAS Language: Reference, Version 6, First Edition,* or *SAS Language and Procedures: Usage, Version 6, First Edition* to see the effects of multiple values of the BY variable(s) in one or both of the data sets to be merged.

Merging Data Sets That Contain Variables with the Same Name, Not Used as BY Variables

Time for one more complication before getting on to the last topic in this chapter. If both data sets being merged contain a variable of the same name other than the BY variable, the rule is that the variable in question in the resulting merged data set will take on values from the last data set named in the MERGE statement. This potentially can present a problem if there are missing values in the last named data set. There are numerous ways to code around this problem, such as using the RENAME= data set option to keep both versions of the duplicated variable by renaming one of them, or by using a series of IF-THEN/ELSE statements to check on missing values. There is one specialized situation, however, where the SAS System provides a method that deals with this, as well as other possible problems. This is covered in later examples in this chapter.

Example 7

> ### Performing "Fuzzy" Merges
>
> *FEATURES:* "Fuzzy" Merges, SOUNDEX Function, Merging with Two BY Variables, IN= Option

The present example is slightly more advanced than others in this book, and it covers a somewhat esoteric topic. You may want to skip it for now (or forever), and that's just fine.

We use the term "fuzzy" in this example to refer to the merging of similar but not exact matches between two files. The most common use for "fuzzy" merges is when you use a name as the matching variable. In this example, we merge data from two files, using similar sounding names, and date of birth as the matching variables. SAS System Releases 6.07 and higher support a SOUNDEX function which follows the algorithm described in D. E. Knuth's book, "The Art of Computer Programming, Volume 3. Sorting and Searching," Reading, MA: Addison-Wesley. This algorithm discards most vowels and substitutes numbers for groups of like-sounding consonants. The result is that like-sounding words or names will translate to the same SOUNDEX description.

In the following program, you use the SOUNDEX function to translate the names in both data sets to their SOUNDEX equivalents and then merge the two data sets by the SOUNDEX name and the date of birth. The use of another variable such as date of birth is necessary since there may be too many like-sounding names in the two data sets to be merged, but it would be unlikely to have like-sounding names with the same date of birth in both data sets. Depending on the size of the two files, you may need to use additional variables to add in the merge.

Data sets ONE and TWO are used to illustrate a "fuzzy" merge.

```
         Data set ONE                    Data set TWO

   NAME      DOB      HEIGHT       NAME       DOB      WEIGHT

   CODY    10/21/46     68       MCKLEARY   9/01/55    200
   CLARK    5/01/40     70       COTY      10/21/46    152
   CLARKE   5/10/45     72       CLARK      7/02/60    160
   ALBERT  10/01/46     69       ALBIRT    10/01/46    200
                                 CLARKE     5/01/40    210
```

The program is shown next:

Example 7

```
DATA ONE_TEMP;
   SET ONE (RENAME=(NAME=NAME_ONE));
   S_NAME = SOUNDEX(NAME_ONE);
RUN;

DATA TWO_TEMP;
   SET TWO (RENAME=(NAME=NAME_TWO));
   S_NAME = SOUNDEX(NAME_TWO);
RUN;

PROC SORT DATA=ONE_TEMP;
   BY S_NAME DOB;
RUN;

PROC SORT DATA=TWO_TEMP;
   BY S_NAME DOB;
RUN;

PROC PRINT DATA=ONE_TEMP NOOBS;
   TITLE 'Data Set ONE_TEMP';
RUN;

PROC PRINT DATA=TWO_TEMP NOOBS;
   TITLE 'Data Set TWO_TEMP';
RUN;

DATA BOTH;
   MERGE ONE_TEMP (IN=ONE)
         TWO_TEMP (IN=TWO);
   BY S_NAME DOB;
   IF ONE = 1 AND TWO = 1;
   FORMAT DOB MMDDYY8.;
RUN;

PROC PRINT DATA=BOTH NOOBS;
   TITLE 'Data Set BOTH';
RUN;
```

You start out by creating two new data sets, ONE_TEMP and TWO_TEMP, from the two data sets you want to merge, ONE and TWO. Each of the new data sets contains all the variables from the original plus a new variable, S_NAME, which is the SOUNDEX equivalent of NAME.

You rename the variable NAME in each of the data sets (to NAME_ONE and NAME_TWO) so that you can maintain the original names from the original data sets and, thereby, see which names were actually matched. If you did not rename the variable NAME, then only the value of NAME from data set TWO would remain in the merged data set. The new data sets are used for your merging process but are not saved.

Here are the two data sets ONE_TEMP and TWO_TEMP followed by the resulting merged data:

```
                Data Set ONE_TEMP

NAME_ONE     DOB      HEIGHT    S_NAME

ALBERT     10/01/46    69       A4163
CODY       10/21/46    68       C3
CLARK      05/01/40    70       C462
CLARKE     05/10/45    72       C462


                Data Set TWO_TEMP

NAME_TWO     DOB      WEIGHT    S_NAME

ALBIRT     10/01/46    200      A4163
COTY       10/21/46    152      C3
CLARKE     05/01/40    210      C462
CLARK      07/02/60    160      C462
MCKLEARY   09/01/55    200      M246


                   Data Set BOTH

NAME_ONE     DOB     HEIGHT   S_NAME   NAME_TWO   WEIGHT

ALBERT     10/01/46    69     A4163    ALBIRT      200
CODY       10/21/46    68     C3       COTY        152
CLARK      05/01/40    70     C462     CLARKE      210
```

There are three matches between these two data sets where both the SOUNDEX equivalent and the date of birth are the same.

Keep in mind that this program is only an example of how to match observations from multiple files on inexact criteria and is only intended to serve as a model of how "fuzzy" matching is performed. You can expect a certain percentage of incorrect matches with procedures such as this, and careful testing must be performed to determine how to perform such a matching task.

Example 8

> ## Updating a Master File from a Transaction File
>
> *FEATURE:* UPDATE Statement

The UPDATE statement is designed to update a master data set from a transaction data set. An example of a master data set would be a data set containing all employee records or a data set of product numbers, descriptions, inventory levels, and prices. A typical transaction data set would contain only the information to identify the record to be updated and the new updated information; for example, a product number and the new price. An update would be accomplished by substituting the new information in the transaction file for the old information in the master file.

One main difference between the UPDATE and MERGE statements is that if there is a missing value for a variable in the transaction data set, that variable is untouched in the master data set. Things can get messy when there are multiple values of the BY variable(s) in either the master data set, the transaction data set, or both, so we will stick to basic examples.

Suppose you have a master and a transaction data set, both of which contain the variables ID, DEPT, and SALARY. Contents of the data sets are as follows:

```
    Data set MASTER            Data set TRANS

ID   DEPT    SALARY        ID   DEPT    SALARY

1    PARTS   13,000        2            22,000
2    PERSON  21,000        3    SALES   24,000
3    PARTS   15,000        5    RECORDS
4    EXEC    55,000
5            18,000
```

You want to apply the transaction data set to the master data set to update the records. If you assume the records are already sorted by ID, you can write:

Example 8.1

```
DATA NEWMAST;
   UPDATE MASTER TRANS;
   BY ID;
RUN;

PROC PRINT DATA=NEWMAST;
   TITLE 'Updated Data Set - NEWMAST';
RUN;
```

The syntax is obvious. The new data set created, NEWMAST, is the old data set, MASTER, updated with the data from TRANS. Output is as follows:

Output from Example 8.1 - Updating a Master File from a Transaction File

```
              Updated Data Set - NEWMAST

              OBS ID DEPT     SALARY

               1   1  PARTS    13,000
               2   2  PERSON   22,000
               3   3  SALES    24,000
               4   4  EXEC     55,000
               5   5  RECORDS  18,000
```

Notice that observations 1 and 4 in the original MASTER data set are unchanged since these ID's are not present in the TRANS data set. In observation 2, the value for SALARY in the TRANS data set (22,000) replaced the corresponding value in the MASTER data set (21,000). The missing value for DEPT in observation 2 of the TRANS data set did not, however, replace the corresponding value for DEPT in the MASTER data set. In observation 3, both values in the TRANS data set replaced the corresponding values in the MASTER data set. In observation 5, the TRANS data set value of RECORDS for variable DEPT replaced the originally missing value in the MASTER data set, while the missing TRANS data set value for SALARY did not replace the MASTER value (18,000).

If a value of the BY variable (ID) is present in the transaction data set which is not present in the master data set, the new observation will be added to the new master data set. For example, if MASTER and TRANS were as follows:

```
    Data set MASTER                  Data set TRANS

ID     DEPT    SALARY            ID     DEPT    SALARY

1     PARTS    13,000            2               22,000
2     PERSON   21,000            3     SALES     24,000
3     PARTS    15,000            5     RECORDS
4     EXEC     55,000            9     SUMMER    10,000
5              18,000
```

The resulting data set, NEWMAST, would contain:

```
Data set NEWMAST

ID  DEPT     SALARY

 1  PARTS    13,000
 2  PERSON   22,000
 3  SALES    24,000
 4  EXEC     55,000
 5  RECORDS  18,000
 9  SUMMER   10,000
```

If a transaction data set has fewer variables than a master data set, the update process only affects the variables contained in the transaction data set and leaves the remainder of the variables in the master data set unchanged. Suppose data set TRANS only held data for ID and SALARY, as follows:

```
Data set MASTER                Data set TRANS

ID  DEPT     SALARY            ID   SALARY

 1  PARTS    13,000             2   22,000
 2  PERSON   21,000             3   24,000
 3  PARTS    15,000             5
 4  EXEC     55,000             9   10,000
 5           18,000
```

The result would be that DEPT would be left unchanged, and SALARY would be updated.

```
Data set NEWMAST

ID  DEPT     SALARY

 1  PARTS    13,000
 2  PERSON   22,000
 3  PARTS    24,000
 4  EXEC     55,000
 5           18,000
 9           10,000
```

Notice that the new observation, ID=9, is added to NEWMAST. If a transaction data set has more variables than a master data set, the update process adds the additional variables to the updated data set. Suppose data set TRANS contained data for a new variable, GENDER, in addition to updated data for old variables, as follows:

Data set MASTER				Data set TRANS			
ID	DEPT	SALARY		ID	DEPT	SALARY	GENDER
1	PARTS	13,000		1			M
2	PERSON	21,000		2		22,000	F
3	PARTS	15,000		3	SALES	24,000	M
4	EXEC	55,000		4			F
5		18,000		5	RECORDS		M

The variable GENDER, along with its values, is added to NEWMAST as follows:

Data set NEWMAST

ID	DEPT	SALARY	GENDER
1	PARTS	13,000	M
2	PERSON	22,000	F
3	SALES	24,000	M
4	EXEC	55,000	F
5	RECORDS	18,000	M

Until now, you have always been using a transaction data set called TRANS to update a master data set called MASTER, and you have been keeping the updated data in a new data set called NEWMAST. This is not absolutely necessary, however. The following code will update data set MASTER "in place":

Example 8.2

```
DATA MASTER;
   UPDATE MASTER TRANS;
   BY ID;
RUN;

PROC PRINT DATA=MASTER;
   TITLE 'Updated Data Set - MASTER';
RUN;
```

There is always some risk of losing data when using this "in place" method of updating, and in a true production environment, you would probably want to use a backup scheme incorporated into your update process.

Conclusion

In this chapter, you have seen several ways of extracting selected variables and/or records from an existing SAS data set and how to combine data from multiple data sets. You will find these techniques are powerful, useful, and used frequently. In the next chapter, we show how merging can be used to perform table lookup, but now it's time for practice. Here are the problems:

Problems

3-1. You have three data sets, ONE, TWO, and THREE. Each data set contains the variables ID, SEX, DOB, and SALARY. In addition, data set TWO contains TAXRATE and WITHHOLD; data set THREE contains HEIGHT and WEIGHT. Some sample observations are shown below:

```
                Data set ONE

    ID  SEX    DOB      SALARY
    1    M   10/21/46   70000
    2    F   11/01/55   68000
    7    M   01/27/59   47000


                Data set TWO

    ID  SEX    DOB      SALARY   TAXRATE   WITHHOLD
    3    F   01/01/33   78000      .36      23000
    5    M   03/07/29   37000      .25       9000


               Data set THREE

    ID  SEX    DOB      SALARY  HEIGHT   WEIGHT
    4    M   10/23/49   65000     68       158
    6    F   07/04/65   55000     74       202
```

Write a program to create a single SAS data set ALL which combines the observations from data sets ONE, TWO, and THREE and contains the variables ID, DOB, and SALARY. A listing of the resulting data set is shown below:

```
            Data set ALL

    ID    DOB      SALARY
    1   10/21/46   70000
    2   11/01/55   68000
    3   01/01/33   78000
    4   10/23/49   65000
    5   03/07/29   37000
    6   07/04/65   55000
    7   01/27/59   47000
```

3-2. Using the data sets in Problem 3-1, write a program to create a new SAS data set for those people born on or before January 1, 1960, and who earn $50,000 or more per year. For this problem, assume that data set TWO uses the variable name IDNUM instead of ID. You may want to refer to "Example 2" in Chapter 6, "SAS Dates," to see how to use a SAS date literal before starting this problem.

3-3. You have a SAS data set, MASTER, which contains records on all your employees. Included in the data set are ID, LASTNAME, FIRSTNAM, GENDER, and AGE. You want to find the name of an employee, but you can only remember that his last name ends in 'fly' and you know he is at least 40 years old.

Data set MASTER

ID	LASTNAME	FIRSTNAM	GENDER	AGE
12	Butterfly	Roger	M	57
39	Cline	Grove	M	44
23	McFly	Clive	M	42
34	Lane	Alice	F	35
44	Hopperfly	Frank	M	21
77	Elfly	Leslie	M	64
13	Kline	Mary	F	29

a) Write a program that will list all the possible names meeting these criteria.

b) Using the same data set, write a program to extract all last names that sound like "Klein" and with first names beginning with 'G' followed by 4 other letters. (Yes, we know this sounds ridiculous but we want to give you some practice with the WHERE operators.)

3-4. You have two SAS data sets. Data set DEMOG contains ID, DOB, and GENDER; data set SCORES contains SSN (which is equivalent to ID in data set DEMOG), IQ, and GPA (grade point average). Write a program to compute the mean IQ and GPA for each value of GENDER. Do this for all the data and then for employees born before January 1, 1972. Some sample data are displayed below: (Please refer to Chapter 10 for examples using the MEANS procedure.)

```
        Data set DEMOG                    Data set SCORES

     ID        DOB     GENDER        SSN         IQ      GPA

 101-45-2343  10/01/44    M      104-38-6686    110      3.9
 123-45-6789  09/13/77    F      788-77-7777    120      3.7
 104-38-6686  12/25/46    M      123-45-6789    106      3.8
 111-22-3333  02/02/89    F      101-45-2343    115      2.9
 555-55-5555  03/03/35    F      666-66-6666    118      3.8
 666-66-6666  12/04/42    F
```

Notes: 1. Data are not in ID order.
 2. There are some IDs that are in one file only.

3-5. You have a MASTER file which contains PART (part number), NUMBER (number in stock), PRICE, and SIZE. The file is sorted by PART. You want to update this file as follows:

For PART 222, you now have 15 in stock.
For PART 123, you have a new price of $1,500.
For PART 333, you have a new price of $2,000 and 20 in stock.

```
        Data set MASTER

PART    NUMBER    PRICE    SIZE
111       34       8000     A
123       87       1200     B
124       45        800     A
222       19       1300     C
234       20       2000     A
333       30       1800     B
```

Chapter 4   Table Lookup Tools

Relating Information from Multiple Sources

EXAMPLES

Introduction

Table lookup is a name given to the process of relating information from multiple sources. An example of a table lookup would be looking up a part description from a lookup table containing part numbers and descriptions, given a part number in another file which did not contain a part description. Some of the table lookup techniques we demonstrate here are based on merging techniques you learned in the last chapter. Here, we extend these techniques to multiple BY variables and introduce alternative ways of performing table lookup that do not use merging.

Example 1

Simple Table Lookup (Method 1 - Merging)

FEATURES: MERGE (including IN= Option) and Subsetting IF Statements

Suppose you have a table of part numbers and descriptions in a SAS data set called PARTS. (Assume this data set is already sorted by PART_NO.) You want to read a part number from a data set called INVOICE and add the variable PARTNAME from the PARTS data set to your INVOICE data set. First, here are the two data sets:

```
     Data Set PARTS              Data Set INVOICE
   (Sorted by PART_NO)


 PART_NO   PARTNAME      INV_NO  PART_NO  COMPANY  QUANTITY

   123     HAMMER          1       123      ABC       3
   232     PLIERS          1       333      ABC       2
   333     SAW             2       999      TOPHAT    2
   432     NAILS           3       432      XYZ       20
   587     SCREWS
```

You can use a MERGE statement to perform the lookup as follows:

Example 1

```
PROC SORT DATA=INVOICE;
   BY PART_NO;
RUN;

DATA LOOKUP1;
   MERGE INVOICE (IN=INCLUDE) PARTS;
   BY PART_NO;
   IF INCLUDE = 1;
   IF PARTNAME = ' ' THEN PARTNAME = 'NOT ENTERED';
RUN;

PROC PRINT DATA=LOOKUP1;
   TITLE 'Resulting File';
RUN;
```

Output from the PRINT procedure is shown next:

Output From Example 1 - Simple Table Lookup (Method 1 - Merging)

			Resulting File		
OBS	INV_NO	PART_NO	COMPANY	QUANTITY	PARTNAME
1	1	123	ABC	3	HAMMER
2	1	333	ABC	2	SAW
3	3	432	XYZ	20	NAILS
4	2	999	TOPHAT	2	NOT ENTERED

This program merges the two SAS data sets, PARTS and INVOICE, using the variable PART_NO as the BY variable. Notice that we first sort the INVOICE data set by PART_NO since it is necessary that both data sets be sorted by the same variable. The PARTS data set was previously sorted, and there is no sense in wasting CPU cycles in sorting it again. (Remember that in SAS System Releases 6.07 and higher, a sort flag is set when a data set is sorted, and a redundant SORT procedure will *not* be executed.) The IN= option assures you that only invoiced items (those in the INVOICE data set) will be kept. (See Chapter 3, "SET, MERGE, and UPDATE," for a more detailed explanation of the MERGE statement.) To denote the case where a PART_NO value in the INVOICE data set is not in the PARTS data set, you substitute the term NOT ENTERED for your missing value.

Example 2

> ### Simple Table Lookup (Method 2 - Formats)
>
> *FEATURES:* **PROC FORMAT and PUT Function**

You can accomplish the same goal as the previous example did by using a format and a PUT function instead of merging the PARTS data set and the INVOICE data set. The code looks like this:

Example 2

```
PROC FORMAT;
   VALUE PARTDESC
      123 = 'HAMMER'
      232 = 'PLIERS'
      333 = 'SAW'
      432 = 'NAILS'
      587 = 'SCREWS'
      OTHER = 'NOT ENTERED';
RUN;

DATA LOOKUP2;
   SET INVOICE;
   PARTNAME = PUT (PART_NO,PARTDESC.);
RUN;

PROC PRINT DATA=LOOKUP2;
   TITLE 'Resulting File';
RUN;
```

The resulting listing is identical to the last output except that the order of the observations is different since the technique shown here did not require the INVOICE data set to be sorted by PART_NO. This has two advantages: first, you save some CPU time; second, you maintain the INVOICE data set in its original order (by invoice number for example). The PUT function (described in Chapter 5, "Example 6," and in Chapter 2, "Example 4") assigns the formatted value for PART_NO to the variable PARTNAME. (See Chapter 11, "PROC FORMAT," for an explanation of the FORMAT procedure.) In a real inventory system, the format PARTDESC would probably be made permanent and stored in a permanent format library.

As you will see in Chapter 11, "Example 11," if you have a large number of part numbers and descriptions where creating the desired format would be tedious, you can create the format by reading part numbers and descriptions from a raw file or from a SAS data set, and requesting the SAS System to create the format for you using what is called a control data set.

Example 3

> ## Looking Up Two Variables (Method 1 - Merging)
>
> *FEATURES:* MERGE (including IN= Option) and Subsetting IF Statements

Let's extend Example 1 by looking up a unit price as well as a product description, then multiplying the price by the quantity ordered to obtain a value for TOTAL. First, include PRICE (a numeric variable) in the PARTS data set:

```
        Data set PARTS
     (Sorted by PART_NO)
```

PART_NO	PARTNAME	PRICE
123	HAMMER	25.00
232	PLIERS	8.50
333	SAW	18.00
432	NAILS	.01
587	SCREWS	.05

The program to look up the part description and price is shown next:

Example 3

```
PROC SORT DATA=INVOICE;
   BY PART_NO;
RUN;

DATA LOOKUP1;
   MERGE INVOICE (IN=INCLUDE) PARTS;
   BY PART_NO;
   IF INCLUDE = 1;
   IF PARTNAME=' ' THEN PARTNAME='NOT ENTERED';
   TOTAL = QUANTITY * PRICE;
    FORMAT TOTAL DOLLAR6.2;
RUN;

PROC PRINT DATA=LOOKUP1;
   TITLE 'Resulting File';
RUN;
```

Output from the PROC PRINT is shown next:

Output from Example 3 - Looking Up Two Variables (Method 1 - Merging)

```
                           Resulting File

OBS    INV_NO    PART_NO    COMPANY    QUANTITY    PARTNAME      PRICE    TOTAL

 1       1         123       ABC          3        HAMMER        25.00   $75.00
 2       1         333       ABC          2        SAW           18.00   $36.00
 3       2         432       XYZ         20        NAILS          0.01    $0.20
 4       3         999       TOPHAT       2        NOT ENTERED
```

The first step in this example, as it was in Example 1, is to sort the INVOICE data set by PART_NO. (Remember that the PARTS data set was previously sorted.) As was done before, the IN= option is used to output only those observations in the merged data set for which an INVOICE is written and missing values for PARTNAME are replaced with the text NOT ENTERED. The total price (TOTAL) for each item is simply QUANTITY times (unit) PRICE. Finally, the DOLLAR6.2 format is applied to TOTAL so that it prints with dollar signs and commas.

Since part number 999 made by the TOPHAT company is not in the PARTS data set, there is a missing value for PRICE, and therefore for TOTAL as well.

Example 4

Looking Up Two Variables (Method 2 - Formats)

FEATURES: **Table Lookup, PROC FORMAT, PUT and INPUT Functions**

You can use the same approach as was used in Example 2 to solve the previous problem by creating another format to associate the prices with the corresponding parts. However, formatted values are always character variables, and you need a numeric variable for PRICE so that you can multiply it by QUANTITY to get TOTAL. One more function (INPUT) and you're done:

Example 4

```
PROC FORMAT;
   VALUE PARTDESC
   123 = 'HAMMER'
   232 = 'PLIERS'
   333 = 'SAW'
   432 = 'NAILS'
   587 = 'SCREWS'
   OTHER = 'NOT ENTERED';
   VALUE PRICE
   123 = '25'
   232 = '8.50'
   333 = '18'
   432 = '.01'
   587 = '.05'
   OTHER = ' ';
RUN;

DATA LOOKUP2;
   SET INVOICE;
   PARTNAME = PUT (PART_NO,PARTDESC.);
   PRICE = INPUT (PUT(PART_NO,PRICE.),5.);
   TOTAL = QUANTITY * PRICE;
   FORMAT TOTAL DOLLAR6.2;
RUN;

PROC PRINT DATA=LOOKUP2;
   TITLE 'Resulting File';
RUN;
```

The output is shown next:

Output from Example 4 - Looking Up Two Variables (Method 2 - Formats)

```
                            Resulting File

 OBS   INV_NO   PART_NO   COMPANY   QUANTITY   PARTNAME      PRICE     TOTAL

  1      1        123      ABC          3       HAMMER        25.00    $75.00
  2      1        333      ABC          2       SAW           18.00    $36.00
  3      2        432      XYZ         20       NAILS          0.01     $0.20
  4      3        999      TOPHAT       2       NOT ENTERED
```

Although the PUT and INPUT functions are described in Chapter 5, "SAS Functions," we briefly explain the use of the INPUT function in this example. The result of the PUT function is a string which is the character representation of the price of each item (technically called a numeral). The INPUT function instructs the system to take the value of the first argument (PUT(PART_NO,PRICE.)) and "read it again" according to the informat listed as the second argument (5.). Therefore, the value of PUT (PART_NO,PRICE.) is a character string such as 25.00; the result of the line, INPUT (PUT(PART_NO,PRICE.),5.) is then number 25. After reading this paragraph a few times (and maybe taking a walk around the block a few times), if things are still unclear, wait until Chapter 5, "Example 6," for a more detailed explanation (it's the next chapter!).

Example 5

A Two-way Lookup Table

FEATURE: **MERGE Statement Using Two BY Variables**

For this example you have two SAS data sets. DAILY contains subject ID number, YEAR, SEASON, and RAINFALL; TEMP contains TEMPER (mean temperature), YEAR, and SEASON.

Here are some sample data:

		DAILY				TEMP	
ID	YEAR	SEASON	RAINFALL		YEAR	SEASON	TEMPER
1	1989	SUMMER	20		1989	WINTER	28
2	1990	FALL	15		1989	SPRING	52
3	1990	SUMMER	25		1989	SUMMER	80
4	1989	WINTER	11		1989	FALL	63
					1990	WINTER	33
					1990	SPRING	56
					1990	SUMMER	78
					1990	FALL	65

You want to read the DAILY data set, look up the temperature in the TEMP data set corresponding to the matching YEAR and SEASON, and create a new data set called COMBINED. Here is the code:

Example 5

```
PROC SORT DATA=TEMP;
   BY YEAR SEASON;
RUN;

PROC SORT DATA=DAILY;
   BY YEAR SEASON;
RUN;

DATA COMBINED;
   MERGE DAILY (IN=INDAILY) TEMP;
   BY YEAR SEASON;
   IF INDAILY;
RUN;

PROC PRINT DATA=COMBINED;
   TITLE 'Listing of the Combined Data Set';
RUN;
```

The resulting output is:

Output from Example 5 - A Two-way Lookup Table

```
            Listing of the Combined Data Set

     OBS    ID    YEAR    SEASON    RAIN    TEMPER

      1      1    1989    SUMMER     20       80
      2      4    1989    WINTER     11       28
      3      2    1990    FALL       15       65
      4      3    1990    SUMMER     25       78
```

By match-merging the two data sets on the variables YEAR and SEASON, you are able to associate the mean temperature with the amount of rainfall for each year-season combination. In this example, it's ambiguous as to which data set serves as the lookup table and which one serves as the data. Usually, a lookup table has one record for each unique value of the lookup variable. In this case, they both do.

Conclusion

Now when you hear the term "table lookup," you will realize that it is a fairly simple process and you have two alternate approaches, using MERGE statements or formats, to accomplish your goal. Merging techniques are very straightforward and usually quite easy to accomplish. Creating a format may be a bit more work but is usually more efficient, especially if you can avoid sorting large files.

Problems

4-1. You have company data in three SAS data sets. Data set EMPLOY contains ID (employee number), GENDER, and DOB (date of birth). Data set PARTS contains PART_NO and PRICE. Data set SALES contains ID (employee number), TRANS (transaction number), PART_NO, and QUANTITY (for each sales call completed). You want to generate reports which contain:

a. a listing, sorted by ID, showing ID, the transaction number, and the total sales for each transaction.

b. a summary showing the total sales for each employee.

c. a summary showing the total company sales for each GENDER.

Here are some sample data values from each data set: Note that data set EMPLOY is already sorted in ID order and data set PARTS is already sorted in PART_NO order.

```
Data Set EMPLOY        Data Set PARTS        Data Set SALES

ID  GENDER  DOB      PART_NO  PRICE     ID TRANS PART_NO QUANTITY
01    F    10/21/46    123     15       03   1    234       5
02    F    09/02/44    234     25       03   1    123       9
03    M    04/23/55    237     20       03   2    237       4
04    F    11/11/38    355     28       01   1    355       5
                       789     55       01   1    234       3
                                        01   1    123       9
                                        01   2    355       5
                                        02   1    237      11
```

Hints: Since this is a difficult problem, let us suggest a few hints. First, merge the PARTS and SALES data sets to create a new data set (call it NEWSALES) that contains ID, TRANS, and TOTAL (PRICE*QUANTITY). Notice that there are some part numbers in the PARTS file that were not sold and need not be included in the listing. This is enough for part A.

Next, merge the NEWSALES data set just created with the EMPLOY data set so that GENDER information can be added. Consider using PROC MEANS to compute totals by ID for part B, and totals by GENDER for part C. You can accept output from PROC MEANS or, if you want to be fancy, create a report from an output data set created by PROC MEANS (discussed in Chapter 10, "PROC MEANS and PROC UNIVARIATE"). We show both solutions.

4-2. You have clinical data in a SAS data set called CLINICAL which contains information on patient visits. Included in the data set are patient ID, DATE, BILLING (billing number), and DX (diagnosis code). You also have a list of DX codes and their descriptions. Using the following CLINICAL data and the list of DX codes and descriptions, create a new data set, NEW, which contains all the variables in CLINICAL plus a new variable (DESCRIP) which contains the DX description. Use PROC FORMAT and a PUT function as in Example 2 to solve this problem.

```
Data Set CLINICAL                DX Code Descriptions

ID    DATE    BILLING   DX        DX    Description
01  01/02/94    123      3         1    Cold
02  01/02/94    127      6         2    Flu
03  01/03/94    231      4         3    Asthma
04  01/03/94    344      3         4    Chest Pain
05  01/04/94    765      1         5    Maternity
                                   6    Diabetes
```

Chapter 5

SAS® Functions

Data Translation Tools

EXAMPLES

Introduction

You have seen how to create SAS data sets and various ways of combining multiple data sets. In this chapter, you see how to use SAS System functions to modify values of existing variables and to create new variables in the DATA step. There are virtually limitless applied uses for SAS System functions. We demonstrate a few examples in this chapter, including the following representative situations:

- You may want to compute AGE as a variable in a DATA step and represent its values as of the last birthday by dropping any fractional part of AGE. SAS functions can handle this as well as many more arithmetic manipulations readily.
- You may want to compute the average of several variables in a data set or find the largest and smallest value of a variable. SAS functions can do this as well as a vast number of other statistical calculations.
- You may want to write a program to help you choose a lottery number. The SAS System provides you with several functions that can generate random numbers.
- You may want to remove specific characters from a character variable, convert one set of characters to another, or create a new variable whose value is a specific part of a larger value. The SAS System provides a large collection of very powerful string functions that can manipulate character variables.
- You may want to convert back and forth between character and numeric values. The SAS System provides ample tools for these conversions.

There are so many useful functions for manipulating SAS dates and times that we have devoted a separate chapter just for them. (See Chapter 6, "SAS Date Functions".) This chapter covers some of the other useful and frequently used functions. We describe some of the simpler functions first, followed by some of the more powerful and/or complex ones later. Even if you don't plan to use a particular function, studying the examples in this chapter will allow you to use many of the other SAS functions not covered here. A complete list of SAS functions can be found in the manual, *SAS Language: Reference, Version 6, First Edition.*

Example 1

Mathematical Transformations of Numeric Variables

FEATURES: **LOG, ARSIN, and SQRT Functions**

Suppose you have a SAS data set (HOSP) which contains LOS (length of stay) and PROP (proportion of the time spent in bed). Many hospital patients spend a relatively short time (about a week) in the hospital, but there are some patients who spend several months or more. To compare length of stay among different treatments or diagnoses, some statistical tests require that something be done with the extreme values (called outliers). (Actually, when the variable in question is AGE, we have outliers and outright liars.)

One way to "pull in" distributions of variables like length of stay is to take the logarithm of the value and use this in the analysis. With this in mind, let's assume that you want to create two new variables. One will be the natural (base *e*) logarithm of LOS; the other, a popular transformation of a proportion called the arcsine square-root *x* transform. This latter transformation involves first taking the square-root of a value, and then taking the arcsine of the result. Here is the SAS code:

Example 1

```
DATA TRANSFRM;
   SET HOSP;
   LOGLOS=LOG (LOS);
   XPROP=ARSIN (SQRT(PROP));
RUN;
```

The general syntax for a SAS function is the function name followed by one or more arguments in parentheses. Even a function like TODAY(), which returns the current SAS date and which actually has no arguments, is followed by a set of parentheses. Notice in the example above that a function can have as its main argument the result of another function.

Example 2

> ## Choosing Every *n*th Observation from a SAS Data Set
>
> *FEATURES:* MOD Function and _N_ (Observation Counter)

Here is an example where you find a useful application of the MOD function. Most people would skip right over this function when reading their SAS manuals, hardly remembering that they once knew what a modulus was (eleventh grade math?). To review, a number *n* modulo *m*, is the remainder when *n* is divided by *m*. For instance, 5 mod 3 is 2 (when you divide 5 by 3, you get 1 with a remainder of 2). And 17 mod 3 is also 2 (3 goes into 17 five times with a remainder of 2). How is this useful? Suppose you want to select every third observation from a SAS data set. The very simple code following, using the MOD function, does just that:

Example 2

```
DATA THIRD;
   SET OLD;
   IF MOD (_N_,3)=1;
RUN;
```

The function MOD(*n,m*) (read *n* mod *m*) is used here with the automatic SAS System variable _N_. This variable is automatically created when a SAS data set is built and is incremented by 1 for each iteration of the DATA step. _N_ is loosely referred to as the observation counter and is used here as the first argument with 3 (the selection criteria) as the second. MOD (_N_,3) is equal to 1 when _N_ is 1, 4, 7, etc. (i.e. every third record beginning with the first observation).

Caution: Don't automatically accept _N_ as a true observation counter in all DATA steps (that's why we said loosely). _N_ is incremented by 1 at each iteration of the DATA step. DATA steps that contain loops and OUTPUT statements may cause the relationship of the observation number and the internal variable _N_ to fall apart. This is not a problem with the system—it's the way it was designed to work. You may very well want to include code such as N+1; in a program to create your own observation counter.

Example 3

> ## Rounding and Truncating Numbers
>
> *FEATURES:* ROUND and INT Functions

Suppose you want to convert pounds to kilograms and inches to centimeters, and you want the results rounded to the nearest kilogram and the nearest tenth of a centimeter (millimeter) respectively. You can use the ROUND function to accomplish this task.

Example 3.1

```
DATA NEW;
   SET OLD;  *Assume OLD has variables WEIGHT and HEIGHT;
   WEIGHT=ROUND (WEIGHT/2.2 , 1);
   HEIGHT=ROUND (2.54*HEIGHT , .1);
RUN;
```

The ROUND function takes two arguments: the first is the variable to be rounded, the second is the rounding unit. By the way, the second argument of the ROUND function does not have to be a power of 10. For example, to create a new variable X, which is Y rounded to the nearest 20, you could write:

```
X=ROUND (Y,20);
```

You can have the same variable on both sides of the assignment statement. Thus, to round Y to the nearest 10, you would write:

```
Y=ROUND (Y,10);
```

To truncate a number (drop off the fractional part), you use the INT function. To truncate WEIGHT and HEIGHT instead of rounding, you would rewrite the program as follows:

Example 3.2

```
DATA NEW;
   SET OLD;  *Assume OLD has variables WEIGHT and HEIGHT;
   WEIGHT=INT (WEIGHT/2.2);
   HEIGHT=INT (2.54*HEIGHT);
RUN;
```

Example 4

Computing Means and Sums of Variables within an Observation. Counting the Number of Non-Missing Values in a List of Variables.

FEATURES: N, MEAN, and SUM Functions

In this example, each subject answered 50 items in a psychological survey. Each question is scored on a 1 to 5 scale. To ensure that an accurate assessment is made, the mean score is computed only if 40 or more items were answered. Your job (should you choose to accept it) is to compute the mean of the 50 scores (ITEM1-ITEM50), but *only* if at least 40 items are non-missing. Here is the program:

Example 4

```
DATA NEWTEST;
   SET OLDTEST;
   IF N (OF ITEM1-ITEM50) GE 40 THEN
      SCORE=MEAN (OF ITEM1-ITEM50);
RUN;
```

As you probably figured out by inspecting this program, the N function returns the number of non-missing values in the variable list, and the MEAN function returns the mean of the non-missing values in the variable list.

Actually, you may not have figured out the importance of the way the MEAN function deals with non-missing values, and this is quite important. If you calculate SCORE by simply adding up all the items and then dividing by 50 as follows:

```
SCORE=(ITEM1 + ITEM2 + ITEM3 + ... + ITEM50)/50;
```

you would be in big trouble if any of the items had missing values. When a SAS statement tries to do arithmetic operations on missing values, the result is always missing. Countless hours have been (and undoubtedly will be) spent trying to figure out why seemingly perfect code continues to yield empty results. Now you know why. You also know that the MEAN function computes the mean of the *non-missing* values and, therefore, always yields a valid result (unless of course all the data values are missing).

In addition to the N and MEAN functions, the functions NMISS and SUM operate in a similar manner, with NMISS returning the number of variables with missing values and SUM returning the sum of the non-missing values. The complementary pair of functions MIN and MAX are also useful and, as you would expect, return the minimum and maximum values in the argument list respectively.

Example 5

Character-to-Numeric Conversion, Using the INPUT Function

FEATURES: INPUT Function and @@ (Double Trailing At Sign)

One of the most extremely useful (and poorly understood) SAS System functions is the INPUT function. It takes the form:

```
variable=INPUT (variable,informat);
```

The traditional use is to reread a character variable with a numeric format, executing a character-to-numeric conversion.

In this example you have a collection of human temperatures (in degrees F.). Instead of entering 98.6, the letter N was used (for Normal). The following program reads the data and converts the N's to 98.6:

Example 5

```
DATA TEMPER;
   INPUT DUMMY $ @@;
   IF DUMMY='N' THEN TEMP=98.6;
      ELSE TEMP=INPUT (DUMMY,5.);
   DROP DUMMY;
DATALINES;
99.7 N 97.9 N N 112.5
RUN;
```

Since you have a mixture of numeric and character data, you have to read all the values as character data. Otherwise, reading N as a numeric value would result in a missing value for that observation. Let's see what happens when the program reads the first few data values. DUMMY is first assigned a value of 99.7 (remember that this is a character string). Since this is not equal to N, the variable TEMP is set to 99.7 and stored as a numerical value because of the 5. informat. The next value for DUMMY is N. The IF statement is true, and the variable TEMP is set to 98.6 (a numeric value).

See Chapter 1, "Example 11," for a refresher on the double trailing @@. See "Problem 2" in Chapter 8, "Retain," for another example of the INPUT function. For an elegant method of reading a mixture of numeric and character data, see Chapter 11, "Example 10".

Example 6

Numeric-to-Character Conversion, Using the PUT Function

FEATURES: PUT Function, SSN11. Format, and RENAME Option (SET Statement)

This rather interesting example came from a real problem that passed the desk of one of the authors. You have two SAS data sets that contain Social Security numbers. Data set ONE has them stored in a variable called ID as 9-digit numerics. Data set TWO has them stored in the variable ID as 11-byte character values (in the form 123-45-6789). You want to merge the two files. You have a choice: convert the numeric ID variable in ONE to character or the character ID variable in TWO to numeric. We show the former method:

Example 6

```
DATA ONE_CHAR;
   SET ONE (RENAME=(ID=SS));
   ID=PUT (SS,SSN11.);
   DROP SS;
RUN;
```

The built-in SAS format SSN11. writes numerics as 11-byte character strings in the standard Social Security number format with dashes and leading zeros. By using the PUT function, you assign this character string to the variable ID. It is necessary to rename ID to SS temporarily since you want the 11-byte character variable to be called ID. The RENAME option on the SET statement allows you to rename variables being read from the incoming data set. (See Chapter 3, "Example 6.2," for more on the RENAME data set option.) You can rename a number of variables using the syntax:

SET *dataset* (**RENAME**=*(oldvar1=newvar1 oldvar2=newvar2 ...)*);

You can now sort and merge the two files. (See Chapter 2, "Example 4," to see how to use a user-created format with the PUT function.)

Example 7

Computing a Moving Average

FEATURE: **LAG Function**

Performing computations between observations in a DATA step is far more difficult than within-observation processing. (See Chapter 8, "RETAIN," for examples of how to manipulate values from previous observations.) For example, to compute the mean of X1, X2, and X3, within a single observation, you would write:

```
MEANX=MEAN (OF X1-X3);        or        MEANX=(X1+X2+X3) /3;
```

However, computing the mean of X for the present observation and the two previous observations presents more of a challenge—without the LAG function, that is. Economists often compute a "moving average" to smooth out trends in their data. For example, stock indices such as the Dow-Jones Average can change considerably from month to month. To see the trend in this index, economists plot the average of the index for the past three months for each month of interest. This smooths out the data so that longer-term trends are more apparent.

In this example, you use the LAG function to compute a moving average. LAG*n* returns the value of the *n*th previous execution of the LAG function. That is, every time the LAG function executes, it "remembers" the current value of the argument, which will be the lagged value the next time the function executes. An example will make this clear. Here is the code to compute the moving average just described:

Example 7

```
DATA MOVING;
    SET OLD;
    X1=LAG (X);
    X2=LAG2 (X);
    AVE=MEAN (OF X X1 X2);
    IF _N_ GE 3 THEN OUTPUT;
RUN;
```

The variable X1 is the value of X from the previous observation; X2 is the value of X from the observation before that. The MEAN function is used to compute the average (mean) of the three values. For the first iteration of the DATA step, LAG(X) and LAG2(X) are missing since there was no previous execution of the LAG function. For the second iteration of the DATA step, LAG(X) is assigned the value of X for observation 1, and LAG2(X) is missing. Finally, for the third through the last iteration of the DATA step, LAG(X) and LAG2(X) are assigned values. In this example, you do not output an observation in the new data set unless AVE is actually based on three values. The _N_ variable is useful for testing this condition. You output an observation for the third through last iteration of the DATA step only.

A Special Caution When Using the LAG Function

CAUTION! Do not execute the LAG function conditionally unless you are purposely doing something very tricky and really know what you are doing. To prove our point, look at the following code:

```
DATA ERROR;
    INPUT X @@;
    IF X GE 5 THEN Y=LAG(X);
DATALINES;
1 8 3 9 2
RUN;
```

What are the values of Y? (Answer: missing, missing, missing, 8, missing.) The IF statement instructs the system to execute the LAG function only when X is greater than or equal to 5. It is therefore first executed when the second observation (X=8) is read. The next time the LAG function executes (observation number 4, X=9), the value of LAG(X) is 8, the value of X the last time the LAG function executed. Did you get that point? If not, don't fret. This is not easy stuff.

Example 8

Taking Substrings

FEATURES: **SUBSTR Function and LENGTH Statement**

The SUBSTR function is the first of the various character functions we demonstrate. A brief review is in order. A "string" in computer parlance is a collection of characters that are assigned to a variable. For example, a character variable called ID could have a value of 427NJ or 12345. Notice that a character string may consist solely of numerals as long as it has been declared as a character variable to the program.

Suppose you have ID's of length 5, and the last two characters represent a state code (such as 427NJ above). Data set OLD, following, contains some sample ID's:

```
Data Set OLD

   ID

   427NJ
   125NY
```

Here is a program to extract the state code from the ID:

Example 8

```
DATA NEW;
   SET OLD; *OLD CONTAINS ID;
   LENGTH STATE $ 2;
   STATE=SUBSTR (ID,4,2);
RUN;
```

The values for STATE are NJ and NY in this example.
The general form of the substring function is:

SUBSTR (*char_variable*, *starting_position*, *length*);

The *char_variable* can also be a character expression or a character constant.
It is a good idea to use a LENGTH statement to assign a length to the substring variable as is done here. The dollar sign in the LENGTH statement indicates that STATE is a character variable and the 2 indicates its length. If you don't take the trouble to do this, the length of the substring is the same as the length of the variable from which you are extracting the substring. This is both wasteful and potentially dangerous in that it can lead to erroneous results.

Example 9

> ### Taking Substrings, "Unpacking" a String
>
> *FEATURES:* SUBSTR and INPUT Functions, ARRAY Statement

In this example, you have a string which represents 10 single-digit scores for a person. This "packing" of data is done to either save space or to reduce the number of variables per person. In many database packages (especially those for PC's), there is a limit to the number of variables that may be contained in a single database. By using a single variable to represent multiple scores, you can "trick" the program into functionally holding more variables than the actual maximum.

After you transfer this data set into a SAS System file, you have a 10-byte character variable from which you want to extract the 10 scores. The SUBSTR function, placed in a loop with the index "pointing" to each of the scores in turn, accomplishes your goal. Here it is: (Data set OLD contains a character variable STRING which holds the 10 scores.)

Example 9

```
DATA SCORE;
   SET OLD;
   ARRAY X[10] X1-X10;
   DO J=1 TO 10;
      X[J]=INPUT (SUBSTR (STRING,J,1),1.);
   END;
   DROP STRING J;
RUN;
```

Here you place the SUBSTR function inside a DO loop which gets executed 10 times, once for each value of the counter J (1 to 10). Each time the loop is executed, another byte is extracted from STRING. Each of the X variables is equal to the value of one of the bytes in the 10-byte variable STRING. (DO loops and ARRAYS are covered in more detail in Chapter 7.) Since you want the variables X1 to X10 to be numeric, you create the array that holds them as a numeric array. Since the original variable STRING is character, you use the INPUT function to make the character-to-numeric conversion (see Example 5). If you omit the INPUT function, the SAS System performs an automatic character-to-numeric conversion. We prefer programming the conversion ourselves.

Example 10

> ### Reading Combinations of Numeric and Character Data
>
> *FEATURES:* **INDEX, LENGTH, SUBSTR, and INPUT Functions, @@**
> **(Double Trailing At Sign)**

For this example you have measurements in a file that are expressed either in inches or centimeters. Each measurement is followed directly by its unit of measurement (I or C). Here is a program to read this combination of data and create a variable that represents all measurements in centimeters:

Example 10.1

```
DATA CONVERT;
    INPUT DUMMY $ @@;
    DUMMY2=SUBSTR (DUMMY,1,LENGTH(DUMMY)-1);   ❶
    IF INDEX (DUMMY,'I') NE 0 THEN   ❷
        CM=2.54*INPUT (DUMMY2,5.);
    ELSE IF INDEX (DUMMY,'C') NE 0 THEN   ❸
        CM=INPUT (DUMMY2,5.);
    ELSE CM=.;   ❹
    DROP DUMMY DUMMY2;
DATALINES;
23C 100I 12I 133C
35I 45C  35  47I
RUN;
```

There are many solutions to this problem. We present one solution which illustrates the use of several string functions. After we discuss the present code, we show an alternative solution, also using string functions.

The LENGTH function ❶ returns the position of the right-most nonblank character in a string. Since you read in DUMMY with list-directed INPUT and do not supply a LENGTH statement, it has a default length of 8 bytes. The LENGTH function returns the actual number of non-blank bytes for you. For the first data value (23C), the LENGTH function returns a 3.

DUMMY2 ❶ is created with the SUBSTR function with a starting position of 1 and a length of one less than the length of the string, which is the numeral part of the string.

To check for a trailing I, you use the INDEX function ❷. This function returns the first position in the first argument (DUMMY) that contains the second argument (letter I). You don't care what position this is, but if there is no I in the string, the INDEX function returns a 0. So, any result from the INDEX function which is non-zero indicates an I in the string. Just to be careful, you also test for a C ❸ in the data and set any measurement without an I or a C to missing ❹.

Another, perhaps easier and cleaner, solution to this example which does not use the INDEX function is shown next. (We presented the previous example to demonstrate a use of the INDEX function.) These examples show that with the large variety of string functions available, there are many ways to solve problems such as this one.

Example 10.2 (Alternate Solution to Example 10.1)

```
DATA CONVERT;
   INPUT DUMMY $ @@;
   LENGTH LAST $ 1;
   LENGTH=LENGTH (DUMMY);  ❶
   LAST=SUBSTR (DUMMY,LENGTH,1);  ❷
   FIRST=SUBSTR (DUMMY,1,LENGTH-1);  ❸
   IF LAST EQ 'I' THEN CM=2.54*INPUT (FIRST,5.);  ❹
      ELSE IF LAST EQ 'C' THEN CM=INPUT (FIRST,5.);  ❺
      ELSE CM=.;
   KEEP CM;
DATALINES;
23C 100I 12I 133C
35I 45C  35  47I
RUN;
```

First, you read in the data value and store it as a character value in DUMMY. Next, you use the LENGTH function ❶ to find the number of non-blank characters in the measurement. Statement ❷ assigns a value to the variable LAST equal to the rightmost byte of the string in DUMMY. (The LENGTH statement sets the length of LAST to 1 byte.) To separate the "number part" from the trailing character, you use the SUBSTR function in statement ❸. This statement creates FIRST and assigns to it a value equal to all but the last byte of the string in DUMMY. It is then straightforward to test if the trailing letter is an I or a C, and perform a conversion or not. The INPUT functions ❹,❺ are used to do the character-to-numeric conversions.

Example 11

Validating Data Values

FEATURES: VERIFY Function, DATA _NULL_ , RETAIN and PUT Statements

The VERIFY function, as its name implies, can be used to verify that a character variable contains only valid characters. It takes the following form:

VERIFY (*char_var*, *verify_string*);

If all the characters in *char_var* are present in *verify_string*, the VERIFY function returns a 0. Otherwise, it returns the position of the first character in *char_var* that is *not* in *verify_string*.

Sound confusing? Yes, we think so too. Here is an example to help clarify it:

Suppose you want to verify that only the characters A, B, C, D, E are present in the variable ANSWER. (Assume that ANSWER has been defined with a length of 1 in data set OLD.) Using the VERIFY function, you have:

Example 11

```
DATA _NULL_;
    SET OLD;
    RETAIN CHECK 'ABCDE';
    IF VERIFY (ANSWER,CHECK) NE 0 THEN PUT
        'ERROR IN RECORD ' _N_ ANSWER=;
RUN;
```

There's actually much going on in this small program that deserves explanation. To begin with, there is that funny data set name _NULL_. This is a SAS System reserved name. It instructs the system to go through all the motions of creating a data set called _NULL_, but not to actually create it. Since the only purpose of the program is to check for errors and report on them, there's no need to create a real data set. The _NULL_ data set name is often used in conjunction with the PUT statement, as it is here. Data values are read in with an INPUT or a SET statement, and they are written (in this case to the SAS log) with the PUT statement. Notice that the PUT statement here first writes the literal 'ERROR IN RECORD ' (including the trailing blank), then it writes the observation number of the offending record and, finally, it writes the value of the variable ANSWER prefixed with the string ANSWER=. The use of DATA _NULL_ is highly recommended as an efficiency measure. No need to take up resources (CPU and storage) to write a data set that you don't really need.

The next feature needing explanation is the RETAIN statement (a short preview here of a full explanation in Chapter 8). You want to verify that the 1-byte value of ANSWER is contained in the string CHECK. You could have written the statement

```
CHECK='ABCDE';
```

in the code, and that would have created the identical value for CHECK for each observation, but you used an alternate method instead. You told the system to initialize a variable called CHECK with the value ABCDE and to retain it for each succeeding observation.

Now for the heart of the example, the VERIFY statement. It's really very simple. For each observation, if the value of ANSWER is not contained in one of the characters making up the string contained in variable CHECK (remember, the string is ABCDE for each observation), the value returned by VERIFY is not equal to 0 (0 is good!). The IF statement then produces a report of the "bad" observation.

Example 12

Translating One Set of Character Values to Another

FEATURES: **TRANSLATE Function and ARRAY Statement**

The TRANSLATE function does just what the name implies—it translates one character to another. The function takes the form:

*new_char_var=***TRANSLATE** (*char_var, to_string, from_string*);

The *to_string* and *from_string* can be one or more characters in length; each byte of the *to_string* is substituted for the corresponding byte in the *from_string*. Suppose you have an optical mark reading machine which scans multiple choice exams. Each question has five possible answers, 'A' through 'E', but the machine can only produce a file of answers containing the numerals '1' through '5'. In order to take the file produced by the machine and translate the numerals '1' through '5' to the letters 'A' through 'E' respectively, you code the following:

Example 12

```
DATA TRANS;
   ARRAY QUES[10] $ 1 QUES1-QUES10;
   INPUT (QUES1-QUES10)($1.);
   DO J = 1 TO 10;
      QUES[J]=TRANSLATE (QUES[J],'ABCDE','12345');
   END;
   DROP J;
DATALINES;
2412552134
1234512345
   .
   .
   .
RUN;
```

The resulting values for QUES1-QUES10 for the observation 1 are: B, D, A, B, E, E, B, A, C, D. Please refer to Chapter 7 for a discussion on using ARRAYS.

Example 13

> ## Removing Blanks or Other Characters from a String
>
> *FEATURES:* COMPRESS Function, COMPBL Function

You may want to remove certain characters from a string (such as blanks) before you test, process, or store the string in a data set. A very useful function, COMPRESS, makes this job almost trivial.

To demonstrate blank removal, suppose that you want to merge two files, keying on last names. Unfortunately, the data entry clerks were not consistent in their use of blanks. For example, you might have 'Mc Lauglin' in one file and 'McLauglin' in the other. Create a new MASTER file by removing all blanks from the variable LASTNAME.

Example 13

```
DATA NEWDATA;
   SET MASTER;
   LASTNAME=COMPRESS (LASTNAME);
RUN;
```

The first argument of the COMPRESS function is the variable to operate on. The second argument contains the characters to be compressed out of the string. Using the COMPRESS function with only a single argument removes all blanks (the default compressable character) from the first argument. If you want to remove characters other than blanks, you place all characters to be removed as the second argument in quotes. For example, to remove parentheses, dashes, and blanks from telephone numbers you would write:

```
TELEPHON=COMPRESS (TELEPHON,' ()-');
```

If you like to live mildly dangerously, you could modify the values of LASTNAME in the original data set (MASTER) without having to create a new data set. By using the same data set name on the DATA and SET statements, you can accomplish this somewhat risky operation:

```
DATA MASTER;
   SET MASTER;
   LASTNAME=COMPRESS (LASTNAME);
RUN;
```

Remember that recovery from such a program may be difficult or impossible.

A related function, COMPBL, converts occurrences of multiple contiguous blanks into single blanks. If a variable ADDRESS contained the value '123   SESAME   ST. KIDSTOWN,   NY   10101', the code COMPBL(ADDRESS); would yield, '123 SESAME ST. KIDSTOWN, NY 10101' with one blank between each set of non-blank characters.

Example 14

> ## Joining (Concatenating) Two Strings
>
> *FEATURES:* || (Concatenation operator) and TRIM Function

You have a SAS data set (NAMES) which contains the variables FIRST and LAST. As you can guess, these variables represent first and last names. You would like to create a new variable, NAME, which is the full name (first, a blank, and last). You need to join (in computer jargon— concatenate) the first name, a blank, and the last name. Using the concatenation operator (||) you can proceed as follows:

Example 14

```
DATA NEW;
   SET NAMES;
   NAME=TRIM (FIRST) || ' ' || LAST;
   KEEP NAME;
RUN;
```

Since the concatenation operation does not remove blanks, you need to use the TRIM function (which removes trailing blanks) before concatenating the single blank and the last name. Otherwise, the variable NAME could contain more than a single blank between the first and last names.

For example, if FIRST was equal to Ron_____ (5 blanks) and LAST was equal to Cody____(4 blanks), the value of FIRST || ' ' || LAST would be Ron_____Cody____ (6 blanks between the first and last name). The TRIM function removes all the blanks in FIRST, so we need to concatenate the single blank between the first and last names.

Conclusion

We hope this sampling of functions has demonstrated to you that spending some time thumbing through the full list of functions may provide you with some efficient and powerful ways to approach a variety of programming problems. Now that you have finished this chapter, you can consider yourself "functionally" literate! Enjoy the problems.

Problems

5-1. You have a SAS data set, ORIG, which contains ID (5 digit numeric), SCORE, PROP (a proportion), and IQ. You want to create the following new variables:

a. The natural (base *e*) log of SCORE.
b. The arcsine of the square root of PROP.
c. IQ rounded to the nearest 10 points.

d. A character variable which is derived from the first two digits and the last two digits of the *numeric* variable ID. For example, if ID=12345, the new *character* variable would be the string 1245.

Here are some sample data for you to work with:

```
        Data Set ORIG

  ID      SCORE     PROP      IQ
12345      95        .8      110
13579      72        .6       90
24680      98        .2      140
11223      92        .3      106
```

5-2. You have a SAS data set, SCORES, which contains the variables X1-X20, Y1-Y20. The X and Y variables may contain missing values. Write a SAS program to accomplish the following:

a. Compute the sum of the non-missing values in variables X1-X20.
b. Compute the mean of Y1-Y20. If there are 5 or more missing values of Y1-Y20, set the mean equal to a missing value.
c. Find the minimum and maximum of the X's.

5-3. You have a raw data file called TEMPER which contains temperature measurements taken at one hour intervals. Each raw data line contains several pairs of the variables HOUR (hour of the day) and TEMP (temperature). All temperatures are in degrees Fahrenheit unless they are written in the form *n*C (the number *n* followed by a C, no spaces), in which case they are expressed in degrees Celsius. In addition, a value of N was coded when a temperature was not obtained. Write a SAS program to read this data file, express all temperatures in degrees Fahrenheit, and convert each N to a numeric missing value.

Hint: The conversion from Celsius to Fahrenheit is:

F=9*C/5+32

Some sample records from file TEMPER are as follows:

```
1 68  2 67  3 N  4 20C
5 72  6 23C 7 75 8 N
```

5-4. You have a raw data file of phone numbers and want to verify that all the numbers are in the following format:

(nnn)nnn-nnnn

where *n* must be a digit 0-9. Extra spaces are permitted, but assume all numbers will be 15 characters or less. Have your program place the valid numbers in data set VALID, and the invalid numbers in data set INVALID.

Hint: Our solution used the following SAS functions: INDEX and VERIFY, but there are many other possible solutions.

Some sample raw data records are as follows:

```
(988)463-4490      (valid)
(241) 343-2233     (valid)
456-5034           (invalid)
(123)456-7890      (valid)
(271)SH4-1234      (invalid)
(592)2578362       (invalid)
```

5-5. You have two SAS data sets, ONE and TWO. Data set ONE contains a variable called DATE1 which is a character variable in the form MM/DD/YY. (i.e. variable DATE1 is *not* a SAS date, which is a numerical quantity, but rather a character string of length 8.) Variables HEIGHT and WEIGHT are also contained in data set ONE. Data set TWO contains a character variable called DATE2 which is in the form ddMONyy. Data set TWO also contains the variable HR (heart rate). Write a program to merge these data sets by date, and assume that there are no duplicate dates in each of the data sets. Solve this problem two ways:

a) Use the PUT function to create a new variable in one of the data sets so that the two data sets have an identical variable to use.

b) Use an INPUT function to create a real SAS date variable in both data sets for merging.

Some sample data are shown below:

Data Set ONE				Data Set TWO	
DATE1	HEIGHT	WEIGHT		DATE2	HR
10/21/46	58	155		21OCT46	58
09/05/55	66	220		11JAN44	68
01/11/44	63	205		05SEP55	72

5-6.   You have a SAS data set called STOCKS which contains variables XXX and YYY
(daily prices of two stocks). Write a SAS program to compute a moving average of
these two stocks, taking 4-day intervals. For days 1 to 3, where you do not have 4
days of data, use as many of the previous days as you have to compute the average
(i.e., for day 1, use the daily price; for day 2, use the average of day 1 and day 2,
etc.). Some sample data values are shown:

```
Data Set STOCKS

DAY     XXX     YYY
 1      43      57
 2      39      58
 3      45      56
 4      38      54
 5      40      55
 6      44      59
```

Hint: Use the LAG*n* family of functions.

5-7.   You have a SAS data set SCORES, which contains an ID variable and a variable
called STRING which holds five 1-digit scores. Write a SAS program to read this
data set and create a new data set which contains an ID and five numeric variables X1
to X5, where the X's are each of the digits in STRING. Following are some sample
data:

```
Data Set SCORES

ID      STRING
1       12345
2       13243
3       53421
```

Hint: You may want to use arrays. We provide solutions with and without them.

Chapter 6

SAS® Dates

Reading, Writing, and 'Rithmetic with Date Values

EXAMPLES

Introduction

SAS software has a wealth of features for working with dates. Date values are commonly found in many applications in many different forms—and SAS software can read them all into SAS data sets and work with them. Dates may be found in MM/DD/YY, YY/MM/DD, or DD/MM/YY formats, with or without the slashes (or just about any delimiter such as dashes, commas, spaces, periods, etc. for that matter). Dates may also be encountered in Julian format. A Julian date consists of the year (either two digits, such as 94, or four digits, such as 1994) followed by the number of days since January 1. As an example, February 1, 1995, is written as 95032 (or 1995032) in Julian format. Dates are also found in ddMMMyy format, such as 01FEB95. Whatever the original format, the SAS System can read the date and convert it to a SAS date value. More about that in a paragraph or two.

Once you've read dates with your SAS program, you can perform any number of operations on them, including formatting them for output as well as for arithmetic operations. You may want to

- sort a data set in date order
- find the elapsed number of intervals between two dates in days, months, years, etc.
- extract the day of the week, month of the year, or the year for a particular date
- print dates in reports in a variety of formats.

To help you accomplish these goals, SAS software provides you with informats, formats, and date functions. In this chapter, we show you how these powerful features can assist you in all of these tasks.

Now, let's get back to those SAS date values. All SAS dates are stored as the number of days from January 1, 1960 (day 0, picked somewhat arbitrarily). This allows you to find the interval between any two dates and to have a uniform way of storing all dates. It is very important to remember that once a date has been read in and converted to a number, it is treated as any other numeric quantity in a SAS data set. For example, if you read in a date of January 1, 1990, a value of 10,958 will be stored. SAS programs have no way of knowing if a number is a date or not. With these points in mind, let's proceed to our first example.

Example 1

Reading a Date from Raw Data

FEATURES: **SAS Dates, SAS Date Formats and Informats**

There are many ways to represent dates in a raw data file. For example, February 13, 1982, could be found as:

```
02/13/82
02-13-82
02+13,82
13FEB82
021382
02/13/1982
13/02/82
82044 (Julian Date)
1982044 (Julian Date)
```

SAS software can read all these forms and more. For example, if each of these date values starts in column 8, you can read each of them with the appropriate informat as follows:

Date	INPUT Statement
02/13/82	INPUT @8 DATE MMDDYY8.;
02-13-82	INPUT @8 DATE MMDDYY8.;
02+13,82	INPUT @8 DATE MMDDYY8.;
13FEB82	INPUT @8 DATE DATE7.;
021382	INPUT @8 DATE MMDDYY6.;
02/13/1982	INPUT @8 DATE MMDDYY10.;
13/02/82	INPUT @8 DATE DDMMYY8.;
82044 (Julian Date)	INPUT @8 DATE JULIAN5.;
1982044 (Julian Date)	INPUT @8 DATE JULIAN7.;

Now, here is the first example. You want to read in the following raw data:

```
                        Raw data file HOSP

Variable    Description                  Starting Column    Length
─────────────────────────────────────────────────────────────────
ID          Patient ID                         1              2
ADMIT       Date of Admission (MM/DD/YY)        5              8
DISCHRG     Date of Discharge (MM/DD/YY)       15              8
COST        Cost of the Hospitalization        25              5

Here are some sample raw data:

Column 1---5----10---5----20---5----30---5----40
       01  10/11/92  10/15/92   5000
       07  09/01/92  10/02/92  84500
       23  9/2/92    9/4/92     1200
       33  12/25/92  01/01/93   3400
```

Write a SAS program to read in these data and compute the number of days between the admission and discharge dates. You will then print out a report showing: ID, ADMIT, DISCHRG, LOS, and COST, where LOS is the length of stay that you computed. Here is the program:

Example 1

```
DATA PATIENT;
   INFILE 'HOSP';
   INPUT @1  ID      $2.
         @5  ADMIT   MMDDYY8.
         @15 DISCHRG MMDDYY8.
         @25 COST    5.;
   LOS = DISCHRG-ADMIT+1;
   LABEL ADMIT  ='Admission Date'
         DISCHRG='Discharge Date'
         COST   ='Cost of Treatment'
         LOS    ='Length of Stay';
   FORMAT ADMIT DISCHRG MMDDYY8. COST DOLLAR8.;
RUN;

PROC PRINT LABEL DATA=PATIENT;
   TITLE 'Hospital Report';
   ID ID;
   VAR ADMIT DISCHRG LOS COST;
RUN;
```

Why do we add one day (ADMIT + 1) to the LOS calculation? This is something that most people forget to do when calculating a range in general. In this case, when patients come in for same-day surgery, if you just take DISCHRG-ADMIT as the LOS, you would lose all of those days. Now, here is the output:

Output from Example 1 - Reading a Date from Raw Data

```
                           Hospital Report


              Admission     Discharge     Length      Cost of
      ID         Date          Date       of Stay    Treatment

      01       10/11/92      10/15/92         5        $5,000
      07       09/01/92      10/02/92        32       $84,500
      23       09/02/92      09/04/92         3        $1,200
      33       12/25/92      01/01/93         8        $3,400
```

The FORMAT statement assigning the format MMDDYY8. to the variables ADMIT and DISCHRG is necessary to make the displayed date values understandable. Also note the use of the DOLLAR8. format applied to COST to enhance its readability. Had you omitted the FORMAT statement, the listing would have looked like this:

```
                           Hospital Report


              Admission     Discharge     Length      Cost of
      ID         Date          Date       of Stay    Treatment

      01        11972         11976           5         5000
      07        11932         11963          32        84500
      23        11933         11935           3         1200
      33        12047         12054           8         3400
```

The numbers you see under the Admission Date and Discharge Date columns are the number of days from January 1, 1960, corresponding to each of the dates. When you see output like this, you should be reminded to include date formats for your date variables. Also note that the values for COST are not easily readable without the dollar signs and commas.

Example 2

> ## Creating a SAS Date from Month, Day, and Year
>
> *FEATURES:* MDY Function, WORDDATE Format

Suppose you have a data file containing dates in a format for which SAS software does not have an informat. Suppose further that you can extract the month, day, and year of each date. To make it still more gruesome, suppose that the month, day, and year information are not even in contiguous columns. Enter the MDY function. This function, which takes as its arguments month, day, and year, will create a SAS date for you. For example, suppose you have DAY in columns 1-2, MONTH in columns 10-11, and YEAR in columns 20-23. To create a SAS date, you would code:

Example 2

```
DATA MDYEXAMP;
    INPUT DAY    1-2
          MONTH 10-11
          YEAR  20-23;
    DATE=MDY (MONTH,DAY,YEAR);
    FORMAT DATE WORDDATE.;
DATALINES;
12        11        1992
11        09        1899
;

PROC PRINT DATA=MDYEXAMP;
    TITLE 'Example of MDY Function';
RUN;
```

Output from Example 2 - Creating a SAS Date from Month, Day, and Year

```
                   Example of MDY Function

         OBS    DAY    MONTH    YEAR          DATE

          1     12      11      1992     November 12, 1992
          2     11       9      1899     September 11, 1899
```

The WORDDATE format prints the month name, the day of the month, and the year as seen in the above output.

Example 3

> ## Computing Age
>
> *FEATURES:* **Date Literals, TODAY function**

Suppose you have a SAS data set EMPLOYEE which contains variables ID, DOB (date of birth), and several other variables. One requirement is to compute AGE from a date of birth. You have several choices to make. You can round the age to the nearest year or drop all fractional parts and take the age as of the last birthday. You also need to consider as of what date you want the age computed. The example that follows is technically an approximate value for age, using the fact that an "average" year has 365.25 days (1 leap year every 4 years). More sophisticated programming is needed to compute exact ages. First, let's look at ways to compute ages using the approximate method.

Here is a program to compute a person's age several different ways:

Example 3

```
DATA AGE;
   SET EMPLOYEE;
   AGE1=INT (('01JAN95'D-DOB)/365.25);
   AGE2=ROUND (('01JAN95'D-DOB)/365.25,1);
   AGE3=INT ((TODAY()-DOB)/365.25);
   AGE4=ROUND ((TODAY()-DOB)/365.25,1);
RUN;
```

AGE1 and AGE2 represent the age as of January 1, 1995, with AGE2 rounded to the nearest year. These assignment statements use a date literal which is of the form:

'DDMMMYY'D

DD is a two-digit day of the month, MMM is a month abbreviation, and YY is a two- or four-digit year (it would be 'DDMMYYYY'D in the latter case). This string is placed in single or double quotation marks, followed by an upper-or lower-case D. SAS software will convert this literal into a SAS date (i.e. the number of days since January 1, 1960). Variables AGE3 and AGE4 are ages computed as of the current date which is represented by the TODAY() function. The null parentheses () following the function name are required by SAS System syntax; all functions, even ones without any arguments, need parentheses so that the software can distinguish variable names from functions names. (Question: What did the TODAY function say to the MEAN function? Answer: "Don't give me any arguments!") Finally, AGE1 and AGE3 compute age as of the last birthday—the INT function truncates (throws away) the decimal part of the number. AGE2 and AGE4 use the ROUND function to compute age to the nearest year. These functions are described in more detail in Example 3 in Chapter 5, "SAS Functions." We demonstrate an exact method to compute age later in this chapter.

Example 4

> ## Extracting Day of Week and Day of Month from a SAS Date
>
> *FEATURES:* DAY and WEEKDAY Functions

The SAS System contains functions to compute day of the week and day of the month from a SAS date. It is easy to confuse the two. The DAY function returns a number from 1 to 31 which represents the day of the month corresponding to a given date; the WEEKDAY function returns a number from 1 to 7, corresponding to the day of the week. Suppose you want to chart the frequency of hospital admissions by day of the week and day of the month using the HOSP data from Example 1. Here is the program:

Example 4

```
PROC FORMAT; ❶
   VALUE DAYFMT 1='SUN' 2='MON' 3='TUE' 4='WED'
                5='THU' 6='FRI' 7='SAT';
RUN;


DATA PATIENT;
   INFILE 'HOSP';
   INPUT @1 ID      $2.
         @5  ADMIT   MMDDYY8.
         @15 DISCHRG MMDDYY8.
         @25 COST    5.;
   DAY_WEEK = WEEKDAY (ADMIT); ❷
   DAY_MON  = DAY (ADMIT); ❸
   LABEL ADMIT   ='Admission Date'
         DISCHRG ='Discharge Date'
         COST    ='Cost of Treatment'
         DAY_WEEK='Day of the Week'
         DAY_MON ='Day of the Month';
   FORMAT ADMIT DISCHRG MMDDYY8. COST DOLLAR8.
          DAY_WEEK DAYFMT.;
RUN;


PROC CHART DATA=PATIENT;
   VBAR DAY_WEEK DAY_MON/DISCRETE;
RUN;
```

Line ❷ computes DAY_WEEK which is the day of the week, a number from 1 to 7. Line ❸ computes DAY_MON, the day of the month, a number from 1 to 31. PROC FORMAT ❶ creates a format for DAY_WEEK. (We cover the FORMAT procedure in Chapter 11, "PROC FORMAT.")

As is usually the case with the SAS System, there is more than one way to achieve the same results. In the current example, DAY_WEEK could have been calculated in an alternative manner which would not necessitate the PROC FORMAT step. The following line of code,

```
DAY_WEEK=PUT(ADMIT,WEEKDATE3.);
```

creates a three-character variable (DAY_WEEK) which has as its value SUN, MON, TUE, etc. The only other difference is that DAY_WEEK is now a character variable as opposed to the earlier method which yields a numeric value for DAY_WEEK. In all likelihood, however, this would not present a major difficulty, if at all. This is just another testament to the versatility and power of the SAS System.

Example 5

Extracting Month and Year from a SAS Date

FEATURES: YEAR and MONTH Functions, PROC CHART (with the SUMVAR and DISCRETE Options)

What day of the week was July 4, 1776? How can you create variables that represent the YEAR and MONTH for a given date? SAS software has a number of very useful date functions to answer these and other questions. The next two examples demonstrate representative situations.

Suppose you have a SAS data set FUND which contains fund drive information. Included are variables DATE (date of donation, stored as a SAS date value) and AMOUNT (amount of donation). You would like charts showing donation AMOUNT by year and month. Here is the program:

Example 5

```
DATA TEMP;
   SET FUND;
   YEAR=YEAR (DATE);
   MONTH=MONTH (DATE);
RUN;

PROC CHART DATA=TEMP;
   VBAR YEAR/SUMVAR=AMOUNT DISCRETE;
   VBAR MONTH/SUMVAR=AMOUNT DISCRETE;
RUN;
```

You need only use the YEAR and MONTH functions to extract the appropriate information from DATE. The YEAR function returns a four-digit year; the MONTH function returns a number from 1 to 12. You might want to create a user-defined format for MONTH with 1='JAN', etc. Chapter 12, "PROC CHART," has more details on the CHART procedure.

Computing Date Intervals

The remaining examples in this chapter cover the INTCK and INTNX functions. These functions are used to compute the number of intervals between two dates and the date after which a given number of intervals has occurred, respectively. Interval units can be one of the following: DAY, WEEK, TENDAY, SEMIMONTH, MONTH, QUARTER (QTR), SEMIYEAR, or YEAR. There is also a WEEKDAY interval which allows you to count the number of working days, specifying which day(s) of the week will be days off. These functions can be quite complicated and we refer you to *SAS Language: Reference, Version 6, First Edition,* SAS Technical Report P-222, *Changes and Enhancements to Base SAS Software, Release 6.07,* and a paper in the 1994 Northeast SAS Users Group Proceedings, by Alan Dickson entitled "Blind Dates & Other Lapses of Reason: Handling Dates in SAS." We demonstrate some elementary applications of these functions in Examples 6, 7, and 8.

Example 6

Counting the Number of Years, Months, and so on, from a Given Date

FEATURES: INTCK and TODAY Functions

Suppose you have a company SAS data set EMPLOY which contains, among other variables, EMP_NUM (employee number) and DATEHIRE (date of hire). You want to know how many years each employee has worked. One approximate method is to count how many year intervals have passed between the date of hire and the current date. The SAS function INTCK can be used to count how many times the period of employment has entered a new year (i.e. how many January 1st's have passed). This is accomplished using the following code:

Example 6

```
DATA NEW_EMP;
   SET EMPLOY;
   CURRENT=TODAY();
   WORK_YRS=INTCK ('YEAR',DATEHIRE,CURRENT);
RUN;
```

Using 'YEAR' for the first argument of the INTCK function gives you the number of times a yearly boundary has passed. For example, if an employee were hired on November 3, 1993, and the value for CURRENT is February 1, 1994, the program above would set WORK_YRS equal to 1 since there is one yearly boundary (January 1st) between November 3, 1993, and February 1, 1994. If an employee were hired on January 2, 1994, and the value for CURRENT is December 31, 1994, the value of WORK_YRS would be 0, even though the employee had worked almost a full year. Be cautious when using these functions and interpret your results very carefully.

If you want to count the number of months between the current month and the month of hire you can use the INTCK function with MONTH as the appropriate interval. In general, the code to determine the number of months between the DATEHIRE date and the CURRENT date is:

```
WORK_MON=INTCK ('MONTH',DATEHIRE,CURRENT);
```

In the first case where the date of hire is 11/3/93 and the CURRENT date is 2/1/94, the calculation gives you 3 (you have passed 3 month boundaries: Dec., Jan., and Feb.).

Example 7

Computing Exact Age in Years

FEATURES: **INTCK Function, Combining Numeric and Logical Operations**

In Example 3, age in years (as of the last birthday) was computed using an approximate calculation based on the fact that an average year contains 365.25 days. While this is usually good enough, an exact method is shown next in case you need to use it someday. It also serves as another example of the INTCK function.

This calculation involves counting the number of months between two dates (e.g. date of birth and the current date) and subtracting one month if the current day of the month is less than the day of the month of the person's birthday. This calculation was originally posted on a public SAS bulletin board (SAS-L) by William Kreuter, and we present it here (with a slight modification) with his permission:

```
AGE=INT( (INTCK('MONTH',BIRTH,CURRENT) -
        (DAY(CURRENT)<DAY(BIRTH)))/12 );
```

BIRTH is the date of birth and CURRENT is the date of the age that you want to compute. The result is the age as of the last birthday. Note the clever use of the logical expression (DAY(CURRENT) < DAY(BIRTH)) in the equation. If the current day of the month is less than the person's birthday, the logical expression is true and you subtract 1 from the number of months. If the current day of the month is greater than the birthday day of the month, the expression is false, which means you subtract 0 from the number of months (you count the current month in the total). Dividing by 12 converts the months to years, and the INT function drops any fractional part of the year.

Let's test this with several current dates. If a person were born on October 21, 1992, and the current date is November 23, 1994, the AGE will be 2 years since INT ((25 - 0)/12) = 2. If the current date is September 15, 1994, the number of months is 23. You subtract 1 since the current day of the month (15) is less than the day of the month at birth (21). The result is AGE=1. Finally, if the current date is October 3, 1994, the number of months is 24, but you subtract 1 (3 is less than 21 and the logical expression is true) to get 23. Dividing this number by 12 and than applying the INT function to the result yields the correct answer, 1.

One situation where this exact method differs from the approximate method in Example 3 is when you are computing ages and the current date is a person's birthday. For example, if the date of birth is 10/21/92, and you compute the age in years for a current date of 10/21/93 by the approximate method (using the INT function), the age will be computed as 0; by the exact method it will be 1 year. The reason for the bogus number is the .25 in the divisor. In this example, the difference in days is 365. Dividing this by 365.25 yields a number less than 1, and applying the INT function to that result yields 0. Be careful.

Example 8

Computing the Date after a Number of Intervals

FEATURE: **INTNX Function**

The companion function to INTCK is the INTNX function. This function returns a SAS date value which is a given number of intervals after a base date value. Suppose you want to find the date 10 months after a patient's initial visit so a follow-up office visit can be arranged. Working from the initial visit date, VISIT, you can easily generate the date 10 months hence as:

```
FOLLOWUP=INTNX ('MONTH',VISIT,10);
```

For example, if the date of VISIT is 10/21/94, the FOLLOWUP date will be August 1, 1995. Once again, realize that this function, like INTCK, works with internal boundaries (in this case, the 1st of each month). As long as you are fully cognizant of what the code is doing, you can't go wrong. Remember one of Murphy's laws: When working toward solving a problem, it always helps when you know the answer.

Conclusion

SAS software provides you with very powerful tools for working with dates. You have seen in this chapter how to read dates in various formats, extract day, month, and year information from a date, and calculate intervals between two dates. As you work with dates, you will become more comfortable with the date informats, formats, and functions. And now, here are the problems.

Problems

6-1. You have an instream raw data file of patient hospital stays with the following file layout:

Starting Column	Length	Format	Description
1	3	character	Subject ID
4	6	mmddyy	Admission date
10	6	mmddyy	Discharge date
16	8	mmddyyyy	Date of birth

Here are some sample data:

```
0010105920107921 0211946
0021112921115920 9011955
0030512920609921 2251899
0040101930107930 4051952
```

a) Write a program to create a SAS data set called DATES1, and list the resulting data set with PROC PRINT. Create variables ID, ADMIT, DISCH, and DOB from the given data, and also create the following new variables:

AGE   age in years on the date of admission (as of the last birthday)
DAY   numeric day of the week of admission date (1=Sun, 2=Mon, etc.)
MONTH numeric month of year of admission date (1=Jan, 2=Feb, etc.)

Set up the DATA step so that the variables print with the following formats:

ADMIT mm/dd/yy
DISCH mm/dd/yy
DOB   ddMMMyyyy
AGE   no decimals
DAY   3 letter names (SUN, MON, etc.)
MONTH numeric (1=Jan, 2=Feb, etc.)

b) Compute the mean age of all patients (use PROC MEANS — see Chapter 10, "PROC MEANS and PROC UNIVARIATE").
c) Create a chart showing the frequency of admissions by day of week (use PROC CHART—see Chapter 12, "PROC CHART").
d) Compute frequencies on the number of visits by month of year (use PROC FREQ — see Chapter 10).

6-2. You have a SAS data set, DATES2, that contains variables MONTH and YEAR (of birth), but not day. Create a new data set based on DATES2 and include AGE as of the date the program is run, using the 15th of the month as an approximate day for the date of birth. Round the value of AGE in years to the nearest year. Store the MMDDYY8. format with DOB.

6-3. You have a SAS data set, DATES3, which contains the variables ID, DOB (date of birth), VISIT_D, VISIT_M, and VISIT_Y (visit day, month, and year respectively). Write a program to create a new data set which includes a variable called AGE (approximate age rounded to the nearest year at the time of visit.) Try to calculate the value of AGE with one statement.

6-4. You have a set of raw data showing the number of crayons produced at Company X on certain sample dates. The company started producing crayons in the beginning of 1990.

Here is the raw data file layout:

Starting Column	Length	Format	Description
1	8	mm/dd/yy	Date of manufacture
11	6	numeric	Number of crayons produced

Here are some sample data:

```
02/01/90  12,500
02/08/90  12,600
04/01/90  13,000
05/05/90  12,800
08/05/90  14,000
12/12/90  14,200
02/18/91  14,400
02/22/91  14,100
05/01/91  15,000
```

You want to compute the mean number of crayons produced in each quarter, starting from 01/01/90. For example, the mean number of crayons produced in quarter 0 (from 01/01/90 to 03/31/90) is 12,550. There are various ways to do this, but try using the INTCK function. Also, see Chapter 10 for the syntax for PROC MEANS.

6-5. You are assigned the job of "match-making" for a dating firm. The firm has its data in a SAS data set called CLIENTS, consisting of variables ID (ID number), GENDER (M or F), and DOB (date of birth.) The astrologer on staff suggests that there are two compatible groups of clients, one being males born on a Wednesday or Thursday in either January or March, and the other being females born on Fridays in either August or September. First, write a program to create a subset of CLIENTS which contains clients fitting the astrologer's suggestions. Next, print out two lists, one for females and one for males, listing the clients by ID and showing the DOB, the DAY of the week on which they were born, and the MONTH of the year in which they were born.

Here is part of the CLIENTS data set:

ID	GENDER	DOB
18	M	03/07/62
28	F	07/12/67
38	M	03/19/59
53	M	01/25/62
72	F	09/01/67
75	F	08/07/59
77	M	05/17/55
80	F	09/07/62

Programming Tips and Techniques

CHAPTERS

Chapter 7

SAS® Arrays

Avoiding Repetitious DATA Step Coding

EXAMPLES

Introduction

Now that you are becoming an experienced SAS programmer, it's time to show you how to save some time and write more compact SAS code. Whenever you find yourself writing many repetitive lines of SAS code, you should consider using an array. SAS arrays are used to represent lists of variables. Writing a single line of SAS code using an array can be equivalent to writing hundreds (or thousands, or millions) of lines of code without using an array. (OK, so we got a little carried away!) This chapter shows you how to save time and typing using SAS arrays.

Example 1

Substituting One Value for Another in a Group of Variables

FEATURES: ARRAY Statement, DO Loop, DIM Function

Suppose you have 105 variables (X1-X100, A,B,C,D, and E) in SAS data set OLD, and a value of 999 is used to represent missing data. It is a common practice in some other database systems to use values such as 99, 999, etc., to represent missing values. Suppose further that you want to substitute a SAS System missing value (.) for the value of 999. You can proceed as follows:

Example 1.1 - Hard Way

```
DATA HARDWAY;
   SET OLD;
   IF X1=999 THEN X1=.;
   IF X2=999 THEN X2=.;
   .
   .
   .
   IF X100=999 THEN X100=.;
   IF A   =999 THEN A   =.;
   IF B   =999 THEN B   =.;
   .
   .
   .
   IF E   =999 then E   =.;
RUN;
```

Pretty tedious eh? You say, "There must be a better way!" And there is—it's called an array. An array is used in the SAS System to represent a list of variables, or elements. The SAS System then allows you to perform an operation, or a set of operations, on the entire list by referring to the array. Using an array, the above program can be rewritten as follows:

Example 1.2 - Easy Way

```
DATA EASYWAY;
   SET OLD;
   ARRAY NARNIA[105] X1-X100 A B C D E;
   DO I=1 TO 105;
      IF NARNIA[I]=999 THEN NARNIA[I]=.;
   END;
   DROP I;
RUN;
```

Here you create an array with the ARRAY statement, name it NARNIA, and define it to represent all 105 variables. (You know where this array name came from if you have young children, and if you've read the C.S. Lewis collection, "The Chronicles of Narnia" to them.) By placing the IF statement in a DO loop, and operating on the array NARNIA, which represents 105 variables, you can accomplish with one statement exactly the same objective as the first program in Example 1.1 did with 105 repetitive statements. To repeat ourselves (we do that often because repetition is a cornerstone of good teaching), you simply assign the variables in question to the array, write one of the repetitive lines using the subscripted array name in place of a variable name, and place the code in a DO loop so that it will execute as many times as there are variables in the array. Notice that you should drop the DO loop index (I) from the data set you create. You really don't need to keep it around after it has served its purpose. This is good coding practice in general.

In addition to using an array to represent an entire group of variables, you can refer to any one of the variables individually by using a bracketed subscript, ([I] in this example). Thus, NARNIA[3] refers to the variable X3, NARNIA[104] refers to the variable D, etc. The time to start using arrays is when you notice that you are coding the same line over and over again, with the only change being the variable name.

An alternate way to code the above ARRAY statement is:

```
ARRAY NARNIA[*] X1-X100 A B C D E;
```

The * indicates that the SAS System will count the number of variables in the array for you. Of course there are always ways for you to get the count yourself, but here you just take the easy way. The DO loop is:

```
DO I = 1 TO DIM(NARNIA);
```

DIM is the dimension function. This returns the length of the array (i.e. the number of variables in the list). Don't worry about the extra CPU time it takes to use this method—it is negligible.

Example 2

Substituting One Value for Another in All Numeric Variables

FEATURES: **ARRAY Statement, DO Loop, DIM Function, _NUMERIC_ Variable**

You can easily extend the program above to substitute a SAS missing value for all the numeric variables in your data set. The internal SAS term _NUMERIC_ can be used to refer to all the numeric variables in a SAS data set (either in a DATA or PROC step). This is a good place to mention that the terms _CHARACTER_ and _ALL_ are also available and represent all character variables and all variables respectively. Here is a program to set a value of 999 to missing for all numeric variables:

Example 2

```
DATA NEW;
   SET OLD;
   ARRAY XXX[*] _NUMERIC_;
   DO I=1 TO DIM (XXX);
      IF XXX[I]=999 THEN XXX[I]=.;
   END;
   DROP I;
RUN;
```

Easy enough! The only "trick" here is to use the term _NUMERIC_ instead of an actual variable list. The DIM function is especially useful in this program because you don't have to count the number of numeric variables. (Be sure that you don't give your array the same name as a variable in your data set.)

Example 3

> ## Substituting One Value for Another in All Character Variables
>
> *FEATURES:* Character Array, DO Loop, _CHARACTER_ Variables

Let's use the previous technique here to set values of NA (Not Applicable) to blanks (character missing value) for all character variables in a data set. (Yes, some people do code things like this.) Here is the program:

Example 3

```
DATA NEW;
   SET OLD;
   ARRAY YYY[*] $ _CHARACTER_;
   DO I=1 TO DIM (YYY);
      IF YYY[I]='NA' THEN YYY[I]=' ';
   END;
   DROP I;
RUN;
```

This program needs very little explanation. To declare array YYY a character array, place a dollar sign ($) after the array name. As we mentioned before, the term _CHARACTER_ is used to represent all the character variables in the data set.

Specifying Lengths in an ARRAY Statement

To specify the length of the variables in an array of numeric variables, follow the array name with the number of bytes for the variables. To specify the length of variables in an array of character variables, place the length after the dollar sign. Here are two examples:

To specify an array X of numeric variables X1-X10, all of length 4, use this code:

```
ARRAY X[10] 4 X1-X10;
```

To specify an array Y of character variables Y1-Y10, all of length 1, use this code:

```
ARRAY Y[10] $ 1 Y1-Y10;
```

Example 4

Restructuring a SAS Data Set: Creating Multiple Observations from a Single Observation

FEATURES: **ARRAY Statement, DO Loop, OUTPUT Statement, Restructuring a SAS Data Set**

When you collect multiple measurements on a subject at different times or under different conditions, you have a choice of how to structure your data set. For example, if you measure X at times 1, 2, and 3, you can choose to have a single observation containing SUBJECT, X1, X2, and X3, where X1 is the value of X at time 1, etc. Or, you can decide to make three observations with SUBJECT, TIME, and X. For some analyses the first structure is more convenient; for others, the second structure is preferred. In this example, we show you how to convert from the first structure to the second.

Suppose you have SAS data set OLD with one observation per subject containing values for three variables, X1 - X3, which represent measurements taken at three different times.

```
     Data set OLD

 SUBJECT   X1  X2  X3
       1    4   5   6
       2    7   8   9
```

You wish to create a SAS data set NEW with three observations per subject (one for each measurement), and a variable TIME denoting the measurement (1, 2, or 3) as follows:

```
Data set NEW

SUBJECT   TIME   X
   1       1     4
   1       2     5
   1       3     6
   2       1     7
   2       2     8
   2       3     9
```

This can be easily accomplished using an array as follows:

Example 4

```
DATA NEW;
    SET OLD;  ❶
    ARRAY XX[3] X1-X3;  ❷
    DO TIME=1 TO 3;  ❸
        X=XX[TIME];  ❹
        OUTPUT;  ❺
    END;
    DROP X1-X3;  ❻
RUN;
```

There are a few new things to notice in this program. First, you cannot use the same name for an array and a variable in the same DATA step. In this example you use XX for the array name, so X will be available for the name of the newly created single variable in data set NEW. Next, you create another new variable TIME to identify which measurement time each observation in data set NEW represents. You can use a shortcut and create TIME in the DO loop, and then use it as the index or subscript of the array XX.

Let's take some TIME to explain exactly what is happening here. The DATA step is executed for each observation read in (SET) from data set OLD ❶. At each iteration, the following happens: Array XX has three elements, the three variables X1-X3 ❷. The DO loop is operated repetitively over TIME by setting TIME equal to 1, then 2, and finally 3 ❸. At each repetition, X is set equal to the value of the element of XX referred to by XX[TIME] ❹, and is then OUTPUT ❺ to create a new observation in data set NEW, along with the other new variable TIME, and the variable SUBJECT from data set OLD.

Note that X1-X3 are not included in data set NEW because they are dropped ❶. As an example, during the first iteration of the DO loop in the first execution of the DATA step, TIME=1 and X is set equal to the value of XX[1], which is the value of X1 (4) in the current observation of data set OLD. These values are then written (using the OUTPUT statement) to data set NEW, and the next iteration of the DO loop is set to go, with TIME=2, etc.

Now if that wasn't bad (or good) enough, you can do better. Arrays don't only come in one flavor - unidimensional. They can also be multidimensional in nature, yielding much more power and many more headaches. Let's plow ahead.

Example 5

Restructuring a SAS Data Set: Creating Multiple Observations from a Single Observation (Multidimensional Example)

FEATURES: Multidimensional ARRAY Statement, Nested DO Loops

In the previous example you created 3 observations from a single observation using an array. In this example, you have 6 values of X (X1 to X6) which represent X at 3 times recorded under 2 different methods. This requires a change from a simple array to a multidimensional array.

Suppose, again, that you have the data set OLD with one observation per subject. This time, however, you have recorded both the time of the observation as well as the method under which the measurement was taken. Each record contains variables X1-X6. Variables X1-X3 represent values of measurements taken for method 1, at times 1 to 3; variables X4-X6 represent values for method 2, also at times 1 to 3. You now want to create data set NEW with six observations per subject, one for each time-method combination. You also wish to create two new variables, METHOD and TIME, for each observation.

The OLD data set looks like this:

```
        Data set OLD

SUBJECT  X1  X2  X3  X4  X5  X6
      1   3   4   6   9  10  11
      2   4   5   5   8   7   9
```

You want the NEW data set to look like this:

```
         Data set NEW

SUBJECT   METHOD   TIME    X
   1        1        1      3
   1        1        2      4
   1        1        3      6
   1        2        1      9
   1        2        2     10
   1        2        3     11
   2        1        1      4
   2        1        2      5
   2        1        3      5
   2        2        1      8
   2        2        2      7
   2        2        3      9
```

Here is the program that accomplishes your goal:

Example 5

```
DATA NEW;
    SET OLD;
    ARRAY XX[2,3] X1-X6;  ❶
    DO METHOD=1 TO 2;  ❷
        DO TIME=1 TO 3;  ❸
            X=XX[METHOD,TIME];  ❹
            OUTPUT;  ❺
        END;
    END;
    KEEP SUBJECT METHOD TIME X;
RUN;
```

This program is much like the previous one, except it is in two dimensions, so it must be twice as good - certainly twice as complicated and twice as powerful. Once again, you use XX for the name of the array and X for the name of the new variable in data set NEW which will represent the measurements ❶. This time you create METHOD as a new variable as well as TIME. You do this in DO loops as before, but this time you use two nested loops, one for each dimension in the array. In nested DO loops, inner loops change faster than outer loops. In your OLD data, the measurements occur in the order: method1-time1, method1-time2, method1- time3, method2-time1, method2-time2, and method2-time3, contained in variables X1-X6.

Since time is changing from 1 through 3 within each static method, time is said to vary faster than method. This pattern can be represented in a multidimensional "2 by 3" array.

Multidimensional arrays are identified by a list of array dimensions, separated by commas, with slower changing dimensions preceding faster changing ones in the list from left to right. Array XX has dimensions [2,3], and is made up of variables X1- X6. This means that XX[1,1] represents X1 (method1-time1), XX[1,2] represents X2 (method1-time2), and so forth, up to XX[2,3] which represents X6 (method2-time3).

The nested loops read through the data in OLD sequentially from X1 through X6 and assign the proper values to variables METHOD and TIME before outputting each observation to data set NEW. First the outer DO METHOD loop sets the variable METHOD to 1 or 2 ❷. Next, the inner DO TIME loop cycles through the three times for each method ❸. Each element of the array is therefore selected, identified as to method and time ❹, and output as X to data set NEW.❺

Easy? Not necessarily. Powerful? Definitely! Maybe you should LOOP through this section a few more TIMEs using different METHODs until you've got it.

Example 6

> ### Restructuring a SAS Data Set: Creating a Single Observation from Multiple Observations
>
> *FEATURES:* **ARRAY, RETAIN, and SET Statements, PROC SORT, FIRST.***byvar* **and LAST.***byvar* **Variables**

Now you do Example 4 in reverse! You again restructure a data set, but this time you are going from a data set with multiple observations per subject to a data set with a single observation per subject. Your original data set OLD contains one observation for each subject-time combination, with a measurement value, X, as follows:

```
Data set OLD

SUBJECT   TIME   X
   1        1    5
   1        2    6
   1        3    7
   2        1    8
   2        2    9
   2        3    4
```

You want a data set NEW that contains one observation per subject, with all measurements on each record, as follows:

```
Data set NEW

SUBJECT   X1   X2   X3
   1       5    6    7
   2       8    9    4
```

X1 in data set NEW is the value of X at time 1 in data set OLD, etc. Here's how to do it:

Example 6

```
PROC SORT DATA=OLD;  ❶
   BY SUBJECT TIME;
RUN;

DATA NEW;
   SET OLD;  ❷
   BY SUBJECT;
   ARRAY XX[*] X1-X3;
   RETAIN X1-X3;          ❸
   IF FIRST.SUBJECT=1 THEN DO I=1 TO 3;  ❹
      XX[I]=.;
      END;
   XX[TIME]=X;     ❺
   IF LAST.SUBJECT=1 THEN OUTPUT;  ❻
   KEEP SUBJECT X1-X3;        ❼
RUN;
```

This program uses a number of powerful SAS System programming features. You start by sorting the data by SUBJECT, and TIME within SUBJECT ❶. If you are really sure the data set is already in SUBJECT- TIME order, the sort is unnecessary. Next, you create a new data set NEW by reading in observations from data set OLD ❷. In general, a BY statement following a SET statement sets up special temporary variables called FIRST.*byvar* and LAST.*byvar* for each of the variables in the BY list. They are temporary because they are not saved with the data set, but rather they exist for the duration of the DATA step only; FIRST.*byvar* has a value of 1 (true) for every observation that is the first occurrence of a new BY group, and a value of 0 (false) for all other occurrences. Likewise, LAST.*byvar* has a value of 1 for the last occurrence of a BY group, and a value of 0 for all other occurrences.

In our example, the temporary variables work as follows. After being sorted, data set OLD exists in the sorted order of TIME within SUBJECT. Using the BY statement following the SET statement in the DATA step, you instruct the SAS System to create the internal variables FIRST.SUBJECT and LAST.SUBJECT. Each time you begin a new SUBJECT BY group (begin reading observations for a new subject), the variable FIRST.SUBJECT ❹ is true (set equal to 1).

At all other times, FIRST.SUBJECT is false (equal to 0). When you encounter the last observation for a subject, LAST.SUBJECT ❻ is true (1). At all other times, it is false (0). You use these logical (true or false) FIRST.*byvar* and LAST.*byvar* variables to accomplish different goals.

The program works by accumulating values for all times for each subject from OLD before outputting an observation to NEW. It's a little tricky, so pay attention. A RETAIN statement ❸ is used to "remember" the values of X1-X3 until it's time to output them. (See Chapter 8, "RETAIN," for details on the RETAIN statement.) When the first observation from OLD is read, SUBJECT=1, TIME=1, X=5, FIRST.SUBJECT=1, and LAST.SUBJECT=0. The elements of ARRAY XX, (X1, X2, X3) are initialized to missing (.) ❹. Although this initialization step is not necessary here, if you are missing an observation for one or more times for a subject, you would retain the values from the previous subject if you did not initialize X1 to X3 to missing. This initialization is done each time a new subject is read in (FIRST.SUBJECT=1).

Statement ❺ instructs the program to set the element of XX with a subscript equal to the current value of TIME, equal to the current value of X. For the first observation, TIME=1 and X=5. Since TIME = 1, XX[TIME] is the same as XX[1] which represents the variable X1 (set equal to 5, the value of X).

The next observation from OLD is then read (SUBJECT=1, TIME=2, X=6, FIRST.SUBJECT=0, and LAST.SUBJECT=0.) Values of X1-X3 are retained from the previous observation (X1=5, X2=., X3=.) and XX[TIME], or XX[2], or X2, is set equal to 6, the current value of X in OLD. This happens again for the next observation resulting in X1=5, X2=6, and X3=7. This time however, since LAST.SUBJECT ❻ is true (equal to 1), the observation is ouput to NEW. Only the variables SUBJECT, X1, X2, and X3 are kept ❼. The process is then repeated for SUBJECT 2.

Conclusion

Although using arrays can get complicated, you should begin to use them in any of your programs where there are many repetitive lines of SAS code. Remember the rule: If you seem to be writing the same line of code over and over again with the only change being variable names, consider using an array. If you need to restructure a SAS data set from one to many or from many to one, consider using an array. Here are some problems for you to try out your newly learned skills:

Problems

7-1. You have SAS data set OLD which contains the variables ID, HTIN1-HTIN10 (10 height measurements in inches), and WTLB1-WTLB10 (10 weight measurements in pounds.) Write a program using arrays to create a new data set NEW with variables ID (same ID), HTCM1-HTCM10 (same 10 heights - now in centimeters), and WTKG1-WTKG10 (same 10 weights - now in kilograms.) The conversions are:

(Height in CM) = 2.54 * (Height in inches)
and
(Weight in KG) = (Weight in pounds) / 2.2.

7-2. You have a SAS data set SURVEY which uses missing value codes of –1 for variables X1-X100, 99 for variables Y1-Y50, and the literal string 'NO DATA' for the character variables A, B, C, D, and E. Use arrays to replace these missing values with standard SAS missing values.

7-3. Given the SAS data set ONEPER as shown, use an array to restructure this data set into the SAS data set FOURPER:

Data Set ONEPER

ID	HR1	HR2	HR3	HR4
1	60	62	64	68
2	80	84	90	98

Data Set FOURPER

ID	TREAT	HR
1	1	60
1	2	62
1	3	64
1	4	68
2	1	80
2	2	84
2	3	90
2	4	98

7-4. Modify your program in Problem 7-3 so that the values for TREAT are translated from numeric values 1, 2, 3, and 4 into character strings 'A', 'B', 'C', and 'D', respectively.

Hint: Use another variable in the DO loop and compute TREAT inside the loop.

7-5. Given the SAS data set THREEPER as shown, use arrays to restructure this data set into the SAS data set ONEPER.

Notes: 1. There are no missing values in the data set.
2. The data set is already sorted in ID order.

Data Set THREEPER

ID	TIME	SBP	DBP
1	1	120	80
1	2	122	84
1	3	128	90
2	1	116	70
2	2	118	74
2	3	122	80

Data Set ONEPER

ID	SBP1	SBP2	SBP3	DBP1	DBP2	DBP3
1	120	122	128	80	84	90
2	116	118	122	70	74	80

Chapter 8 RETAIN

"Remembering" Values from Previous Observations

Introduction

Performing computations within an observation in a SAS DATA step is relatively straightforward; performing computations across observations is not. For example, finding a sum of variables in a single observation is accomplished easily by using simple addition or the SUM function. Adding values across multiple observations involves either using the LAG function (see Chapter 5, "SAS Functions," Example 7) or a RETAIN statement. This chapter acquaints you with the RETAIN statement—its use and abuse.

Basically, RETAIN works as follows: prior to the reading of each new record of data in a DATA step, the SAS System normally initializes each variable to a missing value. A RETAIN statement can be used, however, to instruct the system not to assign a missing value to a variable, but rather to "remember" its value from the previous observation. This value may then be used to calculate running totals, or it may be compared to values in the current observation, or it may be changed within the DATA step in many ways. The examples that follow should help you understand how the RETAIN statement works and will make you aware of some subtle problems that can occur if you are not careful in its use.

Example 1

Creating a Subject Number in the DATA Step: A Common Mistake

FEATURE: **Assignment Statement**

Suppose you have a source of raw data which consists of one record per subject with scores on two variables for each subject. The records are not identified by subject number, but you want to print out each subject by sequential number with the accompanying data. You, therefore, want a program to generate incremental subject numbers. The following program almost does the job.

Example 1

```
******* INCORRECT PROGRAM *******;

DATA NOGOOD;
   SUBJECT=SUBJECT+1;
   INPUT SCORE1 SCORE2;
DATALINES;
 3 4
 5 6
 7 8
;

PROC PRINT DATA=NOGOOD;
   TITLE1 'Incorrect Program';
RUN;
```

The resulting output shows a data set that contains three observations, but they have missing values (.) for subject numbers.

Output from Example 1 - Creating a Subject Number in the DATA Step: A Common Mistake

```
                    Incorrect Program

         OBS    SUBJECT    SCORE1    SCORE2

          1        .          3         4
          2        .          5         6
          3        .          7         8
```

This program did not perform as desired for the following reason: For each iteration of the DATA step, all variables, including SUBJECT, were initialized to missing (.). Values for SCORE1 and SCORE2 were then read in, but no values were read in for SUBJECT. When you add 1 to a missing value, as you do in the following line, the result is also missing (see Chapter 5, Example 4):

```
SUBJECT=SUBJECT+1;
```

Example 2

> ## Creating a Subject Number in the DATA Step Using RETAIN
>
> *FEATURE:* **RETAIN Statement**

To correct the problem in Example 1, you can use a RETAIN statement to initialize the value of SUBJECT to a non-missing value (0 for the first observation), and then bring forward the previous value of SUBJECT to each new observation being added to the data set you are building. You then increment the value of SUBJECT by 1 for each observation. If you place the following line anywhere in the DATA step, the program executes as desired and produces the results shown in Output 2:

```
RETAIN SUBJECT 0;
```

Example 2

```
DATA BETTER;
   RETAIN SUBJECT 0;
   SUBJECT=SUBJECT + 1;
   INPUT SCORE1 SCORE2;
DATALINES;
3 4
5 6
7 8
;

PROC PRINT DATA=BETTER;
   TITLE1 'Correct Program';
RUN;
```

Output from Example 2 - Creating a Subject Number in the DATA Step Using RETAIN

```
                    Correct Program

          OBS   SUBJECT   SCORE1   SCORE2

           1       1        3        4
           2       2        5        6
           3       3        7        8
```

You may be asking yourself why you went through the trouble of producing the variable SUBJECT when the system provides OBS in the PROC PRINT output, and this is exactly the value you worked so hard to obtain. The answer is that OBS is a display variable only. It is not included in the data set; it is only present in the PROC PRINT output. By using the method shown here, you have the value of SUBJECT as part of the data set itself. Of course, if the OBS number on the output is all you'll ever need, by all means use what the system gives you and don't create extra work for yourself.

Example 3

Explicit versus Implicit Retaining of Values

FEATURE: **Sum Statement**

The previous example adequately demonstrates the explicit use of RETAIN. You can achieve the same result by using the following sum statement:

```
SUBJECT+1;
```

This replaces the following lines from the original program:

```
RETAIN SUBJECT 0;
SUBJECT=SUBJECT+1;
```

The sum statement (not to be confused with the SUM function discussed in the next example) is one of those statements in the SAS System that you discover after you've been writing code for a while, and you sit back and say, "Hmmm. I wonder what other goodies there are that I don't know about." Here is the alternate code using the sum statement:

Example 3

```
DATA BEST;
    SUBJECT+1;
    INPUT SCORE1 SCORE2;
DATALINES;
3 4
5 6
7 8
;

PROC PRINT DATA=BEST;
    TITLE1 'Correct Program';
RUN;
```

Notice there is no equal (=) sign in the SUBJECT+1; statement. This sum statement does a few things: It automatically initializes SUBJECT to 0 for the first observation, and then it implicitly retains the previous value for each new observation before performing its function (in this case, adding 1 to the retained value). The output from this program is identical to the output from Example 2.

Example 4

Scoring a Multiple-Choice Test Using RETAIN

FEATURES: **RETAIN, ARRAY, DELETE, and KEEP Statements, SUM Function, _N_ Variable**

Here we use a simple example of test-scoring code to demonstrate a variety of DATA step statements in addition to RETAIN. (You may also want to actually score a test sometime!) The use of arrays and the ARRAY statement is explained in detail in Chapter 7, "SAS Arrays."

Suppose you have a data file in which the first record is the answer key and subsequent records contain student answers. The tasks are to read the answer key data in from the first record, read the student answers in from all the other records, calculate scores for each student answer by comparing key data to answer data, and then derive summary scores for each student. Here is the code to accomplish this:

Example 4

```
DATA SCORING;
    ARRAY KEY[5] $ 1 KEY1-KEY5;        * ANSWER KEY           ;
    ARRAY ANS[5] $ 1 ANS1-ANS5;        * STUDENT RESPONSES    ;
    ARRAY SCORE[5]   SCORE1-SCORE5;    * ITEM SCORES,         ;
                                       *    1=CORRECT,        ;
                                       *    0=WRONG           ;
    RETAIN KEY1-KEY5;    ❶
    IF _N_=1 THEN DO;    ❷
        INPUT (KEY1-KEY5)($1.);  ❸
        DELETE;   ❹
    END;
    ELSE DO;    ❺
        INPUT (ANS1-ANS5)($1.);  ❻
        DO I=1 TO 5;
            IF KEY[I]=ANS[I] THEN SCORE[I]=1;    ❼
            ELSE SCORE[I]=0;
        END;
        RAW=SUM (OF SCORE1-SCORE5);        ❽
        PERCENT=(100*RAW)/5;
    END;
    KEEP RAW PERCENT;
DATALINES;
ABCDE  ❾
ABABA  ❿
ABCDA
;

PROC PRINT DATA=SCORING;
    TITLE1 'Scoring a Test';
RUN;
```

Much is happening in this code. Let's take it step by step. First you read in values for the KEY1-KEY5 variables ❸ (contained in the first record) and make them available for the comparison work which needs to be done for each succeeding student response record. You accomplish this by retaining the KEY1-KEY5 values in the program data vector (PDV) so that they're available for comparison with student answers on each iteration ❶. You then read in the raw data for each student (ANS1-ANS5 = responses to individual questions) ❻, compute a score for each question

(SCORE1-SCORE5) ❼, and then derive two final scores for each student (RAW = number of questions answered correctly; PERCENT = percentage answered correctly. ❽)

Processing Records Differently

Now, how do you treat the first record, which contains the answer key data, differently from the remaining records, which contain student responses? The SAS System supplies the tools for you to accomplish this task. For each iteration of a DATA step, the automatically created SAS System internal variable _N_ ❷ is incremented by 1. For the purposes of this example, you can think of _N_ as an observation counter (see Chapter 5, Example 2 for an important caution note). When the system is set to read in the first data record (the answer key in this example), _N_ equals 1. The IF-THEN/ELSE logic ❸,❻ instructs the system to perform different actions depending on the current value of _N_.

When _N_ equals 1, the first DO ... END; section of code ❸ (this is called a "DO group") is executed and the values for KEY1-KEY5 ❾ are read in. When _N_ is not equal to 1, the lines of code under ELSE DO; ❻ are executed. Values are read in for ANS1-ANS5 ❿ instead of KEY1-KEY5, and SCORE1-SCORE5 values are created from the retained KEY1-KEY5 variables ❼.

Deleting Unneeded Observations

But what about that DELETE statement ❹ in the first DO group? At this point you might be asking, "Why read in a line of data and then delete it?" Good question! Although each record of data is "read in" to the system, it is not actually "written out" to the data set being created until the end of the DATA step. The DELETE statement instructs the program not to write out the first observation (_N_ = 1). You really don't need it because it contains key data only, with no student answer data. Don't worry about losing the key data. Since the first record values for KEY1-KEY5 are retained, they are always available when needed.

Totaling Values (Scoring the Test)

Once you have a score for each item, the total score on the test (RAW) is simply the sum of the number of correct responses. Since all SCORE values are either 1 or 0, RAW is simply the sum of all scores. You use the SUM function ❽ here (not to be confused with the sum statement) to compute this sum. The following line

```
RAW=SUM(OF SCORE1-SCORE5);❽
```

is *almost* equivalent to

```
RAW=SCORE1+SCORE2+SCORE3+SCORE4+SCORE5;
```

Using the SUM function is usually simpler than listing all the sequentially suffixed variables (perhaps not in this simple example, but take our word for it - when you're taking the sum of 2,347 variables, it's simpler!). The reason that it is *almost* equivalent is that the SUM function returns the sum of the non-missing elements, whereas the simple arithmetic expression will return a missing value if any of the elements are missing. The SUM function and other useful SAS System functions are covered in Chapter 5.

The last step is to calculate the PERCENT score. This is simply 100 times the raw score divided by the number of items on the test.

Another tidbit in this already too long example is the KEEP statement. You should make a habit of using this basic storage efficiency technique whenever you are programming in the SAS System. In this example, the KEEP statement instructs the system to keep only the RAW and PERCENT variables in the RESULTS data set you are building. All the KEY, ANS, and SCORE variables which were needed in intermediate steps are not kept around for posterity and do not take up valuable space.

The results of this simple and elegant (or simply elegant) code are shown in Output 4.

Output from Example 4 - Scoring a Multiple-Choice Test Using RETAIN

```
                    Scoring a Test

              OBS   RAW   PERCENT

               1     2      40
               2     4      80
```

More Elegant Techniques

As long as you are getting elegant in your coding (a good goal to strive for), let's go on a digression and get a little fancy. Instead of using the IF-THEN/ELSE ❼ coding to set the value of SCORE to either 1 or 0, you can use the following line of code to accomplish the same results:

```
SCORE[I]=(KEY[I]=ANS[I]);
```

This is a complex statement. The parentheses are optional and are put in for clarity (a procedure that we highly recommend for beginners). The right equal sign could have been written as EQ since it is a logical operator and not part of the assignment statement syntax. The left equal sign, however, must be written as is. The statement is actually saying, "Set the value of SCORE[I] equal to the result of performing the logical operation KEY[I] = ANS[I]." The result of any logical operation is either true (1) or false (0). SCORE[I] is therefore set to 1 if KEY[I] is equal to ANS[I], and 0 if it is not.

While we're off on a tangent (this is actually a tangent to a tangent, and if we keep going, we're bound to come full circle), here is another example which combines a logical expression with an arithmetic one. Suppose you are reading in birthdate data in MMDDYY format, and you have a separate variable (CENTURY) which has values of 1800 or 1900 denoting the century of birth. To compute a person's age (as of January 1, 1995), you can write

```
AGE=('01JAN95'D-DOB)/365.25+100*(CENTURY EQ 1800);
```

DOB is date of birth stored as a SAS System date value. If CENTURY = 1800, then you add 100*(1) to the age; if not, then you add 100*(0). (Refer to Chapter 6, "SAS Dates," Example 3 for more on computing ages.) And now back to our regularly scheduled topic...

Example 5

Using Caution When Coding with RETAIN

FEATURE: RETAIN Statement

This example shows one of the pitfalls you can encounter when using RETAIN. Suppose you have recorded the date of birth and weight of each subject on three different weigh-ins. However, the date of birth was only recorded at the first weigh-in, and you were a little sloppy in your data collection and failed to get it for one of your subjects.

You want to create a SAS data set that contains the subject's date of birth and weight in each observation. If any data are missing, they should be so noted. Here is the raw data file:

```
    File HTWT

SUBJ     DOB      WEIGHT
1     10/21/50    155
1                 158
1                 162
2     11/01/46    102
2                 108
2                 105
3                 200    NOTE: DOB is missing for this subject
3                 202
3                 198
```

Here is a program that has all good intentions but doesn't give you exactly what you want:

Example 5

```
DATA DANGER;
   RETAIN OLD_DOB;  ❶
   INFILE 'HTWT';
   INPUT @1  SUBJ    $2.
         @7  DOB      MMDDYY8.
         @17 WEIGHT  3.;
   IF DOB NE . THEN OLD_DOB=DOB;  ❷  * SET OLD_DOB TO DOB ;
   ELSE DOB=OLD_DOB;  ❸               * SO WE CAN           ;
   FORMAT DOB MMDDYY8.;               * REMEMBER IT         ;
   DROP OLD_DOB;
RUN;

PROC PRINT DATA=DANGER;
   TITLE1 'Incorrect DOB Solution';
RUN;
```

Here is the output:

Output from Example 5 - Using Caution When Coding with RETAIN

```
                    Incorrect DOB Solution

          OBS   SUBJ    DOB     WEIGHT

           1     1    10/21/50     55
           2     1    10/21/50    158
           3     1    10/21/50    162
           4     2    11/01/46    102
           5     2    11/01/46    108
           6     2    11/01/46    105
           7     3    11/01/46    200
           8     3    11/01/46    202
           9     3    11/01/46    198
```

What Went Wrong?

The program was supposed to work in the following way: For each observation being added to the data set, DOB is read in from the raw data and OLD_DOB is created via a RETAIN statement ❶. In this example, you do not supply an initial value for the retained variable as was done in Example 2. As each record is built for the data set, the values of DOB and OLD_DOB have an effect on each other. If DOB as read in is not missing (a new subject), then OLD_DOB is set to DOB ❷. If DOB is missing (another record for the previous subject), then DOB is set to the retained value of OLD_DOB ❸. Sounds reasonable. So what went wrong? Since DOB was missing entirely for Subject 3, the retained value of OLD_DOB for Subject 2 was used (again).

Example 6

> ### Checking for a New Subject Number Using a LAG Function
>
> *FEATURES:* **RETAIN Statement, LAG Function**

To prevent the previous situation from happening, you cannot merely rely on the presence of a value for DOB. Instead, you need to set the variable OLD_DOB equal to DOB each time you read data from what you know to be a new subject. How do you tell when you have reached a new subject? One approach is to compare the current value of SUBJ to the previous value by using the LAG function. (See Chapter 5, Example 7 for more information on the LAG function.) This function is another powerful and easily misunderstood (and misused) feature of the SAS System. The LAG function works by returning the value of its argument last time it (the LAG function) was executed. If you execute the LAG function for every observation, its value is the value of the variable from the previous observation. The statement

```
IF SUBJ NE LAG(SUBJ) THEN OLD_DOB=DOB;  ❶
```

sets OLD_DOB equal to DOB each time a new subject is encountered (even if DOB is missing).

Here is the code that works:

Example 6

```
DATA WORKS;
   RETAIN OLD_DOB;
   INFILE 'HTWT';
   INPUT @1    SUBJ $2.
         @7    DOB  MMDDYY8.
         @17  WEIGHT 3.;

*CHECK IF WE HAVE A NEW SUBJECT NUMBER. IF SO,
 SET OLD_DOB TO THE DOB VALUE FOR THE NEW SUBJECT;

   IF SUBJ NE LAG(SUBJ) THEN OLD_DOB=DOB; ❶
   ELSE DOB=OLD_DOB;
   FORMAT DOB MMDDYY8.;
   DROP OLD_DOB;
RUN;

PROC PRINT DATA=WORKS;
   TITLE1 'Correct DOB Solution';
RUN;
```

The correct results are shown in Output 6.

Output from Example 6 - Checking for a New Subject Number Using a LAG Function

```
                  Correct DOB Solution

         OBS   SUBJ     DOB     WEIGHT

          1     1    10/21/50      55
          2     1    10/21/50     158
          3     1    10/21/50     162
          4     2    11/01/46     102
          5     2    11/01/46     108
          6     2    11/01/46     105
          7     3       .         200
          8     3       .         202
          9     3       .         198
```

Example 7

Checking for a New Subject Number Using a LAG Function and a Trailing @

FEATURES: **RETAIN Statement, LAG Function, Trailing @**

A truly compulsive SAS System programmer like at least one of the authors (well, maybe at least two of them) cannot leave this topic without presenting just one more solution. In this last example, the SAS System reads in a value for DOB only when it reaches what it knows to be a new subject. How does it know it's a new subject? It simply reads in a value for SUBJ and then uses the trailing @ ❶ (see Chapter 1, "Input and Infile," Example 10) to hold the line while it tests to see if it has a new subject or not. It uses the LAG function to make the test ❷ and then treats the remainder of the input line accordingly. If it is a new subject, it reads in a new DOB ❸; if not, DOB equals its retained value ❹. Here is the code:

Example 7

```
DATA COMPULSE;
   RETAIN DOB;
   INFILE 'HTWT';
   INPUT @1 SUBJ   $2.   @; ❶
   IF SUBJ NE LAG(SUBJ) THEN ❷
      INPUT @7   DOB      MMDDYY8. ❸
            @17 WEIGHT 3.;
   ELSE                     ❹
      INPUT @17 WEIGHT 3.;
   FORMAT DOB   MMDDYY8.;

PROC PRINT DATA=COMPULSE;
   TITLE 'Another Correct DOB Solution';
RUN;
```

The results are identical to the listing shown in the output from Example 6 (except for the order of the variables).

The examples in this chapter that are based on the LAG function require that all the data for a single subject be grouped together in the input stream. If this is not the case, the data set can be read as is and then sorted with PROC SORT. Of course, the data would not then be input into the new data set being constructed, but rather would be set in from an existing SAS data set. Also, if you actually have to make another pass through the data after they are sorted, you can use the FIRST. and LAST. variables as an alternative to the LAG function (see Chapter 7, "SAS Arrays," Example 6 for the FIRST. and LAST. word on this matter).

One last comment about this example. You use the DROP statement here to drop OLD_DOB from the data set you are building. Either the KEEP or the DROP statement can be used to achieve the same results. Older versions of the SAS System will not allow both in the same DATA step.

Conclusion

This chapter is a rather eclectic collection of programs and techniques which hangs together by each using the RETAIN statement in one way or another. You should consider using a RETAIN statement when you need information from previous observations. Always remember that the LAG function is also available for this purpose, but using RETAIN may give you more flexibility to solve your problem. Finally, remember the trouble you can get into when RETAIN is not used correctly. Now, for some practice.

Problems

8-1. You have a SAS data set DIET which contains variables ID, DATE, and WEIGHT. There are four records per ID, and the records are sorted by DATE within ID. The task is to create a new SAS data set DIET2 from DIET which contains only one record per subject, with each record containing the subject ID and the mean weight for the subject. This problem could be easily solved by using PROC MEANS or other methods, but for the purposes of this exercise, use a DATA step with a RETAIN statement in your solution. As an additional "learning experience," rewrite the code using a sum statement (not a SUM function.)

Hint: Include a BY ID statement after a SET statement in the DATA step, and then use FIRST. and LAST. variables. The data for the first two subjects of data set DIET are shown below:

```
        Data Set DIET

ID     DATE      WEIGHT

 1    10/01/92     155
 1    10/08/92     158
 1    10/15/92     158
 1    10/22/92     158
 2    09/02/92     200
 2    09/09/92     198
 2    09/16/92     196
 2    09/23/92     202
```

8-2. You have a collection of raw data (in external file TESTSCOR) representing reading scores on three groups of subjects: control, method A, and method B (group codes are C, A, and B, respectively). The data are arranged so that a group code is followed by one or more scores for that group, and scores for any group can span more than one record of raw data (unfortunately, this is not at all an uncommon pattern in which data can and do occur in the real world.) Your task (should you chose to accept it) is to write a program which will read these data and create a SAS data set READING with variables GROUP and SCORE, one set per observation.

Hint: Here is one way to get started - there are others. Read every data item in the raw data file as a character value and test if it is an 'A', 'B' or 'C'. If it is one of those values, set GROUP equal to that value and then read the numeric data. If not, convert the character (numeral) you just read to a number using the INPUT function (syntax: SCORE = INPUT (CHARVAR, 5.);) Don't worry, we still left some work for you to do.

Here are some sample data from external file TESTSCOR:

```
C 303 102 150 B 202 C 300 B 450 400 399
420 A 289 280 278
```

Presenting Your Data

CHAPTERS

Chapter 9

PROC PRINT

Writing Simple Reports

Introduction

You have used the PRINT procedure in numerous examples throughout this book in its basic, unadorned, "vanilla" mode simply to display the results of other techniques that were being emphasized at the time. In fact, we strongly recommend "sprinkling" PROC PRINTs liberally throughout your code in any development process to monitor where the development is going. Think of PROC PRINT as a development tool as well as a production tool.

Having said the above, let's now give PROC PRINT its fair shake as a real SAS System production tool. The most frequent use of PROC PRINT is to list the contents of all or part of a SAS data set. In its simplest form, it produces listings of the data set with each column headed by a variable name. By using a few options and additional statements, you can enhance the appearance of the output from PROC PRINT to generate fairly sophisticated reports with titles, descriptive column headings, totals and subtotals, and a count showing the number of observations. For more flexibility in report writing, you can use the more versatile PROC REPORT.

Example 1

> ## Creating a Simple "Bare-Bones" Report
>
> *FEATURES:* **PROC PRINT, VAR Statement**

For this example you use fictitious medical information data stored in a SAS data set called MEDICAL. Here is a description of the data set:

Variable Name	Description
SUB_ID	Subject ID
DIAGCODE	Diagnosis code
ADMIT_DT	Admission date (stored as a SAS date value)
DISCH_DT	Discharge date (stored as a SAS date value)
HOSPCODE	Hospital code
LOS	Length of stay
COST	Total cost of treatment

For this first example, suppose you want to generate a simple report showing all the data. Without using any options (except the data set name), you can write the world's simplest PROC PRINT code. ❶ Actually, this is not true. You could omit the VAR statement ❷ entirely and let the program default to all variables in the MEDICAL data set. In fact, although we frown upon this next suggestion, you can also omit the DATA= option ❶ if the last data set created is the one you want to print. Being explicit here doesn't cost much and is a good habit to build in the great "Battle of Debug."

Example 1

```
PROC PRINT DATA=MEDICAL; ❶
    VAR SUB_ID ❷
        DIAGCODE
        ADMIT_DT
        DISCH_DT
        HOSPCODE
        LOS
        COST;
RUN;
```

Here is the resulting output:

Output from Example 1 - Creating a Simple "Bare-Bones" Report

```
                         The SAS System                      1
                            09:22 Tuesday, October 18, 1994

 OBS     SUB_ID  DIAGCODE  ADMIT_DT  DISCH_DT  HOSPCODE  LOS      COST

  1    30408916    291      11791     11792       19      1       325
  2    90871243    291      11708     11733       14     25      6000
  3   717615543    480      11753     11754       18      1       621
  4   965287298    480      11693     11705       17     12      7051
  5   756534986    493      11700     11714       18     14      5522
  6   967460913    493      11749     11749       15      0       200
```

As you can see, without your doing much work, PROC PRINT generates a listing of your data with a default title and variable names as column headings. Also notice that the dates are presented as SAS date values (i.e., the number of days since January 1, 1960). We'll fix that shortly.

Example 2

Dropping Observation Numbers

FEATURES: PROC PRINT, NOOBS Option, ID and VAR Statements

One of the first changes you may want to make in this listing is to remove the column labeled OBS (observation number). You can do this two ways: First, you can include the PROC PRINT option NOOBS. This is fine when your variables all fit across one page. If this is not the case, your output will be difficult to read since the continued list of variables will not contain any identifying information. (Note: The OBS column is repeated whenever the list of variables does not fit across a single page.) The alternate method is to include one or more ID variables. An ID variable replaces the OBS column and prints on the left side of the page, even if the list of variables is continued on other pages. Here is the program modified to include an ID variable:

Example 2

```
PROC PRINT DATA=MEDICAL;
    ID SUB_ID;
    VAR DIAGCODE
        ADMIT_DT
        DISCH_DT
        HOSPCODE
        LOS
        COST;
RUN;
```

Notice that SUB_ID is removed from the variable list. If you leave it in, it appears twice on the listing, once as the ID variable and once as one of the VAR variables. The output from this example is identical to the output from Example 1 except that the column labeled OBS is removed.

Example 3

Increasing Readability

FEATURES: **PROC PRINT, LABEL Option, TITLE, ID, VAR, LABEL, and FORMAT Statements, DOLLAR*n*. and SSN*11*. Formats**

The next step to improve this simple report is to include format and label information, along with titles. First the code:

Example 3

```
PROC PRINT DATA=MEDICAL LABEL;   ❶
    TITLE   'Hospital Data Base Report';   ❷
    TITLE2  '————————————————';
    ID  SUB_ID;
    VAR DIAGCODE
        ADMIT_DT
        DISCH_DT
        HOSPCODE
        LOS
        COST;
```

(continued on next page)

Example 3 - *continued*

```
        LABEL DIAGCODE='Diagnosis Code'  ❸
              ADMIT_DT='Admission Date'
              DISCH_DT='Discharge Date'
              HOSPCODE='Hospital Code'
              LOS     ='Length of Stay'
              COST    ='Cost of Treatment';
        FORMAT COST DOLLAR7.  ❹
               SUB_ID SSN11.
               ADMIT_DT DISCH_DT MMDDYY8.;
   RUN;
```

The first thing to notice is the use of both a LABEL option on the PROC PRINT statement ❶ and a separate LABEL statement ❸. These do different things. The LABEL statement defines a set of variable labels which can be used instead of variable names as the column headings. The LABEL option tells the system to actually use the labels that are created in the LABEL statement. Just creating the labels in the statement without turning them on with the option will not do the trick. An aside: you created the variables' labels in this PRINT procedure. They also could have been created with a LABEL statement in the DATA step that was used to create the data set MEDICAL. The difference in the two placements is as follows: when a LABEL statement appears in a procedure, it makes available a set of labels for that procedure only. When a LABEL statement is used in a DATA step (when the data set is being created), the labels are available for any subsequent procedures which operate on the data set.

The next enhancement is the formatting of the COST, SUB_ID, ADMIT_DT, and DISCH_DT variables. This is done with the FORMAT statement ❹. This statement, like the LABEL statement, also could have appeared in the DATA step. Unlike the LABEL statement, it does not have to be turned on with a separate option. Notice that the SSN11. format adds the leading zeroes as well as the dashes to the data when displaying them as Social Security numbers. Pretty slick! The DOLLAR7. format also automatically includes the commas.

The final enhancement in this example to make the output more useful and readable is to use titles. ❷ In Example 1 you saw the default SAS System title (the words "The SAS System"), the time and date of the run, and the page number. In this example you create your own custom titles. Titles in TITLE statements are enclosed in quotation marks, either single or double but they must match. You can have up to 10 title lines (TITLE and TITLE1 are equivalent.) Titles are not specifically PROC PRINT statements - they can be used anywhere in a SAS program. They remain in effect until they are replaced or nullified with null TITLE statements of the form TITLE*n*; (this will clear all titles of number *n* or greater.)

Here is the resulting output from Example 3:

Output from Example 3 - Increasing Readability

```
                      Hospital Data Base Report                    1
                   ─────────────────────────────

                                 13:13 Thursday, September 22, 1994

            Diagnosis  Admission  Discharge  Hospital  Length    Cost of
   SUB_ID     Code       Date       Date       Code    of Stay  Treatment

030-40-8916   291     04/13/92   04/14/92      19         1        $325
090-87-1243   291     01/21/92   02/15/92      14        25      $6,000
717-61-5543   480     03/06/92   03/07/92      18         1        $621
965-28-7298   480     01/06/92   01/18/92      17        12      $7,051
756-53-4986   493     01/13/92   01/27/92      18        14      $5,522
967-46-0913   493     03/02/92   03/02/92      15         0        $200
```

Notice that the labels you create are automatically split into multi-row labels by the system as it sees fit. If you want to, you can instruct the system how to split the labels by defining a split-character on the PROC PRINT statement with the SPLIT=*char* option, and then placing your chosen character in the labels where you want the line splits to occur. Note that the SPLIT= option implicitly includes the LABEL option - it is not necessary to code the LABEL option when defining a split-character. This code defines the asterisk (*) as a split character and creates the following labels:

```
PROC PRINT DATA=MEDICAL LABEL SPLIT='*';
   .
   .
   .
LABEL DIAGCODE='Diagnosis*Code'
      ADMIT_DT='Admission*Date'
      DISCH_DT='Discharge*Date'
      HOSPCODE='Hospital*Code'
      LOS     ='Length*of*Stay'
      COST    ='Cost*of*Treatment';
```

Labels produced using the * split-character appear as follows:

```
                                                  Length     Cost
          Diagnosis  Admission  Discharge  Hospital    of       of
SUB_ID      Code       Date       Date      Code      Stay    Treatment
```

Example 4

> ## Adding Column Totals and Subtotals, Observation Counts, and Footnotes
>
> *FEATURES:* **PROC PRINT, N and LABEL Options, TITLE, BY, SUM, SUMBY, ID, VAR, LABEL, FORMAT, and FOOTNOTE Statements, NOCENTER, NODATE, NONUMBER, PAGESIZE, and LINESIZE System Options**

This next example includes summary data of various kinds, footnotes and titles, and some overall system formatting options. In addition, each DIAGCODE group is processed individually. Here is the program:

Example 4

```
OPTIONS NOCENTER NODATE NONUMBER;

PROC SORT DATA=MEDICAL; ❶
    BY DIAGCODE;
RUN;
                            ❷
PROC PRINT DATA=MEDICAL N LABEL;
    BY DIAGCODE; ❸
    TITLE 'Hospital Data Base Report';
    TITLE2 '————————————————';
    FOOTNOTE 'Prepared by RPC and Company'; ❹
    SUM LOS COST;    ❺
    SUMBY DIAGCODE;  ❻
    ID SUB_ID;
    VAR DIAGCODE
        ADMIT_DT
        DISCH_DT
        HOSPCODE
        LOS
        COST;
```

(continued on next page)

Example 4 - continued

```
    LABEL DIAGCODE = 'Diagnosis Code'
           ADMIT_DT = 'Admission Date'
           DISCH_DT = 'Discharge Date'
           HOSPCODE = 'Hospital Code'
           LOS      = 'Length of Stay'
           COST     = 'Cost of Treatment';
       FORMAT COST DOLLAR7.
              SUB_ID SSN11.
              ADMIT_DT DISCH_DT MMDDYY8.;
    RUN;
```

You use PROC SORT to sort the data set by DIAGCODE, assuming that is isn't already in the desired order.❶ Actually, the SAS System does not re-sort a data set if it has been previously sorted by a SORT procedure. It does, however, inform you that a re-sort is not necessary. It is not enough merely to sort the data set; you also have to tell the procedure that you want to process the data set by the BY group as well. This is accomplished with the BY statement in the PRINT procedure. ❸ Keep in mind that the BY statement in the SORT procedure tells the system how to sort the data, and the BY statement in the other procedures tells the system to use the BY groups created by the SORT procedure. Your report appears in multiple sections, one for each BY group, with an identifying BY line above each subgroup.

You add the N option ❷ to obtain the number of observations in the data set. When a BY variable(s) is used, the N option also indicates the number of observations for each value of the BY variable(s). ❸ The FOOTNOTE statement ❹ is like a TITLE statement except that the text following a FOOTNOTE statement appears on the bottom of each page of the report. The SUM statement ❺ prints sums for the listed variables, LOS and COST in this case. The SUMBY statement ❻, which can only be used when you have a BY variable(s), gives the sums of the indicated variables for each value of the SUMBY variable(s). Here is the final output. Note that only selected portions of the output are shown.

Output from Example 4 - Adding Column Totals and Subtotals, Observation Counts, and Footnotes

```
Hospital Data Base Report
_____


Diagnosis Code=291

           Diagnosis Admission Discharge Hospital  Length  Cost of
    SUB_ID    Code      Date      Date      Code   of Stay Treatment

030-40-8916    291    04/13/92  04/14/92     19        1      $325
090-87-1243    291    01/21/92  02/15/92     14       25    $6,000
                                                      ___    _____
DIAGCODE                                               26    $6,325
N = 2


Prepared by RPC and Company

Hospital Data Base Report
_____


Diagnosis Code=493

           Diagnosis Admission Discharge Hospital  Length  Cost of
    SUB_ID    Code      Date      Date      Code   of Stay Treatment

756-53-4986    493    01/13/92  01/27/92     18       14    $5,522
967-46-0913    493    03/02/92  03/02/92     15        0      $200
                                                      ___    _____
DIAGCODE                                               14    $5,722
                                                   ======= =========
                                                       53   $19,719
       N = 2
Total N = 6


Prepared by RPC and Company
```

This example uses some SAS system options that affect the appearance of the listings from PROC PRINT. Your titles are left aligned instead of centered (as they are for most of the sample listings in this book), and you omit the time, date, and page number. You may also want to start page numbering at a number of your choosing. An OPTIONS statement, placed at any point in your SAS program, will alter the selected options from that point on until they are changed. For example, to left align your titles, omit the date and time, and start page numbering at 1, write the OPTIONS statement like this:

```
OPTIONS NOCENTER NODATE PAGENO=1;
```

If at some later point in the program (before another PROC PRINT most likely) you want the title centered and you want to restart the page numbering from 1, you would use:

```
OPTIONS CENTER PAGENO=1;
```

Other useful OPTIONS are PAGESIZE= and LINESIZE= (abbreviated as PS and LS respectively). Use these two options to control the number of lines printed per page and the number of characters per line. Valid values for PAGESIZE are from 15 to 32,767; for LINESIZE from 64 to 256.

Dealing with Multi-Page Reports

PROC PRINT provides options (available since Release 6.07) which allow you some control over column widths and overall column placement on multi-page reports. The PROC PRINT option WIDTH= allows you to choose FULL, MINIMUM, UNIFORM, or UNIFORMBY. To demonstrate some of these options, let's redo a simple version of the above code using WIDTH=FULL and WIDTH=MINIMUM. First we'll set WIDTH=FULL, and then we'll use WIDTH=MINIMUM.

Example 5

Using the WIDTH=FULL Option

FEATURES: WIDTH=FULL Option with PROC PRINT

Example 5

```
PROC PRINT DATA=MEDICAL WIDTH=FULL;
   TITLE 'WIDTH option FULL';
   VAR SUB_ID
       DIAGCODE
       ADMIT_DT
       DISCH_DT
       HOSPCODE
       LOS
       COST;
   FORMAT COST DOLLAR7.
          SUB_ID SSN11.
          ADMIT_DT DISCH_DT MMDDYY8.;
RUN;
```

Output from Example 5 - Using the WIDTH=FULL Option

```
                        WIDTH option FULL

   OBS          SUB_ID        DIAGCODE      ADMIT_DT    DISCH_DT

    1        030-40-8916         291        04/13/92    04/14/92
    2        090-87-1243         291        01/21/92    02/15/92
    3        717-61-5543         480        03/06/92    03/07/92
    4        965-28-7298         480        01/06/92    01/18/92
    5        756-53-4986         493        01/13/92    01/27/92
    6        967-46-0913         493        03/02/92    03/02/92


   OBS         HOSPCODE          LOS         COST

    1              19             1         $325
    2              14            25       $6,000
    3              18             1         $621
    4              17            12       $7,051
    5              18            14       $5,522
    6              15             0         $200
```

Example 6

Using the WIDTH=MINIMUM Option

FEATURES: **WIDTH=MINIMUM and HEADING Options with PROC PRINT**

Here is the same program and output with the WIDTH option set to equal MINIMUM:

Example 6

```
PROC PRINT DATA=MEDICAL WIDTH=MINIMUM;
   TITLE 'WIDTH option MINIMUM';
   VAR SUB_ID
       DIAGCODE
       ADMIT_DT
       DISCH_DT
       HOSPCODE
       LOS
       COST;
   FORMAT COST DOLLAR7.
          SUB_ID SSN11.
          ADMIT_DT DISCH_DT MMDDYY8.;
RUN;
```

Output from Example 6 - Using the WIDTH=MINIMUM Option

```
                     WIDTH option MINIMUM

   OBS    SUB_ID    DIAGCODE ADMIT_DT DISCH_DT HOSPCODE LOS   COST

    1   030-40-8916    291   04/13/92 04/14/92    19     1    $325
    2   090-87-1243    291   01/21/92 02/15/92    14    25  $6,000
    3   717-61-5543    480   03/06/92 03/07/92    18     1    $621
    4   965-28-7298    480   01/06/92 01/18/92    17    12  $7,051
    5   756-53-4986    493   01/13/92 01/27/92    18    14  $5,522
    6   967-46-0913    493   03/02/92 03/02/92    15     0    $200
```

Notice that the WIDTH=FULL option produces a report which takes up more room. Using this option causes PROC PRINT to use the formatted widths cf variables, if supplied, or default widths if you do not supply formats (for character variables, these are the lengths of the variables as defined in the data set; for numeric variables, a width of 12 is used). Since the width of each variable is constant for all observations, reports that span more than one page all have the same total column widths.

The WIDTH=MINIMUM option uses the minimum width necessary to display the data on a given page for each column. Therefore, a multi-page report may use different column widths on different pages and the total column width may vary from page to page. This can cause a quite obvious non-uniformity in the display from page to page.

A nice compromise between the two options shown above is WIDTH=UNIFORM. If a variable is formatted, this option uses the associated format to define the column width. If a variable is not formatted, this option uses the widest data value for a variable to display all values of that variable. The UNIFORM value usually uses narrower column widths than FULL and may use wider widths than MINIMUM, but UNIFORM has the advantage of providing the same individual column width for each variable throughout and, therefore, the same overall page column width throughout, even if the report spans multiple pages. Note that both MINIMUM and UNIFORM take a bit more CPU time than FULL (if you are concerned about such things).

Controlling the Orientation of the Column Headings

The reports so far in this chapter all have the column headings printed horizontally. In certain circumstances (when the column widths are small and the variable names are large), PROC PRINT may decide to print the column headings vertically. If you want to override the orientation of the column headings, use the PROC PRINT options HEADING=HORIZONTAL or HEADING =VERTICAL to specify the orientation. For example, to force PROC PRINT to print the column headings horizontally, write:

```
PROC PRINT HEADING=HORIZONTAL;
```

Conclusion

PROC PRINT is a very useful tool for quick and easy reports. By using some of the options and statements in this chapter, you can customize your reports to a certain extent. If your reporting needs exceed the capability of PROC PRINT, you have to move to the next step; use either PROC REPORT, which gives you much more control over the appearance of the report, or FILE and PUT statements in a DATA step to create reports to meet almost any specification.

Problems

9-1. You have a SAS data set DONOR which contains variables L_NAME, F_NAME, AMOUNT (of donation), and DATE (of donation.) Write the code to produce a simple report from DONOR. The report should list the variables in the following order: F_NAME, L_NAME, DATE (in MM/DD/YY format), and AMOUNT (using DOLLAR8. format).

Here are some sample data to work with:

Data Set DONOR

F_NAME	L_NAME	AMOUNT	DATE
Janet	Bloom	$50	01/14/94
Dora	Chelsea	$35	06/14/94
Walter	Donnelly	$35	01/07/95
Walter	Donnelly	$10	07/06/94
Anne	Farnham	$100	07/07/93
James	Zoll	$45	07/06/94

9-2. Write the code to produce the following report from the DONOR data set described in Problem 9-1, including the two-line title, column headings, date format, observation count, and sum of donations. Note that the title is flush left (starts at the left margin) and does not include the date or page number.

Report on the Donor Data Base
_____

First Name	Last Name	Amount of Donation	Donation Date
Janet	Bloom	$50	14JAN94
Dora	Chelsea	$35	14JUN94
Walter	Donnelly	$35	07JAN95
Walter	Donnelly	$10	06JUL94
Anne	Farnham	$100	07JUL93
James	Zoll	$45	06JUL94
		____	
		$275	

N = 6

9-3. Using the same DONOR data set from Problems 9-1 and 9-2, write the code to generate simple reports with the following characteristics:
a) variable names printed vertically and minimum width assigned to the columns
b) horizontal column headings and uniform printing (if the report actually ran over several pages).

Chapter 10

PROC MEANS and PROC UNIVARIATE

Producing Descriptive Statistics and Summary Data Sets

Introduction

The MEANS and UNIVARIATE procedures can be used to produce reports of descriptive summary statistics such as mean, standard deviation, etc. from SAS data sets. They can also be used to process the data and produce new data sets containing summary statistics. You don't have to be a statistician to use these procedures—they can be very useful for straightforward counting and adding. The examples in this chapter demonstrate several ways in which these procedures can be put to work.

You should note from the outset that the SAS System also contains a procedure called PROC SUMMARY which is identical to PROC MEANS (with a NOPRINT option). PROC MEANS can do much of what PROC UNIVARIATE can do to create a summary data set, but the differences that do exist (see Example 7 in this chapter) make PROC UNIVARIATE a procedure that should also be in your repertoire.

For those of you who are either not familiar or not comfortable with complex statistical terms and procedures, here is a very brief review of all you need to know about means and medians to get through this chapter. In actuality, you've been dealing with arithmetic means since grade school (grade point averages, batting averages, etc.), although you've probably been calling them "averages." An arithmetic mean is actually only one type of average, the one you get by adding up all the numbers and dividing by how many numbers there are. Statisticians use the term "mean" instead of "average" so they can be more specific and sound more intellectual.

The other type of average used in this chapter is the "median." A median in a collection of ordered numbers is the one at the 50th percentile, or half way through. Half the numbers are below the median; half are above. You usually see medians computed on variables such as yearly salaries where extreme values can distort the true picture of "representativeness." For example, if a collection of people in a certain neighborhood contains one or two multi-millionaires among a majority of non-millionaires, the mean salary is affected by the extreme high values, whereas the median salary is not affected. The middle salary (the median) is the same whether the top salary is $100,000 or $100,000,000. There is a wonderful little book by Darryl Huff called *How to Lie with Statistics*, but that's a whole other story. Let's get back to reality with some examples.

Example 1

> **Computing Totals and Using PROC MEANS to Create a Summary Data Set**
>
> *FEATURES:* **PROC MEANS, CLASS and OUTPUT Statements**

This example shows the default printed output from PROC MEANS and how you can use the procedure to create a SAS data set that contains summary information.

Suppose you have a SAS data set SALES which contains sales figures for a mail order company. Each record in the data set represents the sale of a single item. The variables are PO_NUM (purchase order number), ITEM (item description), REGION (region of the country where the item was sold), PRICE (selling price of the item), and QUANTITY (number of items sold).

A listing of all the observations in the data set follows:

```
           Observations from the SALES Data Set

    PO_NUM   ITEM      REGION    PRICE    QUANTITY

    1456     Hammer    NORTH      $10        5
    1458     Saw       NORTH      $15        4
    1511     Pliers    NORTH       $8       35
    1600     Hammer    SOUTH      $10       15
    1711     Hammer    EAST       $10       12
    1712     Hammer    EAST       $10        2
    1713     Saw       EAST       $15       25
    1715     Saw       EAST       $15       24
    1800     Pliers    EAST        $8        7
    1900     Saw       WEST       $15        9
    1901     Saw       WEST       $15        5
```

We use the SALES data set to demonstrate the use of the CLASS statement as well as the two variables _FREQ_ and _TYPE_ that are automatically included in any output data set created by PROC MEANS. In this example, you want to see the summary statistics of the QUANTITY sold (included in the VAR statement) broken down by REGION and ITEM. One way to do this is to use PROC SORT to pre-sort the data set by REGION and ITEM, and then add a BY statement to the PROC MEANS code. A more efficient approach is to use a CLASS statement to specify the two categorizing variables. This does not require a separate procedure to perform the sort. In this example you also want to create an output data set which contains the totals (SUM) of the quantities for the various REGION-ITEM categories. Here is the code:

Example 1

```
PROC MEANS DATA=SALES; ❶
    TITLE 'Sample Output from PROC MEANS';
    CLASS  REGION ITEM; ❷
    VAR    QUANTITY; ❸
    OUTPUT OUT=QUAN_SUM SUM=TOTAL;
RUN;   ❹       ❺              ❻


PROC PRINT DATA=QUAN_SUM;
    TITLE 'Summary Data Set';
RUN;
```

The output from the above program is shown in two sections: first the output from PROC MEANS, then some discussion, then the output from PROC PRINT.

Output from Example 1 - Computing Totals and Using PROC MEANS to Create a Summary Data Set (PROC MEANS Output)

```
                    Sample Output from PROC MEANS

   Analysis Variable : QUANTITY

   REGION  ITEM    N Obs  N  Mean         Std Dev    Minimum     Maximum

   EAST    Hammer    2    2  7.0000000  7.0710678   2.0000000  12.0000000
           Pliers    1    1  7.0000000          .   7.0000000   7.0000000
           Saw       2    2  4.5000000  0.7071068   4.0000000  25.0000000
   NORTH   Hammer    1    1  5.0000000          .   5.0000000   5.0000000
           Pliers    1    1  5.0000000          .   5.0000000  35.0000000
           Saw       1    1  4.0000000          .   4.0000000   4.0000000
   SOUTH   Hammer    1    1  5.0000000          .   5.0000000  15.0000000
   WEST    Saw       2    2  7.0000000  2.8284271   5.0000000   9.0000000
```

The format of the report, including the output statistics and the maximum number of decimal places to use, can be fairly customized. If you do not ask specifically for certain statistics to be produced, as in this example ❶, the procedure automatically gives you the following: N, Mean, Standard Deviation, Minimum, and Maximum. When you ask for the data to be broken down by category as you did here with the CLASS statement ❷, PROC MEANS also throws in number of observations (N Obs). N is the number of non-missing data points and N Obs is the total number of observations per group or sub-group. In the present case, these numbers are equal because there are no missing data (an easy goal to accomplish when you're making up the data, but not always that easy in real life.)

Although the above report is quite useful as is, PROC MEANS can also be used to produce an output data set containing the summary statistics instead of a printed report. The rest of the examples in this chapter do not produce a report directly but, instead, create only an output data set. How do you produce this output data set? With an OUTPUT statement of course.❹ The OUT= option ❺ in the OUTPUT statement specifies the name of the output data set you want to create. Various statistics can be included in this data set (we asked for SUM only) ❻, depending on the OUTPUT statement statistics you choose. Typical OUTPUT statistics are N=, MEAN=, and SUM=. Following each of these keywords is a list of variables to be included in the newly created data set that will contain the values for the N, MEAN, SUM, etc. for each of the variables in the VAR list ❸. The statistics available for the OUTPUT statement are the same as those available for the PROC MEANS statement itself. The creation of the output data set does not produce printed output. In order to see the resulting data set, you add a PRINT procedure which produces the following listing:

Output from Example 1 - Computing Totals and Using PROC MEANS to Create a Summary Data Set (PROC PRINT Output)

```
                                Summary Data Set

        REGION     ITEM      _TYPE_     _FREQ_     TOTAL
                                0          11        143         ❼
                   Hammer       1           4         34      ⎫
                   Pliers       1           2         42      ⎬  ❽
                   Saw          1           5         67      ⎭
        EAST                    2           5         70      ⎫
        NORTH                   2           3         44      ⎬
        SOUTH                   2           1         15      ⎬  ❾
        WEST                    2           2         14      ⎭
        EAST      Hammer        3           2         14      ⎫
        EAST      Pliers        3           1          7      ⎪
        EAST      Saw           3           2         49      ⎪
        NORTH     Hammer        3           1          5      ⎬
        NORTH     Pliers        3           1         35      ⎬  ❿
        NORTH     Saw           3           1          4      ⎪
        SOUTH     Hammer        3           1         15      ⎪
        WEST      Saw           3           2         14      ⎭
```

Output data sets produced by PROC MEANS contain a wealth of information. In addition to the actual summary data values, the procedure automatically produces the variables _TYPE_ and _FREQ_, which can be used to identify the population or sub-population contributing to the statistic. Let's use the actual data to explain these. The first observation ❼ has a _TYPE_ = 0 and represents the entire population. The value of TOTAL here (143) is the sum of QUANTITY for all regions and all items. The _FREQ_ variable shows you that there are 11 observations (purchase orders) that contribute to this sum. The next 3 lines (_TYPE_ = 1) give the sums for each level of the last (rightmost) CLASS variable, ITEM, across regions.❽ Here, _FREQ_ shows how many orders were placed for each ITEM, and TOTAL tells how many of each ITEM were sold in the entire country (across regions). Following these are 4 lines (_TYPE_ = 2) which represent the sums for each level of the next rightmost CLASS variable, REGION, for all items in each region.❾ Finally, the remaining lines (_TYPE_ = 3) are the totals for each combination of all the CLASS variables, REGION and ITEM.❿

While this is fairly clear from the listing, if you are up on your binary numbers you'll recognize that the _TYPE_ value, if expressed in binary notation, shows which variables contribute to each line of information, and how they contribute. The following figure should make this clear.

TYPE	REGION	ITEM
0	0	0
1	0	1
2	1	0
3	1	1
Decimal	Binary	

For each of the _TYPE_ values, if there is a 1 under a variable in the binary listing, the data are presented for each discrete value of the variable; if there is a 0 under the variable, the observation is summed (or meaned, etc.) over that variable. The _TYPE_ = 0 observation therefore represents the SUM for all items and all regions, the _TYPE_ = 1 observations give the sums for each item (across regions), the _TYPE_ = 2 observations show the sums for each region (over all items), and the _TYPE_ = 3 observations contain the sums for each ITEM-REGION combination. It's not really that daunting once you get the hang of it.

Example 2

Computing More Than One Statistic

FEATURES: **N=, MEAN=, and SUM= OUTPUT Options**

If you have more than one variable in your VAR list, the variable names in the OUTPUT statement following the N=, MEAN=, SUM=, etc. represent the variables in the output data set that contain the values of that statistic for each of the variables in the VAR list in the order in which they are listed. A procedure to create an output data set STATS containing the number of observations, means, and sums from a data set ORIGDATA containing CLASS variables A and B and analysis variables X, Y, and Z, is shown here:

Example 2

```
PROC MEANS DATA=ORIGDATA;
    CLASS A B;
    VAR   X Y Z;
    OUTPUT OUT =STATS
           N    =NUM_X   NUM_Y   NUM_Z
           MEAN=MEAN_X   MEAN_Y  MEAN_Z
           SUM =TOT_X    TOT_Y   TOT_Z;
RUN;
```

The variables NUM_X, NUM_Y, and NUM_Z in the output data set STATS contain the values for the number of nonmissing observations for the variables X, Y, and Z; the variables MEAN_X, MEAN_Y, and MEAN_Z contain the means for X, Y, and Z; the variables TOT_X, TOT_Y, and TOT_Z contain the sums of the three variables X, Y, and Z. Note that _FREQ_ indicates the total number of observations, while the variable(s) created with the N= option counts only nonmissing observations.

Example 3

> ## Creating Unweighted Summary Statistics (Step 1)
>
> ***FEATURES:*** **PROC MEANS, NWAY and NOPRINT Options, CLASS Statement**

This example demonstrates how to compute unweighted means for a population containing varying numbers of observations per subject. In other words, you want each subject to contribute equally to the overall mean. You have to process the data twice: the first processing produces a mean for each subject, and the second processing uses the per-subject value to produce a mean over all subjects.

Suppose you have a data set which contains blood pressure readings for a number of subjects, but there are a variable number of observations per subject per year. You want a mean value for your readings per year, but you only want one reading per subject per year. Variables are:

SUBJ, YEAR, SBP (systolic blood pressure), and DBP (diastolic blood pressure). Here are a few sample observations:

SUBJ	YEAR	SBP	DBP
1	1950	130	80
1	1950	132	82
1	1951	140	86
2	1950	118	72
2	1950	120	74
2	1952	122	76
2	1952	116	74

You first have to compute the mean SBP and DBP for each subject for each year and put these values out to a new output data set. You then use this new data set to compute yearly means over all subjects. Note that you cannot simply use PROC MEANS with YEAR as a CLASS variable. Doing this would include all readings over each year, including multiple readings per subject (with different numbers of readings per subject) and would, therefore, produce a weighted mean. Subjects with more measurements per year would make a larger contribution to the overall mean. This is generally not what is wanted.

Here is a set of programs which produce unweighted yearly means. The first program produces a data set, MEANOUT, containing the mean SBP and DBP for each subject for each year.

Example 3

```
PROC MEANS DATA=PRESSURE NOPRINT NWAY;

* Note: Data set PRESSURE does NOT have to be sorted;

   CLASS   SUBJ YEAR;
   VAR     SBP DBP;
   OUTPUT OUT=MEANOUT MEAN=;
RUN;
```

Notice first the NOPRINT option on the PROC MEANS statement. This instructs the system not to print the resulting statistics. You really don't need to see output at this point because you are basically using the procedure to create another data set that will then be processed to produce the values that you really want, the unweighted yearly values.

In this example, you do not specify variable names after MEAN= in the OUTPUT statement. This results in the mean SBP and DBP in the output data set having the same variable names as the individual variables in the original data set as listed on the VAR statement, namely SBP and DBP. This is fine in a simple application like this, but in general, new variables should have new unique names. It makes everything clearer. Also, if you output more than one statistic, you obviously have to give them new names -- you can't use SBP for both the mean and the standard deviation, for example. The resulting output data set, MEANOUT, contains the variables YEAR, SUBJ (the CLASS variables), SBP, DBP, _TYPE_, and _FREQ_. If you had used a PROC PRINT statement to list this data set, you would have obtained the following output:

```
                    Listing of Data Set MEANOUT

         OBS    SUBJ    YEAR   _TYPE_   _FREQ_   SBP    DBP

          1      1      1950      3        2     131    81
          2      1      1951      3        1     140    86
          3      2      1950      3        2     119    73
          4      2      1952      3        2     119    75
```

Why is this output data set so skimpy compared to previous examples? Where are the values for the overall population, and for each individual subject over years, as well as for each individual year over subjects? The answer is the NWAY option. You use this option to tell the system to produce output for only the highest level of class interactions. Here, this results in means for each SUBJ-YEAR combination only (_TYPE_ = 3.) The lower level _TYPE_ values are not included in the output data set. The combination of the NOPRINT and NWAY options makes a very powerful and frequently used data production tool.

Example 4

Creating Unweighted Summary Statistics (Step 2)

FEATURES: PROC MEANS, MEAN and MAXDEC= Options, CLASS Statement

Now you are ready to complete the task by processing your new intermediate summary data set which contains one observation per subject per year. The result will be yearly unweighted means of the variables. Here is the code:

Example 4

```
PROC MEANS DATA=MEANOUT MEAN MAXDEC=2;
    TITLE 'Averages Computed from Person Yearly Means';
    CLASS YEAR;
    VAR SBP DBP;
RUN;
```

The resulting output shows the mean SBP and DBP for each year, computed from the yearly means of each subject. Notice that since you specifically ask for only the MEAN statistic, that's all you get (actually, you also get N Obs because you are using a CLASS variable). Had you not done this, you would have gotten the default set of statistics as you did in the earlier example. Also, the MAXDEC=2 option limits output values to two decimal places.

Output from Example 4 - Creating Unweighted Summary Statistics (Step 2)

```
           Averages Computed from Person Yearly Means


           YEAR   N   Obs Variable       Mean
           ─────────────────────────────────────
           1950    2   SBP            125.00
                       DBP             77.00
           1951    1   SBP            140.00
                       DBP             86.00
           1952    1   SBP            119.00
                       DBP             75.00
           ─────────────────────────────────────
```

Example 5

Producing a Formatted Summary Report

FEATURES: **PROC MEANS, PROC PRINT, N=, NMISS=, SUM=, and CLASS Variables, NWAY, NOPRINT, LABEL, and DOUBLE Options, COMMA*n*. and DOLLAR*n*. Formats**

In this example, you use PROC MEANS to do much of the work that is often done by using extensive data manipulation in a DATA step, such as accumulating sums and counting missing values. You use several of the OUTPUT options in PROC MEANS to create an output summary data set that is then further formatted in a subsequent DATA step. This data set is then processed by PROC PRINT to produce the final report.

The fictitious data in this example were collected as part of a fund drive and then stored in SAS data set FUND. Each observation represents a letter mailed out to a resident asking for a contribution. The variables contained in FUND are NAME, TOWNSHIP, and AMOUNT. When the value for AMOUNT is missing, no donation was made by that person. Here is the SAS data set FUND:

```
          Data Set FUND

   NAME          TOWNSHIP    AMOUNT

   Apple         Raritan       25
   Brown         Raritan       20
   Collins       Readington    25
   Denison       Readington     .
   Early         Raritan        .
   Franks        Raritan       10
   George        Raritan        .
   Harris        Franklin      20
   Ignatz        Raritan       15
   Jackson       Franklin       .
   Kennedy       Franklin      15
   Little        Raritan       25
   Morris        Readington    35
   Nash          Readington    25
   Owens         Franklin       .
   Percy         Franklin       .
   Quincy        Readington    25
   Ripple        Readington     .
   Smith         Readington     .
```

You want to produce a report showing the following information for each township: the number of letters mailed, the total number of donations received, the total amount received, the average amount received per donation, and the average amount received per letter mailed. Sound difficult? Not if you use PROC MEANS. Here is the code:

Example 5

```
OPTIONS LS=72 NONUMBER NODATE;

PROC MEANS DATA=FUND NOPRINT NWAY;
   CLASS TOWNSHIP;
   VAR AMOUNT;
   OUTPUT OUT  =SUMMARY
          N    =RETURNED   ❶
          NMISS=NOT_RETN
          SUM  =TOTAL;
RUN;

DATA REPORT;
   SET SUMMARY;
   MAILED=RETURNED+NOT_RETN; ❷
   *Alternative: MAILED=_FREQ_ ;
   PER_RETN=TOTAL/RETURNED; ❸
   PER_MAIL=TOTAL/MAILED; ❹

   LABEL MAILED  ='LETTERS MAILED'      ❺
         RETURNED='NUMBER OF DONATIONS'
         TOTAL   ='TOTAL DONATION'
         PER_RETN='MEAN DONATION'
         PER_MAIL='MEAN DONATION PER LETTER MAILED';
RUN;
                              ❻
PROC PRINT DATA=REPORT LABEL DOUBLE;
   TITLE 'Fund Drive Summary Report';
   ID TOWNSHIP;
   VAR MAILED RETURNED TOTAL PER_RETN PER_MAIL;
   FORMAT MAILED RETURNED COMMA5.
          TOTAL DOLLAR7.
          PER_RETN PER_MAIL DOLLAR5.;
RUN;
```

The statistics N, NMISS, and SUM in the PROC MEANS code provide you with some of the finished quantities you are looking for. You output N as RETURNED ❶ and eventually label it as "NUMBER OF DONATIONS," ❺ and output SUM as TOTAL and then label that as "TOTAL DONATION." NMISS is output as NOT_RETN. In the DATA step, you calculate the rest of the variables you need. You add N (RETURNED) and NMISS (NOT_RETN) to get MAILED (total number of units mailed per township) ❷ and label it "LETTERS MAILED"❺. SUM (TOTAL) is divided by RETURNED (number of donations) ❸ to get PER_RETN ("MEAN DONATION"), and by MAILED (number of units mailed) ❹ to get PER_MAIL ("MEAN DONATION PER LETTER MAILED") to complete the data you need for the report. The LABEL option of PROC PRINT ❺ instructs the system to use the labels connected to the variables for column headings instead of the variable names, and the DOUBLE option double spaces the report (see details in Chapter 9, "PROC PRINT"). The final listing from the program is shown here:

Output from Example 5 - Producing a Formatted Summary Report

| | | | | | MEAN DONATION |
TOWNSHIP	LETTERS MAILED	NUMBER OF DONATIONS	TOTAL DONATION	MEAN DONATION	PER LETTER MAILED
Franklin	5	2	$35	$18	$7
Raritan	7	5	$95	$19	$14
Readington	7	4	$110	$28	$16

Fund Drive Summary Report

As you can see, this complete formatted summary report was generated with very little effort, using PROC MEANS as the centerpiece of the program.

Example 6

Computing Values as Percentages of All Observations

FEATURES: **PROC MEANS, NOPRINT Option, OUTPUT Statement, Conditional SET Statement (in DATA Step)**

In this example, you want to express individual data values as a percentage of the mean of all subjects in a group. You have a SAS data set TEST containing variables HR (heart rate), SBP (systolic blood pressure), and DBP (diastolic blood pressure) for each subject, and you want to express these values as percents of the mean of all subjects. For example, if the values for heart rate for the group were 80, 70, and 60, the group mean would be 70 and the first subject's HR value of 80 would yield a percentage score of 114.286% (100 x 80/70). The approach here is to use PROC MEANS to compute group means, and then to output them to a data set which you combine with the original data so that you can perform the needed computations. The code follows:

Example 6

```
    DATA TEST;
        INPUT HR SBP DBP;
    DATALINES;
    80 160 100
    70 150 90
    60 140 80
    ;
                        ❶
    PROC MEANS NOPRINT DATA=TEST;
        VAR HR SBP DBP;
        OUTPUT OUT =MOUT
                MEAN=MHR MSBP MDBP;
    RUN;

    DATA PERCENT ; ❷
        SET TEST; ❸
        DROP MHR MSBP MDBP _TYPE_ _FREQ_ ;
        IF _N_=1 THEN SET MOUT; ❹
        HRPER =100*HR/MHR;  ❺
        SBPPER=100*SBP/MSBP;
        DBPPER=100*DBP/MDBP;
    RUN;

    PROC PRINT NOOBS DATA=PERCENT;
        TITLE 'Listing of PERCENT Data Set';
    RUN;
```

You use the NOPRINT option ❶ with PROC MEANS because you do not want the procedure to print anything, only to create a data set of means. In this case, because there is no CLASS statement and you are processing the entire TEST data set as one entity with no subsetting, the output data set MOUT consists of only one observation. This single observation is shown here:

OBS	_TYPE_	_FREQ_	MHR	MSBP	MDBP
1	0	3	70	150	90

You want to combine the data from MOUT (the three mean variables: MHR, MSBP, and MDBP) with the data from every observation in the original data set so that you can divide each single value by the appropriate mean (HR by MHR; SBP by MSBP; DBP by MDBP) and then multiple by 100. Since the original data set TEST has three observations and the mean data set MOUT contains only one observation, you use a trick (that's what this SAS programming stuff is all about). You create a new data set PERCENT ❷ by reading in variables (via SET statements) from existing data sets TEST and MOUT. Each time you loop through the DATA step in creating another observation in PERCENT, you set another observation from the original TEST data set to bring in a new collection of variables HR, SBP, and DBP ❸ (go back to Chapter 3, "SET, MERGE, and UPDATE," for a review of SET if needed). You only have to set the values from the MOUT variables (MHR, MSBP, MDBP) once, however, from the first (and only) observation in MOUT, and then retain the values for all new observations in PERCENT. You do this by using the SAS internal variable _N_ (the observation counter) to execute conditionally the SET MOUT statement only once.❹ Since you do not set a new observation from MOUT with subsequent iterations of the DATA step, the values from the first one are automatically retained into each new obsesrvation being built in PERCENT. This works because the SET statement contains an implicit RETAIN statement within it (you can review RETAIN in Chapter 8, "RETAIN"). Variables that are accessed via a SET statement are not reinitialized with each new observation being built. Values from the previous observation are carried forward and are replaced only with a new execution of the SET statement. Since the SET statement here is only executed once, when _N_=1, the original values for MHR, MSBP, and MDBP are always brought forward (never replaced) and are always available. You divide HR by MHR, SBP by MSBP, and DBP by MDBP, and then multiply each quotient by 100 to get the percentages you want, HRPER, SBPPER, and DBPPER respectively.❺ The final data set created by this program is shown in Ouput 6:

Output from Example 6 - Computing Values as Percentages of All Observations

```
                       Listing of PERCENT Data Set

          HR     SBP     DBP      HRPER       SBPPER       DBPPER

          80     160     100     114.286      106.667      111.111
          70     150      90     100.000      100.000      100.000
          60     140      80      85.714       93.333       88.889
```

Example 7

Creating a Summary Data Set That Contains a Median

FEATURES: PROC UNIVARIATE, BY and OUTPUT Statements, TRANSLATE and INPUT Functions, Merging Data Sets, LAST. Variable, Clever Comment Boxes

In this last example you produce summary statistics and a report which includes a median. You use PROC UNIVARIATE instead of PROC MEANS because you want to compute medians as well as means, and PROC UNIVARIATE is the only SAS procedure that can easily produce medians and then output them to a SAS data set. When you use this procedure to output statistics to a file, the syntax is almost identical to PROC MEANS. PROC UNIVARIATE and PROC MEANS have slightly different sets of statistics that can be output, and you cannot use a CLASS statement with PROC UNIVARIATE -- you are restricted to using a BY statement.

The example that follows was thought up around 3:00 a.m. one night by one of the authors (RC) who had trouble sleeping because of a MEAN head cold. The reader should be able to see the effects of too many clinical symptoms, too much antihistamine and decongestant medication, and too little sleep. The pun in the first line of this paragraph was thought up by the other author (RP) after a full night's sleep and he accepts full responsibility.

You have a SAS data set CLINICAL which contains information on patient visits to a physician. As you can see from the data, there are a variable number of visits for each patient.

Variable Name	Description
PATNUM	Patient Number
DATE	Date of Visit
DRUGGRP	Drug Group (D or P - Drug or Placebo)
CHOL	Cholesterol Level
SBP	Systolic Blood Pressure
DBP	Diastolic Blood Pressure
HR	Heart Rate
ROUTINE	Was Visit Routine? (Y or N)

Here is a listing of the CLINICAL SAS data set:

PATNUM	DATE	DRUGGRP	CHOL	SBP	DBP	HR	ROUTINE
01	01/05/89	D	400	160	90	88	Y
01	02/15/89	D	350	156	88	80	Y
01	05/18/90	D	350	140	82	76	Y
01	09/09/90	D	300	138	78	78	N
01	11/11/90	D	305	142	82	84	Y
01	01/05/91	D	270	142	80	72	N
01	02/18/91	D	260	156	92	88	N
02	02/19/90	D	390	180	100	82	N
02	02/22/90	D	320	178	88	86	Y
02	02/25/90	D	325	172	82	78	Y
02	04/24/90	D	304	166	78	99	N
02	08/25/90	D	299	150	80	80	Y
02	03/13/91	D	222	144	82	72	Y
02	07/16/91	D	243	140	80	68	Y
02	10/10/91	D	242	138	74	62	Y
02	10/30/91	D	230	156	92	88	N
02	12/25/91	D	200	142	82	80	Y
03	01/01/90	P	387	190	110	90	N
03	02/13/90	P	377	188	96	84	Y

(continued on next page)

CLINICAL SAS data set continued

03	05/09/90	P	380	182	88	80	Y
03	08/17/90	P	400	186	92	82	Y
03	10/10/90	P	390	182	90	78	N
03	10/11/90	P	380	178	82	72	Y
03	11/11/90	P	370	160	82	72	Y
03	02/02/91	P	380	156	78	70	Y
04	05/15/91	D	380	120	78	56	Y
04	08/20/91	D	370	122	76	58	N
04	03/23/92	D	355	128	68	60	Y
04	05/02/92	D	306	130	72	68	N
04	07/02/92	D	279	126	74	62	Y
04	07/03/92	D	277	126	74	64	Y
04	07/05/92	D	261	130	80	72	N
05	01/06/90	P	399	188	110	92	N
05	03/06/90	P	377	182	100	88	N
05	04/24/90	P	400	180	92	82	Y
05	04/24/90	P	400	180	92	88	N
05	06/24/90	P	388	176	88	80	Y
05	08/01/90	P	378	162	82	78	Y
05	10/10/90	P	388	156	78	78	Y
05	12/01/90	P	359	156	72	70	Y
06	01/01/92	D	387	128	62	60	N
06	01/03/92	D	379	128	66	62	Y
06	04/24/92	D	375	132	70	58	N
06	05/01/92	D	365	130	76	66	Y
06	05/28/92	D	321	132	78	68	N
06	06/01/92	D	308	128	72	58	Y
07	01/05/90	P	376	118	68	54	Y
07	04/05/90	P	379	124	72	70	N
07	04/07/90	P	389	120	68	62	Y
07	06/28/90	P	388	124	78	60	Y
07	01/04/91	P	400	128	80	66	N
07	03/03/91	P	401	132	70	80	N

For this example, you want to create a new data set which contains one record for each patient. Each record is to contain:

1. patient number

2. date of last visit

3. last cholesterol measurement

4. mean values of the following for each patient:
   cholesterol
   SBP (systolic blood pressure)
   DBP (diastolic blood pressure)

5. median cholesterol value for each patient
6. the proportion of visits that were routine (ROUTINE = Y).

Let's examine the needed items one step at a time. Item 1 is easy and comes as a by-product of some other operations. We'll note it in passing. Items 2 and 3 are obtained by sorting the data set by PATNUM (patient number) and DATE and then selecting the last record for each patient. Items 4 and 5 are computed by PROC UNIVARIATE and written out to a data set. To compute item 6, you need to create a numeric variable that has values of 0 and 1 corresponding to the character values of 'N' and 'Y' in the ROUTINE variable. By doing this, you can calculate the mean of the numeric variable (let's call it RATIO), which will be the proportion of visits that are routine (i.e., the proportion of observations where ROUTINE=Y). The program and accompanying explanation will get it all done, but not necessarily in the order of the items listed here.

Here is the program:

Example 7

```
/*—————————————————————————————————————*\
| First, create a new data set NEW_CLIN from CLIN which |
| contains a numeric variable RATIO which has values    |
| of 0 for 'N' and 1 for 'Y'.                           |
\*—————————————————————————————————————*/

DATA NEW_CLIN;
    SET CLINICAL;
    RATIO=INPUT (TRANSLATE(ROUTINE,'01','NY'),1.);   ❶
/*—————————————————————————————————————*\
|                                                       |
| Two alternatives would be:                            |
|                                                       |
| IF ROUTINE = 'N' THEN RATIO = 0;                      |
|                       ELSE RATIO = 1;                 |
|                                                       |
|          or                                           |
|                                                       |
| SELECT (ROUTINE);                                     |
|    WHEN ('N') THEN RATIO = 0;                          |
|    WHEN ('Y') THEN RATIO = 1;                          |
| END;                                                  |
|                                                       |
\*—————————————————————————————————————*/
RUN;


PROC SORT DATA=NEW_CLIN;     ❷
    BY PATNUM DATE;
RUN;
```

(continued on next page)

Example 7 - *continued*

```
* Create a data set with the last record for each patient;
DATA LAST (RENAME=(DATE=LASTDATE
                   CHOL=LASTCHOL));
   SET NEW_CLIN  (KEEP=PATNUM DATE CHOL);
   BY PATNUM; ❸
   IF LAST.PATNUM;   ❹
RUN;


* Output means and medians for each patient to a data set;

PROC UNIVARIATE DATA=NEW_CLIN NOPRINT;   ❺
   BY PATNUM;
   VAR CHOL SBP DBP RATIO;
   OUTPUT OUT=STATS
          MEAN=MEANCHOL MEANSBP MEANDBP RATIO
          MEDIAN=MEDCHOL;
RUN;


* Combine the LAST data set with the STATS data set;
DATA FINAL;   ❻
   MERGE STATS LAST;
   BY PATNUM;
RUN;


* Print a final report;
PROC PRINT DATA=FINAL LABEL DOUBLE;   ❼
   TITLE 'Listing of data set FINAL in Example 7';
   ID PATNUM;
   VAR LASTDATE LASTCHOL MEANCHOL MEDCHOL
       MEANSBP MEANDBP RATIO;
   LABEL LASTDATE='Date of Last Visit'
         MEANCHOL='Mean Chol'
         MEANSBP ='Mean SBP'
         MEANDBP ='Mean DBP'
         MEDCHOL ='Median Chol'
         LASTCHOL='Last Chol'
         RATIO   ='Proportion of visits that were routine';

   FORMAT MEANCHOL MEANSBP MEANDBP MEDCHOL LASTCHOL 5.0
          RATIO 3.2;
RUN;
```

The first DATA step creates a new data set called NEW_CLIN. The sole purpose of this step is to create a numeric variable RATIO so that you can use the mean of this variable to indicate the proportion of visits that were routine. It's a simple concept. In any population, the sum of a binary variable (values are 0 or 1) is equal to the total number of scores equal to 1, and the mean is equal to the proportion of the scores equal to 1. Try it. The functions TRANSLATE and INPUT are used here to convert the character values of 'N' and 'Y' to 0 and 1 respectively. While the alternative sets of code shown in the comment box are perhaps simpler to understand, the method used here gives you an opportunity to review two of the functions discussed in Chapter 5, "SAS Functions." The TRANSLATE function ❶ converts each character value in the from string ('NY') to the corresponding character value in the to string ('01'). Thus, each 'N' becomes a '0' and each 'Y' becomes a '1'. The INPUT function ❶ then rereads these character values using the numeric 1. format, and turns each character '0' into a numeric 0, and each character '1' into a numeric 1. (See Chapter 5, Examples 5 and 12 for more details on these two functions.) A note about the comment box itself is in order here. It works because the entire box starts with the comment-initiating character string (/*) and ends with the comment-terminating character string (*/) . The rest of the box border is just some fancy comment fingerwork.

You next sort the data set NEW_CLIN by PATNUM and DATE ❷ so that you can use the SET-BY combination in the next DATA step. This DATA step creates the data set LAST by using a SET statement on NEW_CLIN followed by the BY PATNUM statement ❸. The use of the BY statement following the SET statement creates the two internal SAS variables FIRST.PATNUM and LAST.PATNUM (see Chapter 7, "SAS Arrays," Example 6). Since you only want to keep the most recent (i.e. last) observation for each patient, you use the subsetting IF statement, IF LAST.PATNUM ❹. This gives you just what you want, including the PATNUM, which we said we'd note in passing -- here it is.

In the next part of the process, you use PROC UNIVARIATE ❺ to create an output data set STATS which contains the patient means for CHOL, SBP, DBP, and RATIO as well as the median CHOL reading. These are contained in MEANCHOL, MEANSBP, MEANDBP, RATIO, and MEDCHOL respectively. Notice that you had to use a BY statement with PROC UNIVARIATE, whereas PROC MEANS gives you the option of using CLASS or BY.

The data set FINAL ❻ merges the data set STATS, which contains the means and median values, with the data set LAST, which contains the most recent visit date. The merge is done using the BY PATNUM statement to assure that the proper match-merging by PATIENT takes place.

Finally, the PROC PRINT statement ❼ uses the two options DOUBLE and LABEL. You've seen these before, but it doesn't hurt to see them again. DOUBLE, as the name implies, double-spaces the output; LABEL tells the procedure to use variable labels instead of variable names as column headings.

Finally, here is the output. We hope it was worth the wait and the wade (through that deep code).

Output from Example 7 - Creating a Summary Data Set Containing a Median

PATNUM	Date of Last Visit	Last Chol	Mean Chol	Median Chol	Mean SBP	Mean DBP	Proportion of visits that were routine
01	02/18/91	260	319	305	148	85	.57
02	12/25/91	200	278	271	157	84	.70
03	02/02/91	380	383	380	178	90	.75
04	07/05/92	261	318	306	126	75	.57
05	12/01/90	359	384	388	171	89	.71
06	06/01/92	308	356	370	130	71	.50
07	03/03/91	401	389	389	124	73	.50

Listing of Data Set FINAL in Example 7

This example really shows the enormous power of PROC MEANS and PROC UNIVARIATE in creating summary statistics. It also brings together techniques from several chapters of this book (LAST. variables, MERGE, functions, etc.).

Conclusion

In this chapter, you have seen how SAS procedures can produce data sets which contain summary information such as counts, means, medians, and sums. These summary data sets can then be further manipulated in subsequent DATA steps to perform calculations on the summary data. You will find that, with a little practice, you will be able to use many of the techniques demonstrated in this chapter to save significant amounts of time and energy when you need to summarize data. Speaking of practice, here are the end-of-chapter problems:

Problems

10-1. Given the data set GRADES, create a new data set MEAN_GRD which contains the separate mean test scores for boys and girls. Use the same variable name (SCORE) for the mean values in MEAN_GRD as for the raw data in GRADES, and let the procedure produce (print) output. The data set MEAN_GRD should contain only two observations. **Note:** Data set GRADES also contains the variable WEIGHT which will be used in other problems.

Here are some sample data to work with:

```
Data Set GRADES

GENDER   WEIGHT   SCORE

BOY      LIGHT    80
GIRL     HEAVY    90
GIRL     LIGHT    85
BOY      HEAVY    92
BOY      LIGHT    93
BOY      HEAVY    88
GIRL     LIGHT    96
```

10-2. Using the data set GRADES from Problem 10-1, create a new data set PROB2 which contains the mean scores for each combination of GENDER and WEIGHT but does not contain the overall mean score (for the whole data set) or the mean scores for each gender or weight classification. Do not print the results from the procedure you use to create the means, but rather from a subsequent PROC PRINT. Use the variable name MEAN_SCR for the mean values. The new data set should contain 4 observations.

10-3. Using the data set GRADES from Problem 10-1, create a new data set PROB3 which contains the mean scores for each combination of GENDER and WEIGHT, as well as the overall mean score (for the whole data set) and the mean scores for each gender and weight classification. Create an output data set, and then use the _TYPE_ variable to create yet another data set which only contains the mean scores for boys and girls (separately.) No need to print the results of the mean-creating procedure.

10-4. You have a SAS data set EXPER with variables GROUP (A or B), TIME (1 or 2), and SCORE. You want to plot the mean score at each time period for each group with the value of GROUP as the plotting symbol. Your resulting plot should look like the following:

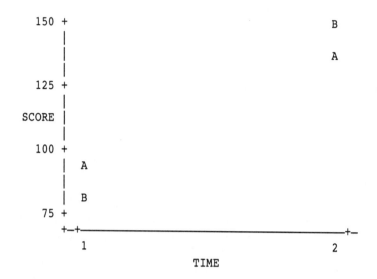

Hint: Use PROC MEANS with a CLASS statement to compute the mean score for each combination of group and time. Use the PLOT procedure to produce the plot (see Chapter 13, "PROC PLOT," for more information on the PLOT procedure). Use a PLOT statement of the form:

```
PLOT y-axis variable * x-axis variable = plotting symbol variable;
```

Here are some sample data to work with:

```
Data Set EXPER

GROUP   TIME    SCORE

  A       1       90
  A       1      100
  A       2      120
  A       2      150
  B       1       80
  B       1       80
  B       2      120
  B       2      180
```

10-5. Create a report similar to the one produced in Chapter 10, Example 7, with the following two changes: 1. Omit the median cholesterol value and the RATIO computation. 2. Include the mean heart rate (HR).

Since you no longer need to calculate a median, use PROC MEANS (with a CLASS statement).

Chapter 11

PROC FORMAT

Using and Creating Formatting Tools

EXAMPLES

Introduction

Very simply put, formats allow you to associate descriptive text with internal values of variables in a SAS data set. You can instruct the SAS System to print "MALE" or "FEMALE" instead of the actual values of "M" or "F". You can also use formats to create new variables as translated versions of other variables. The SAS System provides a plethora of ready-to-use formats and informats, but usually they are not enough. When this is the case, you can use the FORMAT procedure to create your own formats or informats.

The FORMAT procedure is one of the most potentially useful and productive tools available in the SAS System, yet it remains one of the most underused by beginning programmers. Although this chapter does not present an exhaustive in-depth look at this powerful tool, it does cover such topics as creating and storing your own formats and creating a user-defined format from a SAS data set. This latter feature can be extremely useful when you have a long list of values and descriptions stored in a raw data file or a SAS data set and you want to create a format associating the values with their descriptions. Without the automating features of CNTLIN/CNTLOUT, this could be a tedious process.

One of the most basic concepts in the SAS System, and also one of the most commonly misunderstood among beginning SAS programmers, is the notion that formats exist independently of variables and must be associated with them by the use of a FORMAT statement in a procedure or in a DATA step. Just creating formats with some PROC FORMAT code doesn't automatically link the formats you create to any variables you may use in subsequent procedures. The word "subsequent" here is quite important. It may seem obvious (but it's not) that you have to create a format before you can associate it with a variable. This chapter introduces some of the concepts necessary for a basic understanding of the format/informat creation process.

Example 1

Formatting Values in a Questionnaire

FEATURES: **PROC FORMAT, Character Formats, Numeric Formats, Numeric Ranges, PUT Function, OTHER= Option**

In this first example, you have collected questionnaire data and you want to create a finished report showing more meaningful descriptions rather than the numeric codes that were used for data entry. Your raw data file contains:

Variable	Description	Codes	Column(s)	Type
ID	Subject ID No.		1-2	Character
GENDER	Subject Gender	1=MALE, 2=FEMALE, BLANK=missing value All other codes=miscoded	4	Numeric
RACE	Subject Race	C=Caucasian, A=African American, H=Hispanic, N=Native American All other codes=missing or miscoded	6	Character
AGE	Subject Age		8-9	Numeric
SATISFY	Are you satisfied with your job?	Likert 5-point scale	11	Character
TIME	Do you have enough leisure time?	Likert 5-point scale	13	Character

Scales which express a range of attitudes using numbers such as 1 to 5 are sometimes referred to as Likert scales, named after a psychometrician who published studies on how to measure attitudes. The five-point Likert scale you are using is: 1=strongly disagree, 2=disagree, 3=no opinion, 4=agree, 5=strongly agree. You also want to create a new variable called AGEGROUP which groups age into 20 year intervals up to age 60, and includes all ages above 60 in a single group.

The formats you need are not supplied with the system, so you have to create them. This is done with PROC FORMAT, wherein you create one or more formats, each one created with a VALUE statement. Here is the code to produce the formats you need, as well as the DATA step to create the data set and the PROC PRINT to produce the finished report.

Example 1

```
PROC FORMAT;
    VALUE GENDER 1 = 'Male'
                 2 = 'Female'
                 . = 'Missing'
             OTHER = 'Miscoded';
    VALUE $RACE   'C' = 'Caucasian'
                  'A' = 'African American'
                  'H' = 'Hispanic'
                  'N' = 'Native American'
              OTHER = 'Other'
                ' ' = 'Missing';
    VALUE $LIKERT '1' = 'Str dis'
                  '2' = 'Disagree'
                  '3' = 'No opinion'
                  '4' = 'Agree'
                  '5' = 'Str agree'
              OTHER = ' ';
    VALUE AGEGROUP LOW-<20 = '< 20'
                   20-<40  = '20 to <40'
                   40-<60  = '40 to <60'
                   60-HIGH = '60+';

DATA QUESTION;
    INPUT   ID      $ 1-2
            GENDER    4
            RACE    $ 6
            AGE       8-9
            SATISFY $ 11
            TIME    $ 13;
    FORMAT GENDER GENDER.
           RACE    $RACE.
           SATISFY TIME $LIKERT.;
    AGEGROUP=PUT (AGE,AGEGROUP.);
DATALINES;
01 1 C 45 4 2
02 2 A 34 5 4
03 1 C 67 3 4
04   N 18 5 5
```

(continued on next page)

Example 1 - *continued*

```
05 9 H 47 4 2
06 1 X 55 3 3
07 2   56 2 2
08     20 1 1
RUN;

PROC PRINT DATA=QUESTION NOOBS;
   TITLE 'Data listing with formatted values';
RUN;
```

This example demonstrates many of the basic features of PROC FORMAT and the use of formats in general. The first format you create, GENDER, associates the text strings 'Male' and 'Female' (placed in single or double quotation marks) with the numeric data values 1 and 2, respectively. Missing values (.) are represented as 'Missing,' and all other values (OTHER) are identified as 'Miscoded.' This is a numeric format. Note that this format is not connected to any variable in any data set; it just exists waiting to be called into use. This is true of all the formats you create and is a point worth repeating.

The next format you create, $RACE, is a character format. Here you begin the format name with a dollar sign ($) to denote it as a character format (to be used with character variables) and place the data values to be formatted in single or double quotation marks. RACE codes other than 'C', 'A', 'H', or 'N' are associated with 'Other,' and missing values (' ') are associated with 'Missing.' The $LIKERT and AGEGROUP formats are created similarly. In the numeric AGEGROUP format, you assign inclusive ranges of values to specific labels. This is used in the DATA step to create a new grouped variable.

At this point in the code, the formats are created. Now you have to use them. The DATA step reads in the raw data and permanently makes the following format assignments: format GENDER. to variable GENDER, format $RACE. to variable RACE, and format $LIKERT. to variables SATISFY and TIME. Note that $LIKERT. was assigned to more than one variable — perfectly legal. Of much more importance to note is the period (.) after the format names in the FORMAT statement. You do not define the formats with a period in the PROC FORMAT code, but you must include the period whenever you refer to the format in subsequent code. This is a very common beginning mistake, and most of you will make it. We did, and we still do from time to time. Since you link the variables to the formats in the DATA step, you do not have to do so in the PROC PRINT code.

To finish the example, you use the AGEGROUP. format with a PUT function to create a character variable (also conveniently called AGEGROUP) based on the formatted values of the numeric variable AGE (see Chapter 2, "Data Recoding," Example 3, for more information on this technique).

The listing from this program follows:

Output from Example 1 - Formatting Values in a Questionnaire

```
                    Data listing with formatted values

   ID  GENDER    RACE              AGE  SATISFY     TIME        AGEGROUP

   01  Male      Caucasian          45  Agree       Disagree    40 to <60
   02  Female    African American   34  Str agree   Agree       20 to <40
   03  Male      Caucasian          67  No opinion  Agree       60+
   04  Missing   Native American    18  Str agree   Str agree   < 20
   05  Miscoded  Hispanic           47  Agree       Disagree    40 to <60
   06  Male      Other              55  No opinion  No opinion  40 to <60
   07  Female    Missing            56  Disagree    Disagree    40 to <60
   08  Missing   Missing            20  Str dis     Str dis     20 to <40
```

Notice that PROC FORMAT produces no output of its own, with one optional exception which is covered in the last two examples in this chapter.

Example 2

Encountering a Subtle Problem with Missing Values, Formats, and PROC FREQ

FEATURES: PROC FORMAT, PROC FREQ

In the previous example, you used formats to either display a translated version of a variable's values, or to create a new variable as a grouped version of another variable. Formats can also be used to aggregate data values together for group processing and presentation in procedures that operate on groups of values such as PROC FREQ, a procedure that counts the number (frequency) of occurrences for each formatted value of a variable (i.e., for each group. See Chapter 2, Example 3, for another example of PROC FREQ). This process of labeling or grouping data values using a format usually has no adverse side effects; however, unexpected results can occur in PROC FREQ, specifically when formatting a variable that contains missing values. Let's look at an example that demonstrates this rather subtle problem.

Example 2

```
PROC FORMAT;
   VALUE BADFMT   1='ONE'
                  2='TWO'
              OTHER='MISCODED';
RUN;

DATA TEST;
INPUT X  Y;
DATALINES;
1 1
2 2
5 5
3 .
;

PROC FREQ DATA=TEST;
   TABLES X Y;
   FORMAT X Y BADFMT.;
RUN;
```

Output from Example 2 - Encountering a Subtle Problem with Missing Values, Formats, and PROC FREQ

X	Frequency	Percent	Cumulative Frequency	Cumulative Percent
ONE	1	25.0	1	25.0
TWO	1	25.0	2	50.0
MISCODED	2	50.0	4	100.0

Y	Frequency	Percent	Cumulative Frequency	Cumulative Percent
ONE	1	50.0	1	50.0
TWO	1	50.0	2	100.0

Frequency Missing = 2

Notice that Output 2 shows the category MISCODED with a frequency count of 2 for the variable X. This represents the two data values that fall into the special format category called OTHER, namely the 5 in Observation 3, and the 3 in Observation 4. Next, look at the output for the variable Y. Notice that there is no longer a row with a label of MISCODED. Why not? The two values in Observations 3 and 4, namely the 5 and the period (missing), are neither 1 nor 2, and therefore should (you would think) be included in the OTHER category. Instead of this, however, the output shows `Frequency Missing = 2` at the bottom. Even though there was only one observation that contained a missing value for the variable Y (Observation 4), PROC FREQ reports two missing values. The reason for this is a little convoluted, but worth the struggle to understand. In this example, since missing values do not have their own separate range in the BADFMT. format, they automatically fall into the OTHER category. Unfortunately, the inclusion of missing values in this OTHER category declares the entire category as missing. The reason is that when a range of values, or a group of discrete values, are grouped together in a single format, all the values in the range or series are represented by the lowest value in the range or series. Since missing is the lowest value possible, the inclusion of missing in a range, or series, of values translates all the values into missing for formatting purposes. This means that if any observation contains a missing value, all the observations that fall into the OTHER range are treated as missing. PROC FREQ determines the number of missing values after formatting has occurred. Most other procedures that work with grouped data values, such as PROC MEANS and PROC TABULATE, check for missing values before formatting.

Example 3

Resolving the Subtle Problem

FEATURES: **PROC FORMAT, Separate Missing Assignment**

To prevent the intermingling of missing and non-missing values, and the resulting incorrect designation of some non-missing values as missing, simply include a separate range for missing values as follows:

Example 3

```
   .
   .
   .
PROC FORMAT;
   VALUE GOODFMT   . = 'MISSING'
                   1 = 'ONE'
                   2 = 'TWO'
               OTHER = 'MISCODED';
   .
   .
   .
```

The new format is able to distinguish between missing values and out-of-range values, and this solution provides you with acceptable output as shown in Output 3:

Output from Example 3 - Resolving the Subtle Problem

X	Frequency	Percent	Cumulative Frequency	Cumulative Percent
ONE	1	25.0	1	25.0
TWO	1	25.0	2	50.0
MISCODED	2	50.0	4	100.0

Y	Frequency	Percent	Cumulative Frequency	Cumulative Percent
ONE	1	33.3	1	33.3
TWO	1	33.3	2	66.7
MISCODED	1	33.3	3	100.0

Frequency Missing = 1

You are now accurately categorizing the missing value as missing, as is noted in the Frequency Missing = 1 note.

Example 4

Checking for Invalid Values: A DATA Step Approach (Setting Invalid Values to Missing)

FEATURES: IN Operator, Character Missing Values

When you have raw data that you want to turn into a SAS data set, and you want to change the format in which some of the data values are stored, you can do it in one of two ways. You can either read the data as they occur in their raw form, insert them into the SAS data set you are building, and then change the values via conditional assignment statements, or you can "pre-screen" the raw data on the way into the data set and make changes to the values before they are stored as SAS variable values. The latter method is usually used for efficiency purposes. In this example, you use both methods. First, you read raw data into a SAS data set as they appear and change the stored values. Then you use an alternative method to change the data as they are being read in.

Suppose you have data coded as 'M' for male and 'F' for female, and you want to set all values other than 'M' or 'F' to a missing value (blank). A straightforward way to do this is to simply supply some logic statements in the DATA step as follows:

Example 4

```
DATA SCREEN4;
    INPUT    ID      1-3
             GENDER $ 4 ...  ;
    IF GENDER NOT IN ('M','F')
       THEN GENDER = ' ';
         .
         .
         .
```

The IF statement with the IN operator as shown is equivalent to:

```
IF GENDER NOT='M' AND GENDER NOT='F' THEN GENDER=' ';
```

The result of this code is that all values of GENDER other than 'M' or 'F', including missing values (' '), are first read into data set SCREEN4, and then changed into a missing value (blank). Each value already coded as blank is "changed" into itself.

Example 5

> ### Checking for Invalid Values: A DATA Step Approach (Separating Invalid and Missing Values)
>
> *FEATURES:* **IN Operator, Character Missing Values**

The previous strategy might be sufficient, but most likely you would still want to differentiate between invalid data and missing data. An alternative and slightly more sophisticated approach, but one that still has to read in data and then translate them, is to keep track of invalid codes separately from the missing responses. The following code accomplishes this:

Example 5

```
DATA SCREEN5;
   INPUT ID        1-3
         GENDER   $ 4  ... ;
   IF GENDER NOT IN ('M','F',' ')
      THEN GENDER='X';
      .
      .
      .
```

In this revised code, values for GENDER that are invalid and non-missing are coded as an 'X'.

Example 6

Using a User-Created Informat to Filter Input Data (Setting Invalid Values to Missing)

FEATURES: PROC FORMAT, INVALUE Statement, Informats, IN Operator, _SAME_ Value

Now you take a different approach and use a simple and elegant method that yields the same end results as Example 5, but performs the process in a more efficient manner by changing the data on the way into the data set. Here you filter the data values as they are read in and do the necessary conversion at INPUT time by first creating a user-defined informat. As before, you proceed using two alternate methods. First, you will handle all values other than 'M' or 'F' (including missing) as a single group. The next example separates missing from invalid data. Here is the code for the first method:

Example 6

```
PROC FORMAT;
    INVALUE $GENDER 'M', 'F'= _SAME_
                        OTHER=' ';
RUN;

DATA SCREEN3;
    INPUT @1 ID     3.
          @4 GENDER $GENDER1. ;
    .
    .
    .
```

Here's how it works. You first define an informat in the PROC FORMAT code by using an INVALUE statement instead of a VALUE statement. Since you are defining an informat that will result in a character value, you specify an informat name that starts with a dollar sign ($). (If you wanted the result to be a numeric value, you would leave off the beginning $.)

Informat names can only be seven characters in length, including the $ if it is used. This is in contrast to format names, which can be up to eight characters in length (including the $ if it is used.) The reason is that the system needs room to add an internal tag to the front of the name declaring it to be an informat - it actually adds a @ which you can see in system generated messages.

Following the informat name, you indicate specific values and/or ranges of values on the left and their corresponding resultant informatted values on the right (of the =). If a value is read in that matches a value in the list or lies within a specified range, the informatted value gets assigned to the variable. In this example, if you wanted to store expanded versions of the 'M' and 'F', you might have coded 'M' = 'MALE', 'F' = 'FEMALE'. Since you are satisfied with the one- character data values, you choose not to change them. You accomplish this by using the keyword _SAME_ which instructs the system to leave these values intact. Values other than an 'M' or an 'F' are, however, set equal to missing because of the OTHER = ' ' assignment. There are also other special key words that can be used in the range specifications on the left of the = such as HIGH and LOW. These can be used when creating formats as well as informats.

Although you create your informat as $GENDER, you write it as $GENDER1. in the INPUT statement. Just as you do with formats, you must include a period(.) at the end of the informat when you use it in a subsequent DATA step but not when you create it. When creating informats, or formats, you cannot end the name with a number. You can, however, append a number to user-defined, as well as system-supplied, formats and informats when you use them in subsequent DATA or PROC steps. With formats, the number determines the display width of the formatted variable. With informats, the number specifies how many characters to read from the input record. The default length for an informat is the longest informatted value (in this case it is equal to 1). It is good coding practice to follow all user-defined informats with a number to ensure that you read the correct number of columns from the input record. You should, however, realize that like a LENGTH statement, this can also establish the length of a variable.

Example 7

> ### Using a User-Created INFORMAT to Filter Input Data (Separating Invalid and Missing Values)
>
> *FEATURES:* PROC FORMAT, INVALUE Statement, Informats, IN Operator, _SAME_ Value

To keep track of miscoded values separately from missing values, as you did in Example 5, you can write:

Example 7

```
PROC FORMAT;
    INVALUE $GENDER 'M', 'F', ' '=_SAME_
                    OTHER        ='X';
RUN;

DATA SCREEN7;
    INPUT @1 ID     3.
          @4 GENDER $GENDER1. ;
    .
    .
    .
```

Here you add a blank (a missing character value) to the first list and code all other values to 'X'. Thus, the values 'M', 'F', and ' ' (missing) are not modified, while all other values are assigned a value of 'X'.

You can use informats for numeric as well as character values. The next example demonstrates such a use.

Example 8

Checking Ranges for Numeric Variables

FEATURES: **PROC FORMAT, Informats, _SAME_ Value**

In this example you provide two informats for two numeric variables. These informats set values outside of the normal range for the variables equal to missing values. Here is the code:

Example 8

```
PROC FORMAT;
INVALUE SBPFMT 40 - 300= _SAME_
               OTHER  =.;
INVALUE DBPFMT 10 - 150= _SAME_
               OTHER  =.;
RUN;

DATA FORMAT8;
    INPUT @1 ID   $3.
          @4 SBP  SBPFMT3.
          @7 DBP  DBPFMT3.;
DATALINES;
001160090
002310220
003020008
004   080
005150070
;

PROC PRINT DATA=FORMAT8;
RUN;
```

You create two informats, one for SBP (systolic blood pressure — the larger of the two numbers in a blood pressure reading, e.g. the 120 in 120/80) and one for DBP (diastolic blood pressure — the lower of the two numbers). SBP values below 40 or above 300 are set equal to missing (.), as are DBP values below 10 or above 150.

Here is the PROC PRINT output from this code.

Output from Example 8 - Checking Ranges for Numeric Variables

OBS	ID	SBP	DBP
1	001	160	90
2	002	.	.
3	003	.	.
4	004	.	80
5	005	150	70

Notice that the out-of-range values are all set to missing values.

Example 9

Using Different Missing Values to Keep Track of High and Low Values

FEATURES: **PROC FORMAT, INVALUE and VALUE Statements, _SAME_ Value, HIGH, LOW, Alternate Missing Values (.H and .L), MISSING Option Used with a TABLES Statement**

You can easily extend Example 8 to provide additional information concerning out-of-range values. To do this, you use two alternate missing values, namely .H and .L. The use of numeric missing values other than a single period (.) is another underused SAS System feature. Besides the single period that specifies a missing value, there are 27 additional missing value designations: ._ (that's a period followed by an underscore) and .A through .Z. In this example, you use separate missing values to represent high and low out-of-range values. You are then able to produce counts of these out-of-range values, and at the same time, you are able to compute statistics without including them. Here is the program:

Example 9

```
PROC FORMAT;
   INVALUE SBPFMT LOW-<40 =.L              ❶
                  40-300 =_SAME_
                  301-HIGH=.H;
   INVALUE DBPFMT LOW-<10 =.L
                  10-150 =_SAME_
                  151-HIGH=.H;
   VALUE CHECK    .H='High'                ❷
                  .L='Low'
                  . ='Missing'
               OTHER='Valid';
RUN;

DATA FORMAT9;
   INPUT @1 ID   $3.
         @4 SBP  SBPFMT3.
         @7 DBP  DBPFMT3.;
DATALINES;
001160090
002310220
003020008
004   080
005150070
;

PROC PRINT DATA=FORMAT9 NOOBS;    ❸
   TITLE 'Listing from Example 9';
RUN;

PROC FREQ DATA=FORMAT9;
   FORMAT SBP DBP CHECK.;
   TABLES SBP DBP / MISSING NOCUM;   ❹
RUN;

PROC MEANS DATA=FORMAT9 N MEAN MAXDEC=1;
   VAR SBP DBP;
RUN;
```

The output from this program follows.

Output from Example 9 - Checking Ranges for Numeric Variables

```
              Listing from Example 9

            ID    SBP    DBP

            001   160     90
            002    H      H
            003    L      L
            004    .      80
            005   150     70


              Listing from Example 9

         SBP      Frequency    Percent

       High            1         20.0
       Low             1         20.0
       Missing         1         20.0
       Valid           2         40.0


         DBP      Frequency    Percent

       High            1         20.0
       Low             1         20.0
       Valid           3         60.0


       Listing from Example 9

       Variable   N           Mean

       SBP        2          155.0
       DBP        3           80.0
```

You conveniently choose .H and .L as the special missing values for high and low out-of-range values.❶ You alternatively could have chosen any of the 27 available missing values such as .A and .B to represent the low and high values. Values in the valid ranges are untouched because you specify _SAME_ for your informatted value.

In the PROC FORMAT code, you also use a VALUE statement ❷ to create an output format so that you can label the appropriate missing values. You use this format to label the variables SBP and DBP in the PROC FREQ output, but not in the PROC PRINT listing ❸, so that you can see the actual "internal" values stored in the SAS data set. Note that the missing SBP value for ID number 004 is truly missing, whereas the out-of-range missing values are stored as the appropriate special missing values.

In this example, you use the MISSING and NOCUM options ❹ on the TABLES statement of PROC FREQ. Without the missing option, the missing values would only be noted at the bottom of the table in the form Frequency Missing = . When the MISSING option is specified, the missing value(s) are listed in the body of the frequency table, and the frequencies and percentages are calculated based on all the observations, including the ones with missing values. You use the NOCUM option to eliminate the Cumulative Frequency and the Cumulative Percent columns.

PROC MEANS is run to demonstrate that no distinction is made between different missing values when statistical calculations are made. A missing value by any other name is still missing.

Example 10

> ## Creating and Using an Enhanced Numeric Informat
>
> *FEATURES:* **PROC FORMAT, INVALUE Statement, Enhanced Numeric Informat**

Here is an elegant way of reading a mixture of numeric and character data using what is called an enhanced numeric informat. This type of format became available in Release 6.07 of the SAS System. (See Chapter 5, "SAS Functions," Example 5, on how to convert character values to numeric values using the INPUT function.) With this type of informat, you have the ability to specify numeric or character ranges. Here is the temperature example from Chapter 5, using this type of informat:

Example 10

```
PROC FORMAT;
   INVALUE TEMPER 70-110=_SAME_
                     'N' = 98.6
                   OTHER=.;
RUN;

DATA TEST;
   INPUT TEMP : TEMPER. @@;
DATALINES;
99.7 N 97.9 N N 112.5
;

PROC PRINT DATA=TEST NOOBS;
   TITLE 'Temperature Listing';
RUN;
```

Output from Example 10 - Creating and Using an Enhanced Numeric Informat

```
                     Temperature Listing

                            TEMP

                            99.7
                            98.6
                            97.9
                            98.6
                            98.6
                             .
```

As you can see from the listing, the N's were converted to 98.6 and the out-of-range value was set to missing.

Example 11

Using a SAS Data Set to Create a Character Format

FEATURES: **PROC FORMAT, CNTLIN and FMTLIB Options, RETAIN Statement, Creating a Character Format**

In this example, you use a set of variables in an existing SAS data set to create a format. This is most useful when you have a long list of items and expansions, such as ICD-9 codes and descriptions. For those not familiar with the term, ICD-9 stands for the International Classification of Diseases, ninth revision. Here is a very short portion of the entire list.

ICD9	Description
072	Mumps
410	Heart Attack
487	Influenza
493	Asthma
700	Corns

If you have a relatively short list such as this one, you can go ahead and write a VALUE statement list this:

Example 11 - Using PROC FORMAT Directly

```
PROC FORMAT;
    VALUE $ICDFMT '072'='Mumps'
                  '410'='Heart Attack'
                  '487'='Influenza'
                  '493'='Asthma'
                  '700'='Corns';
RUN;
```

When the list of codes is hundreds of entries long as it is with the ICD-9, or even thousands of entries long, this gets to be tedious. There is a better way — the CNTLIN option of PROC FORMAT. By using a SAS data set which contains the codes and descriptions needed, and which meets very rigid structural and naming conventions, you can have PROC FORMAT read this data set (which is called a control data set) and automatically create a format for you. Standard sets of codes and descriptions are usually available in some electronic format which can easily be transformed into a SAS control data set as the first step in creating a very useful data formatting tool.

We demonstrate this technique with two simple examples; the current one creates a character format and the next example creates a numeric format. These two short examples serve merely to introduce this powerful facility.

The following program first converts the previous ICD-9 raw data subset to a SAS data set, then to a SAS control data set, and then to a user-defined SAS format. It then uses the format to associate labels to sample raw data read into another SAS data set and prints out the formatted values. The example is a little cumbersome for educational purposes, and it is explained after the code.

Example 11 - Using a CNTLIN Data Set

```
DATA CODES; ❶
INPUT  @1 ICD9     $3. ❷
       @5 DESCRIPT  $12.;
DATALINES;
072 MUMPS
410 HEART ATTACK
487 INFLUENZA
493 ASTHMA
700 CORNS
;

DATA CONTROL; ❸
   RETAIN FMTNAME '$ICDFMT' ❹
          TYPE    'C' ;
   SET CODES (RENAME=(ICD9=START ❺
                      DESCRIPT=LABEL));
RUN;

PROC FORMAT CNTLIN=CONTROL; ❻
RUN;

DATA EXAMPLE; ❼
   INPUT ICD9 $ @@;
   FORMAT ICD9 $ICDFMT.; ❽
DATALINES;
072 493 700 410 072 700
;

PROC PRINT NOOBS DATA=EXAMPLE; ❾
   TITLE 'Using a Control Data Set';
   VAR ICD9;
RUN;
```

Well now you've seen the code, and if that didn't frighten you away, here is the explanation. The first step is to turn the raw data into the SAS data set CODES to contain the collection of codes and descriptions as SAS variables ❶. Pretty straightforward stuff. You could have made things easier on yourself by naming the variables in the CODES data set START and LABEL, the names required for the control data set and the CNTLIN feature of PROC FORMAT, which is what this example is all about. You choose however, to give them other, more realistic names ❷ and then rename them ❺. This makes the coding more general, and more like the situation you may encounter if you ever need to convert an existing SAS data set with previously assigned variable names into a control data set. The next step is to create the control data set (which you cleverly call CONTROL) ❸. The control data set consists of one observation for each pair of codes and descriptions. Each observation must contain a specific set of variables with prescribed names. These are as follows:

Variable Name	Description of the Variable
FMTNAME	the name of the format name you are creating. Use standard format naming conventions.
TYPE	format type: 'C' for character; 'N' for numeric.
START	the value (code) you want to translate. If you are working with a range of values, use this as the lower value of the range and also include an END variable for the upper end of the range.
LABEL	the label you want to assign to the value(s).

You use a RETAIN statement ❹ to assign values to the variables FMTNAME and TYPE since they are the same on every observation. You could use assignment statements instead, but the RETAIN statement is more efficient (See Chapter 8, "RETAIN," for an explanation of how RETAIN works). After the control data set is created, you merely have to tell PROC FORMAT to use it to create a format. This is done with the CNTLIN option ❺. You don't even have to name the format you are creating; it's all in the control data set. At this point in the example, you have a character format called $ICDFMT. created and waiting to be used.

You test out your new format by creating another SAS data set called EXAMPLE from a collection of sample ICD-9 data ❼. It's important to realize that this represents a set of actually collected data whereas the data used to create data set CODES is a set of all the unique codes that are possible with their descriptions. You permanently assign the formatted values to the codes in the data set EXAMPLE with the FORMAT statement ❽. The last step is to print out the data set EXAMPLE ❾, with the following result:

Output from Example 11 - Using a SAS Data Set to Create a Character Format

```
                    Using a Control Data Set

                         ICD9

                         MUMPS
                         ASTHMA
                         CORNS
                         HEART ATTACK
                         MUMPS
                         CORNS
```

One very useful option with PROC FORMAT is the FMTLIB option, which gives you a descriptive listing of your format. In the previous program, you could have added this option as follows:

```
PROC FORMAT CNTLIN=CONTROL FMTLIB;
```

This would have generated the following output:

FORMAT NAME: $ICDFMT LENGTH: 12 NUMBER OF VALUES: 5		
MIN LENGTH: 1 MAX LENGTH: 12 DEFAULT LENGTH 12 FUZZ: STD		
START	END	LABEL (VER. 6.03 23DEC92:09:51:49)
072	072	MUMPS
410	410	HEART ATTACK
487	487	INFLUENZA
493	493	ASTHMA
700	700	CORNS

Note that the START value is repeated in the END column because you are not using ranges, but rather discrete values.

Example 12

Using a SAS Data Set to Create a Numeric Format

FEATURES: PROC FORMAT, CNTLIN and FMTLIB Options, RETAIN Statement, Creating a Numeric Format

The previous technique can also be used to create a numeric format. In this example, you have a long list of numeric codes and country names, and you want to create a format assigning a country name to each of the numeric codes. You create the CNTLIN data set in one step and (cleverly) use the variable names START and VALUE for the numeric codes and the country names respectively. Here is the program:

Example 12

```
DATA COUNTRY;
RETAIN FMTNAME 'COUNTRY'
       TYPE 'N';
   INPUT START 1-2
         LABEL $ 3-15;
DATALINES;
01UNITED STATES
02FRANCE
03ENGLAND
04SPAIN
05GERMANY
;

PROC FORMAT CNTLIN=COUNTRY FMTLIB;
RUN;
```

Since you do not use the format you create to format actual data, the only output you have is from the FMTLIB option. Here it is:

Output from Example 12 - Using a SAS Data Set to Create a Numeric Format

```
         FORMAT NAME: COUNTRY  LENGTH:   13   NUMBER OF VALUES:    5
   MIN LENGTH:   1  MAX LENGTH:   40  DEFAULT LENGTH  13  FUZZ: STD

   START            END                 LABEL   (VER. 6.08   15JUL94:10:02:42)

   1                1                    UNITED STATES
   2                2                    FRANCE
   3                3                    ENGLAND
   4                4                    SPAIN
   5                5                    GERMANY
```

Although control data sets seem complicated at first, when the alternative is writing hundreds (or thousands) of assignment statements, we strongly recommend you consider using them.

Conclusion

You have seen in this chapter that there are many different uses for PROC FORMAT. Starting from the simple use of creating formats for enhancing the display of character and numeric variables, you progressed to using formats to create new variables, then to screening data by creating user-defined informats, and then to creating formats from specially created data sets called control data sets. You may also want to refer back to Chapter 2, which describes how to recode variables using formats and PUT statements, and Chapter 4, which uses formats to do table lookups.

Problems

11-1. You have a SAS data set containing survey data which is coded as follows:

Variable	Type	Code	Description
GENDER	Character	M	Male
		F	Female
RACE	Character	W	White
		A	African American
		H	Hispanic
	(other codes)		Other
ISSUE1	Numeric	1	Str Disagree
to		2	Disagree
ISSUE5		3	No opinion
		4	Agree
		5	Str Agree
QUES1	Numeric	0	No
to		1	Yes
QUES10			

Write the necessary statements to create SAS formats for these variables. Also, write the FORMAT statement you would include in the DATA step to assign the formats you have created to each of the variables listed.

11-2. You have a collection of raw data (in external file ZIP) with the following file layout:

Starting Column	Length	Format	Description
1	5	character	ZIP code
6	20	character	Town name

Use this raw data file to create a character format called $ZIPCODE which will assign town names to ZIP codes.

Here are some sample data:

```
08822Flemington
08903New Brunswick
78028Kerrville
```

Hint: Use the CNTLIN feature of the FORMAT procedure.

11-3. You have a SAS data set INVENTRY which contains the numeric variable PART_NO (part number) and the character variable DESCRIPT (part description.) Use this existing data set to create a format called PARTS which associates the part numbers with the descriptions.

Here is part of data set INVENTRY:

```
PART_NO     DESCRIPT

    123     Hammer
    124     Nails
    213     Saw
```

11-4. You have a raw data file that contains gender and race data. Valid values for gender are 'M' and 'F', and for race are 'W','A','N', and 'H'. Unfortunately, there are also other invalid values in the data. Create two user-defined informats which will read in all valid data unchanged and set all invalid data to missing values.

Chapter 12

PROC CHART

Charting Your Data

Introduction

PROC CHART can produce a variety of bar, pie, star and three-dimensional block charts. All the output produced by PROC CHART is in character mode as opposed to the camera-ready output that can be produced by SAS/GRAPH software. Therefore, although you cannot produce solid connected lines or textured bars or text output in different fonts, you can use PROC CHART to produce some fairly complex and useful charts with a few simple commands. That's the tradeoff. If refined publication-quality copy is absolutely necessary, graduate to SAS/GRAPH with its myriad of features. For a quick, useful graphical display of your data, PROC CHART may well suffice.

For most of the examples in this chapter, you use two data sets, SALES and CLINICAL. Here are those data sets:

SALES Data Set

PO_NUM	ITEM	REGION	PRICE	QUANTITY
1456	Hammer	NORTH	$10	5
1458	Saw	NORTH	$15	4
1511	Pliers	NORTH	$8	35
1600	Hammer	SOUTH	$10	15
1711	Hammer	EAST	$10	12
1712	Hammer	EAST	$10	2

1713	Saw	EAST	$15	25
1715	Saw	EAST	$15	24
1800	Pliers	EAST	$8	7
1900	Saw	WEST	$15	9
1901	Saw	WEST	$15	5

CLINICAL Data Set

PATNUM	DATE	DRUGGRP	CHOL	SBP	DBP	HR	ROUTINE
01	01/05/89	D	400	160	90	88	Y
01	02/15/89	D	350	156	88	80	Y
01	05/18/90	D	350	140	82	76	Y
01	09/09/90	D	300	138	78	78	N
01	11/11/90	D	305	142	82	84	Y
01	01/05/91	D	270	142	80	72	N
01	02/18/91	D	260	156	92	88	N
02	02/19/90	D	390	180	100	82	N
02	02/22/90	D	320	178	88	86	Y
02	02/25/90	D	325	172	82	78	Y
02	04/24/90	D	304	166	78	99	N
02	08/25/90	D	299	150	80	80	Y
02	03/13/91	D	222	144	82	72	Y
02	07/16/91	D	243	140	80	68	Y
02	10/10/91	D	242	138	74	62	Y
02	10/30/91	D	230	156	92	88	N
02	12/25/91	D	200	142	82	80	Y
03	01/01/90	P	387	190	110	90	N
03	02/13/90	P	377	188	96	84	Y
03	05/09/90	P	380	182	88	80	Y
03	08/17/90	P	400	186	92	82	Y
03	10/10/90	P	390	182	90	78	N
03	10/11/90	P	380	178	82	72	Y
03	11/11/90	P	370	160	82	72	Y
03	02/02/91	P	380	156	78	70	Y
04	05/15/91	D	380	120	78	56	Y
04	08/20/91	D	370	122	76	58	N
04	03/23/92	D	355	128	68	60	Y
04	05/02/92	D	306	130	72	68	N
04	07/02/92	D	279	126	74	62	Y
04	07/03/92	D	277	126	74	64	Y
04	07/05/92	D	261	130	80	72	N
05	01/06/90	P	399	188	110	92	N
05	03/06/90	P	377	182	100	88	N
05	04/24/90	P	400	180	92	82	Y
05	06/24/90	P	388	176	88	80	Y

05	08/01/90	P	378	162	82	78	Y
05	10/10/90	P	388	156	78	78	Y
05	12/01/90	P	359	156	72	70	Y
06	01/01/92	D	387	128	62	60	N
06	01/03/92	D	379	128	66	62	Y
06	04/24/92	D	375	132	70	58	N
06	05/01/92	D	365	130	76	66	Y
06	05/28/92	D	321	132	78	68	N
06	06/01/92	D	308	128	72	58	Y
07	01/05/90	P	376	118	68	54	Y
07	04/05/90	P	379	124	72	70	N
07	04/07/90	P	389	120	68	62	Y
07	06/28/90	P	388	124	78	60	Y
07	01/04/91	P	400	128	80	66	N
07	03/03/91	P	401	132	70	80	N

Example 1

Creating a Vertical Bar Chart

FEATURES: **PROC CHART, VBAR Statement**

The simplest type of chart you can produce is a frequency bar chart. In this type of chart, the bars represent the number of the observations that have the values that are displayed on the X axis. If you simply want to display the number of observations in the data set SALES for each region of the country, you write:

Example 1

```
PROC CHART DATA=SALES;
    TITLE 'Vertical Bar Chart';
    VBAR REGION;
RUN;
```

The VBAR (vertical bar) statement specifies the variable for which you want frequency counts. In this case REGION is a character variable which has the values NORTH, SOUTH, EAST, and WEST. The resulting chart follows. Note that LINESIZE= and PAGESIZE= settings will effect the heights and widths of the bars and scales.

Output from Example 1 - Creating a Vertical Bar Chart

```
                         Vertical Bar Chart

         Frequency

          5 |       *****
            |       *****
          4 |       *****
            |       *****
          3 |       *****        *****
            |       *****        *****
          2 |       *****        *****                     *****
            |       *****        *****                     *****
          1 |       *****        *****        *****        *****
            |       *****        *****        *****        *****
            +----------------------------------------------------------
                    EAST        NORTH        SOUTH         WEST
                                    REGION
```

The bars in the chart represent the frequency of observations for the regions listed on the X axis. PROC CHART uses the asterisk (*) character to build the bars by default. You can specify a different character with the SYMBOL= option. Also, in Example 11, you use the SUBGROUP= option which adds intelligence to the bar-building characters.

Example 2

Creating a Horizontal Bar Chart with Statistics

FEATURES: PROC CHART, HBAR Statement

You can also display the information in a horizontal bar chart by replacing the statement VBAR with HBAR in the program. Here is the code:

Example 2

```
PROC CHART DATA=SALES;
    TITLE 'Horizontal Bar Chart';
    HBAR REGION;
RUN;
```

Here is the output:

Output from Example 2 - Creating a Horizontal Bar Chart with Statistics

```
                        Horizontal Bar Chart

    REGION                                  Cum.              Cum.
                                      Freq  Freq  Percent  Percent
           |
    EAST   |********************       5     5    45.45    45.45
           |
    NORTH  |************             3     8    27.27    72.73
           |
    SOUTH  |****                       1     9     9.09    81.82
           |
    WEST   |********                   2    11    18.18   100.00
           |
         +—|—|—|—|—|
           1   2   3   4   5
              Frequency
```

By default, HBAR charts include the same frequency information as produced by PROC FREQ.

Example 3

Creating a Horizontal Bar Chart without Statistics

FEATURES: **PROC CHART, HBAR Statement**

You can use HBAR options to specify individual statistics to produce (FREQ, CFREQ, PERCENT, CPERCENT) or choose to omit all of the frequency statistics by specifying the

NOSTATS option. These options are separated from the statement to which they apply by a slash (/). If you want a horizontal bar chart with no statistics, code the following:

Example 3

```
PROC CHART DATA=SALES;
    TITLE 'Horizontal Bar Chart without Statistics';
    HBAR REGION / NOSTAT;
RUN;
```

Here is the output:

Output from Example 3 - Creating a Horizontal Bar Chart without Statistics

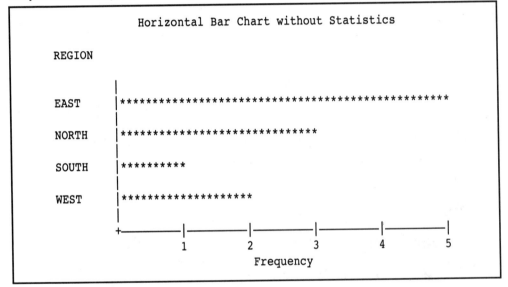

Notice that when statistics are not included in the output, the horizontal scale is adjusted to fill out the page.

Example 4

Creating a Bar Chart That Displays Percentages

FEATURES: PROC CHART, VBAR Statement, TYPE= and PERCENT Options

If you want the height (VBAR) or the length (HBAR) of the bars to represent the frequency in percent of the total observations rather than actual counts, you employ the TYPE=PERCENT option on either the VBAR or HBAR statement. To create a vertical bar chart of REGION using percents, code:

Example 4

```
PROC CHART DATA=SALES;
    TITLE 'Vertical Bar Chart Showing Percents';
    VBAR REGION / TYPE=PERCENT;
RUN;
```

Here is the output:

Output from Example 4 - Creating a Bar Chart That Displays Percentages

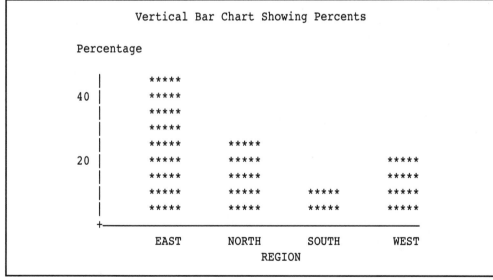

Here the vertical scale represents percentages of occurrences and is appropriately scaled and labeled.

Example 5

> ## Creating a Bar Chart for a Continuous Variable (System-Chosen Midpoints)
>
> *FEATURES:* **PROC CHART, VBAR Statement**

In the examples in this chapter thus far, you have been displaying frequencies, or percentages, of observations with discrete values of a character variable, namely REGION. You can also use continuous numeric variables with the VBAR and HBAR statements. If you want to see the frequency distribution of the variable PRICE, for example, you write:

Example 5

```
PROC CHART DATA=SALES;
   TITLE 'Vertical Bar Chart for a Continuous Variable';
   VBAR PRICE;
RUN;
```

When you use PROC CHART to produce frequencies or percentages for a continuous numeric variable, the procedure creates sub-ranges of values of the variable to use for grouping purposes. You can either let the system decide on the ranges to use, or you can make the decision. In this example, you let the system do the choosing and it automatically selects the ranges of PRICE to be placed on the X axis. The Y axis then represents the number of observations that fit into the selected ranges.

Since PROC CHART can produce both vertical and horizontal charts, the terms "X axis" and "Y axis" may be confusing. SAS Institute publications often refer to the axis representing the height or length of the bars as the "response axis." The explanations here will continue to use X axis and Y axis for vertical charts (there are no more HBAR outputs so it should not be confusing.)

The previous code produces the following chart:

Output from Example 5 - Creating a Bar Chart for a Continuous Variable (System-Chosen Midpoints)

```
             Vertical Bar Chart for a Continuous Variable

        Frequency

        5 |                                              *****
          |                                              *****
        4 |                            *****             *****
          |                            *****             *****
        3 |                            *****             *****
          |                            *****             *****
        2 |           *****            *****             *****
          |           *****            *****             *****
        1 |           *****            *****             *****
          |           *****            *****             *****
          +---------------------------------------------------------
                      9              11            13            15
                              PRICE Midpoint
```

The values on the X axis represent the midpoints of the intervals. For example, the bar labeled 9 represents all observations with amounts between 8 and 10. In actuality, the amounts are greater than 8 and less than 10. That is why the observations with values of 10 fall in the 11 category (GE 10 and LT 12.)

Example 6

Creating a Bar Chart for a Continuous Variable (User-Chosen Midpoints by Range)

FEATURES: PROC CHART, VBAR Statement, MIDPOINTS= Option

If you would like to select your own X axis intervals, you have two options which are discussed in this example and the next one. You can use the MIDPOINTS= option of VBAR or

HBAR to specify your own midpoints. Starting with the previous code, to select midpoints ranging from 8 to 20 that are incremented by a value of 4, you write:

Example 6

```
PROC CHART DATA=SALES;
    TITLE 'Vertical Bar Chart Demonstrating MIDPOINTS Option';
    VBAR PRICE / MIDPOINTS=8 to 20 by 4;
RUN;
```

Here is the output produced:

Output from Example 6 - Creating a Bar Chart for a Continuous (User-Chosen Midpoints by Range)

```
        Vertical Bar Chart Demonstrating MIDPOINTS Option
        Frequency

     5 |                                    *****
       |                                    *****
     4 |                      *****          *****
       |                      *****          *****
     3 |                      *****          *****
       |                      *****          *****
     2 |          *****       *****          *****
       |          *****       *****          *****
     1 |          *****       *****          *****
       |          *****       *****          *****
       +----------------------------------------------------
                   8          12           16          20
                          PRICE Midpoint
```

There are still three bars owing to the particular makeup of the data and the midpoints chosen, but the midpoints and accompanying ranges are now as you chose them, and not as the system decided.

You can specify midpoints several ways. The most common method, which is used in this example, is:

```
MIDPOINTS = lower_bound TO upper_bound BY interval;
```

You can also provide a list of specific midpoints without equal intervals like this:

```
VBAR PRICE / MIDPOINTS=0, 5, 10, 20;
```

Or even like this:

```
VBAR PRICE / MIDPOINTS=0, 10, 100, 1000, 10000, 100000;
```

The third method produces an X axis with intervals based on a log10 scale.

Example 7

Creating a Bar Chart for a Continuous Variable (without DISCRETE Option)

FEATURES: PROC CHART, VBAR Statement

In Example 6 you used the MIDPOINTS= option to specify intervals for a continuous numeric variable. In Example 8 you use the DISCRETE option to specify meaningful intervals, but first you write the code here without using DISCRETE, for comparison.

Suppose you want frequencies on a numeric variable DAY in a data set called OSCAR where the values 1 to 7 represent the days of the week (1=Sun, 2=Mon, etc.). You can simply write:

Example 7

```
PROC CHART DATA=OSCAR;
   TITLE 'Vertical Chart without DISCRETE Option';
   VBAR DAY;
RUN;
```

This code yields the following strange-looking output:

Output from Example 7 - Creating a Bar Chart for a Continuous Variable (without DISCRETE Option)

```
                        Vertical Chart without DISCRETE Option

        Frequency

               |                                                    *****
            12 |                                                    *****
               |                                                    *****
            10 |                                        *****        *****
               |                                        *****        *****
             8 |                                        *****        *****
               |                                        *****        *****
             6 |                                        *****        *****
               |                                        *****        *****
             4 |                                        *****        *****
               |          *****       *****       *****              *****
             2 |          *****       *****       *****       *****  *****
               |          *****       *****       *****       *****  *****
               +---------------------------------------------------------------
                          0.75        2.25        3.75        5.25   6.75
                                        DAY Midpoint
```

The SAS System, unable to read your mind, found reasonable intervals for the numeric variable DAY and represented each interval with a midpoint. How was the system to know that the numeric values supplied in the data set already represented meaningful categories?

Example 8

Creating a Bar Chart for a Continuous Variable (with DISCRETE Option)

FEATURES: PROC CHART, VBAR Statement, DISCRETE Option

To tell the program to treat the X axis values as unique categories, you use the DISCRETE option of VBAR or HBAR statements (you should always try to be discrete when dealing with meaningful data.) To correct the previous bar chart, you modify the program as follows:

Example 8

```
PROC CHART DATA=OSCAR;
   TITLE 'Vertical Chart with DISCRETE Option';
   VBAR DAY / DISCRETE;
RUN;
```

Notice in the following output, that the actual DAY values 1 through 7 are used on the X axis, instead of using system-calculated range midpoints.

Output from Example 8 - Creating a Bar Chart for a Continuous Variable (with DISCRETE Option)

```
                    Vertical Chart with DISCRETE Option

       Frequency

           |                                              *****
        12 |                                              *****
           |                                              *****
        10 |                            *****             *****
           |                            *****             *****
         8 |                            *****             *****
           |                            *****             *****
         6 |                            *****             *****
           |                            *****             *****
         4 |                            *****             *****
           |      *****      *****      *****             *****
         2 |      *****      *****      *****      *****   *****
           |      *****      *****      *****      *****   *****
           +------------------------------------------------------
                    1          2          3          5          7
                                        DAY
```

Example 9

Plotting Sums and Means of Numeric Variables

FEATURES: PROC CHART, VBAR Statement, SUMVAR= and TYPE= Options

---

So far, you have seen bar charts where the Y axis represents the frequency count, or percentage, for values or ranges displayed on the X axis. PROC CHART can also provide charts where the Y axis represents the mean or sum of a numeric variable for each value of another variable shown on the X axis.

For example, suppose you want to see the total (SUM) of the variable QUANTITY for each region of the country from the SALES data set. You use the SUMVAR= option to select the numeric variable on which to compute the sum or mean, and the TYPE= option to indicate the desired statistic. The default type is SUM, but you should always include a TYPE= option whenever you use the SUMVAR= option. So, to produce the chart just described, use the following code:

Example 9

```
PROC CHART DATA=SALES;
    TITLE 'Adding Options SUMVAR= and TYPE=';
    VBAR REGION / SUMVAR=QUANTITY TYPE=SUM;
RUN;
```

The resulting chart follows:

Output from Example 9 - Plotting Sums and Means of Numeric Variables

```
                      Adding Options SUMVAR= and TYPE=

     QUANTITY Sum

        70 |         *****
           |         *****
        60 |         *****
           |         *****
        50 |         *****
           |         *****         *****
        40 |         *****         *****
           |         *****         *****
        30 |         *****         *****
           |         *****         *****
        20 |         *****         *****
           |         *****         *****         *****         *****
        10 |         *****         *****         *****         *****
           |         *****         *****         *****         *****
           +-----------------------------------------------------------
                     EAST          NORTH         SOUTH          WEST
                                        REGION
```

The bars here represent the sum of the variable QUANTITY for each of the regions. If you had done this using an HBAR statement, you could have requested the actual sums to print alongside of the bars; if you used TYPE=MEAN, you could have requested the mean statistic.

Example 10

Representing Two Variables on One Axis

FEATURES: **PROC CHART, VBAR Statement, GROUP= Option**

OK, now for some really neat charts. You can represent two nested categories on the X axis. Suppose you want separate frequency distributions of items for each region of the country using the SALES data set. Use the GROUP= option to accomplish this as follows:

Example 10

```
PROC CHART DATA=SALES;
   TITLE 'Vertical Bar Chart with GROUP= Option';
   VBAR ITEM / GROUP=REGION;
RUN;
```

The resulting chart is:

Output from Example 10 - Representing Two Variables on One Axis

```
                    Vertical Bar Chart with GROUP= Option

      Frequency

      2 |  **       **                                              **
        |  **       **                                              **
        |  **       **                                              **
        |  **       **                                              **
        |  **       **                                              **
      1 |  **   **  **   **   **   **   **                          **
        |  **   **  **   **   **   **   **                          **
        |  **   **  **   **   **   **   **                          **
        |  **   **  **   **   **   **   **                          **
        |  **   **  **   **   **   **   **                          **
        +----------------------------------------------------------------
           H   P   S   H   P   S   H   P   S   H   P   S   ITEM
           a   l   a   a   l   a   a   l   a   a   l   a
           m   i   w   m   i   w   m   i   w   m   i   w
           m   e       m   e       m   e       m   e
           e   r       e   r       e   r       e   r
           r   s       r   s       r   s       r   s

           |- EAST -|   |- NORTH-|   |- SOUTH-|   |- WEST -|   REGION
```

What you get is a series of bar charts showing the frequency of ITEM codes for each of the regions. For example, in the east, there were two purchase orders for hammers, one for pliers, and two for saws. (If this company is not going to go out of business, they're going to have to retool!)

Example 11

Displaying Groups within a Bar — Character Variable

FEATURES: **PROC CHART, VBAR Statement, SUBGROUP= Option**

There is one more way to represent another variable in a chart—you can use the SUBGROUP= option of the VBAR or HBAR statement to specify that you want the bar-plotting symbol (default is *) to represent values of another variable. For example, if you want to see the sales frequencies by REGION and also want to see which items contributed to these sales, you can include ITEM as a subgroup. The modified code is:

Example 11

```
PROC CHART DATA=SALES;
    TITLE 'Vertical Bar Chart with SUBGROUP= Option';
    VBAR REGION / SUBGROUP=ITEM;
RUN;
```

Notice in the following output that the bars are made up of H's (hammers), S's (saws), and P's (pliers). The first letter of each ITEM value is used to create the bars, and the output includes a legend below the graph.

Output from Example 11 - Displaying Groups within a Bar — Character Variable

```
              Vertical Bar Chart with SUBGROUP= Option
      Frequency

         5 |      SSSSS
           |      SSSSS
         4 |      SSSSS
           |      SSSSS
         3 |      PPPPP      SSSSS
           |      PPPPP      SSSSS
         2 |      HHHHH      PPPPP                      SSSSS
           |      HHHHH      PPPPP                      SSSSS
         1 |      HHHHH      HHHHH      HHHHH           SSSSS
           |      HHHHH      HHHHH      HHHHH           SSSSS
           +---------------------------------------------------
                   EAST       NORTH      SOUTH          WEST
                                 REGION


       Symbol   ITEM       Symbol  ITEM      Symbol   ITEM
          H     Hammer        P    Pliers       S     Saw
```

As you can see, the height of the bars shows the total number of items sold in each of the four regions. The subdivisions within each bar show, by the appropriate charting symbol, how many hammers, pliers, and saws make up this total.

Now what, you might ask, would the system do if the inventory included screwdrivers as well as saws, both beginning with "S." It's simple. The system would simply substitute sequential letters starting with A, B, C, etc. until the series was sufficient to account for all the data. Satisfied?

Example 12

Displaying Groups within a Bar — Numeric Variable

FEATURES: **PROC CHART, VBAR Statement, SUBGROUP= Option**

The SUBGROUP= option can also be used with numeric variables. PROC CHART will automatically assign letters (A, B, C, etc.) to each unique value of the SUBGROUP= variable. To demonstrate this, if you want to see how many of each unit price went into the frequencies of the regional sales, you write:

Example 12

```
PROC CHART DATA=SALES;
    TITLE 'Another Vertical Bar Chart with SUBGROUP= Option';
    VBAR REGION / SUBGROUP=PRICE;
RUN;
```

The output from this program is shown next:

Output from Example 12 - Displaying Groups within a Bar — Numeric Variable

```
          Another Vertical Bar Chart with SUBGROUP= Option
          Frequency

        5 |        CCCCC
          |        CCCCC
        4 |        CCCCC
          |        CCCCC
        3 |        BBBBB       CCCCC
          |        BBBBB       CCCCC
        2 |        BBBBB       BBBBB                   CCCCC
          |        BBBBB       BBBBB                   CCCCC
        1 |        AAAAA       AAAAA       BBBBB       CCCCC
          |        AAAAA       AAAAA       BBBBB       CCCCC
          +------------------------------------------------------
                   EAST        NORTH       SOUTH       WEST
                                 REGION


          Symbol   PRICE     Symbol   PRICE     Symbol   PRICE

             A       8         B       10         C       15
```

Note that a letter was assigned to each unique value of PRICE in alphabetical order.

Example 13

Creating Three-Dimensional Block Charts

FEATURES: **PROC CHART, BLOCK Statement**

We could not leave this chapter without showing you a block chart or two. When one of the authors (RP) was designing "PROC NYASUG;", the newsletter of the New York Area SAS Users Group, he relied on the talents of another founding member, Akos Felsovalyi, to create the group logo as a PROC CHART block chart constructed to be reminiscent of a three-dimensional New York City skyline.

For the current example you use the CLINICAL database. Suppose you want to see the relationship between the type of visit (ROUTINE = Y or N) and the year in which the data were collected. You could always use PROC FREQ to generate a two-way table, but we all know how many PROC FREQs a picture is worth. And while you're at it, why not also create a block chart showing the mean SBP for each YEAR and value of ROUTINE.

Before you create the block chart, you need to create the YEAR variable. This code, along with the PROC CHART statements, is shown next:

Example 13

```
DATA BLOCKEG;
   SET CLINICAL (KEEP=DATE ROUTINE SBP);
   YEAR=YEAR(DATE);
RUN;

PROC CHART DATA=BLOCKEG;
   TITLE 'Example of a BLOCK CHART';
      BLOCK YEAR / GROUP=ROUTINE DISCRETE;   ❶
      BLOCK YEAR / GROUP=ROUTINE SUMVAR=SBP TYPE=MEAN DISCRETE;   ❷
   FORMAT SBP 5.;
RUN;
```

The first BLOCK statement ❶ places YEAR on the horizontal axis, ROUTINE on the depth axis (into the page), and the number of visits for the given year and value of ROUTINE on the vertical axis. The DISCRETE option is necessary here since you want the actual YEAR values on the horizontal axis. The block chart produced by the first BLOCK statement is shown next:

Output from Example 13 - Creating Three-Dimensional Block Charts - First BLOCK Statement

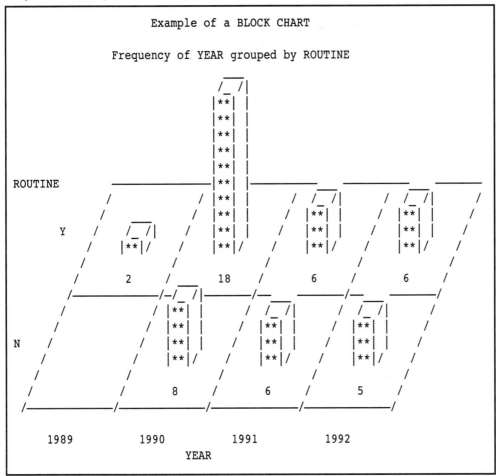

The second BLOCK statement ❷ uses the SUMVAR= and TYPE=MEAN options to give the mean SBP for each combination of YEAR and ROUTINE. You also provide a zero-decimal format for SBP so that you don't have long decimal values in the boxes. This chart is shown next:

Output from Example 13 - Creating Three-Dimensional Block Charts - Second BLOCK Statement

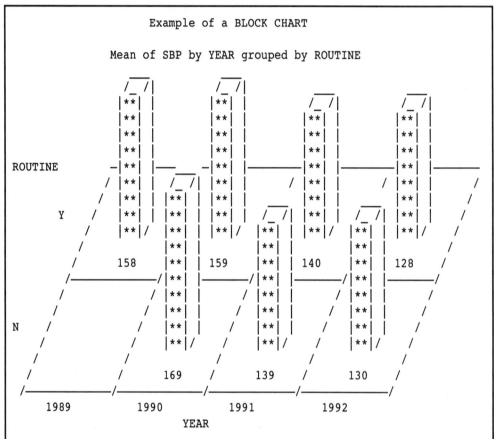

To be honest, we should point out that there are many cases where block charts just don't work. If there are too many levels of the variables on the horizontal or vertical axis, the procedure will not be able to fit the block chart on the page (even with large LINESIZE= and PAGESIZE= options), and you will get an HBAR chart instead. As a matter of fact, we had to try several variables and data sets to find a block chart that we could use here as a demonstration.

PROC CHART can also produce pie and star charts, but we chose not to show examples of them here. For these types of charts, as well as for more refined looking charts of all kinds, we recommend the GCHART procedure which is part of SAS/GRAPH. PROC GCHART can output to true graphics devices unlike PROC CHART, which is designed to produce line-printer style charts.

Conclusion

While the charts created by PROC CHART are not as pretty as those produced by SAS/GRAPH, they are still useful for visualizing your data in a variety of ways. PROC CHART is very flexible and can produce charts showing complex relationships with very little programming. Now, for some practice.

Problems

12-1. Using the SAS data set SALES from this chapter, write the code to produce a simple vertical bar graph showing the frequencies of all the item codes.

12-2. Write the code to produce a horizontal bar graph corresponding to the vertical bar graph in Problem 12-1. Include the appropriate option to omit the frequency statistics.

12-3. Write the code to produce a vertical bar graph showing the frequencies of item codes as percentages from the SAS data set SALES.

12-4. Write the code to generate a vertical bar chart for the continuous numeric variable QUANTITY from the SAS data set SALES. Use the following two methods of laying out the X axis:

a) let the program select the X axis intervals for you
b) choose your own midpoints ranging from 0 to 40 in units of 10.

12-5. Write the code to generate a vertical bar chart for the continuous numeric variable PRICE from the SAS data set SALES. Show each individual value of PRICE (do not create subgroups), and show a separate analysis for each item (all on one chart.)

Hint: You will probably want to use more than one option on the VBAR statement.

12-6. Write the SAS code to create a vertical bar chart showing the mean SBP for each level of drug group (DRUGGRP) using data from SAS data set CLINICAL (shown in the beginning of this chapter).

12-7. Using data from the SAS data set CLINICAL, construct a vertical bar graph showing the frequency distribution of cholesterol for each value of drug group, using the value of ROUTINE as the charting symbol. Your chart should look like the one shown here:

```
Frequency
    |                                             YY
 12 |                                             YY
    |                                             YY
  8 |           YY YY YY                       YY YY
    |        YY YY YY YY                       YY NN
  4 |        YY NN NN YY YY                    YY NN
    |  YY NN NN NN NN NN                       NN NN
    +--------------------------------------------------------
          2  2  2  3  3  4   2  2  2  3  3  4   CHOL Midpoint
          0  4  8  2  6  0   0  4  8  2  6  0
          0  0  0  0  0  0   0  0  0  0  0  0

       |------ D ------|  |------ P ------|   DRUGGRP


Symbol ROUTINE       Symbol ROUTINE

   N   N                 Y   Y
```

12-8. Write the SAS code to produce a block chart using the data from the SAS data set CLINICAL. Show the mean DBP (vertical-axis) for each level of DRUGGRP (horizontal-axis) and ROUTINE (depth-axis). Your chart should look like the one here:

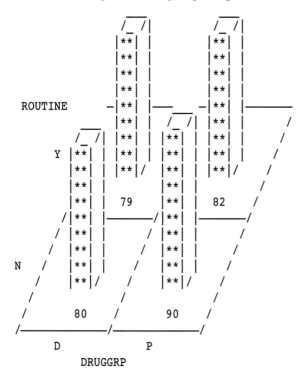

```
Mean of DBP by DRUGGRP grouped by ROUTINE
```

Chapter 13   PROC PLOT

Plotting Your Data

EXAMPLES

Introduction

In Chapter 12, "PROC CHART," you saw how to use the CHART procedure to produce a variety of charts. The PLOT procedure is similar to PROC CHART in that it provides a graphical representation of your data. The procedure produces plots showing the relationship between two (or more) variables. In their simplest form, the plots generated by PROC PLOT are often called scatter plots or x-y plots.

PROC PLOT, like PROC CHART, produces line-printer quality output. However, just as there are SAS/GRAPH procedures to produce true, high-quality charts, there are also SAS/GRAPH procedures to produce high-quality plots. Like PROC CHART, there is a tradeoff involved. You will find PROC PLOT both very easy to use and practical, but limited in output quality.

In this chapter, you use a data set which is based on the CLINICAL data set described in Chapters 10, "PROC MEANS and PROC UNIVARIATE," and 12, "PROC CHART," with some minor changes. To see several features of PROC PLOT you use a smaller data set with only one observation per patient. There are three new patients, and the variable PATNUM (patient number) is replaced by NAME. Here is the new data set, CLIN_2:

CLIN_2 Data Set

NAME	DATE	DRUGGRP	CHOL	SBP	DBP	HR	ROUTINE
George	01/05/89	D	400	160	90	88	Y
Fred	02/19/90	D	390	180	100	82	N
Ron	01/01/90	P	387	190	110	90	N
Ray	05/15/91	D	380	120	78	56	Y
Dave	01/06/90	P	399	188	110	92	N
Jennifer	01/01/92	D	387	128	62	60	N
Carol	01/05/90	P	376	118	68	54	Y
Steven	08/15/94	P	220	160	90	77	Y
John	08/17/94	D	170	128	62	64	N
Mary	11/25/94	P	188	128	64	72	Y

Example 1

Producing a Simple Scatter Plot

FEATURES: **PROC PLOT, PLOT Statement, Multiple Plot Requests**

Suppose you are interested in the relationship between systolic blood pressure (SBP) and diastolic blood pressure (DBP). One useful way to visually detect a relationship between these variables is to plot one versus the other. If you choose to place SBP on the X axis and DBP on the Y axis, use the following SAS statements to create such a plot:

Example 1

```
PROC PLOT DATA=CLIN_2;
   TITLE 'Scatter Plot of SBP by DBP';
   PLOT DBP * SBP;
RUN;
```

Note that even though these basic plots are typically called X-Y plots, the PLOT statement lists the Y axis variable first and then the X axis variable (Y=DBP, X=SBP.) Be careful!

The very basic output from this simple example follows. Like PROC CHART, settings for PAGESIZE and LINESIZE affect the scales and spacing of the plot points.

Output from Example 1 - Producing a Simple Scatter Plot

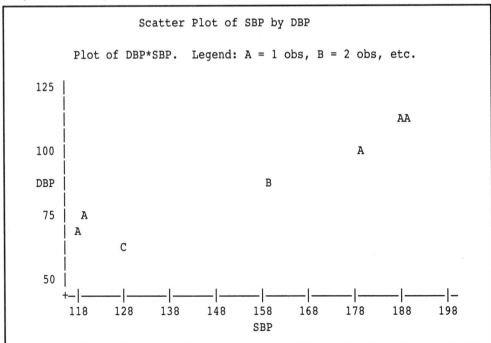

It appears from this plot that there is a relationship between the two measures of blood pressure—the higher the systolic blood pressure, the higher the diastolic blood pressure.

Notice the use of letters (A, B, C, etc.) as plotting symbols. While this seems strange at first, it is quite useful. Because the program is attempting to plot a graph using a character printer, plotting symbols can only be placed in discrete positions on the page, typically with a resolution of 10 characters per inch horizontally and 6 lines per inch vertically. With this resolution, two data points that occupy the same position on the graph, or even data points that are fairly close together, wind up in the same print position. By default, PROC PLOT uses the convention of assigning 'A' for 1 data point, 'B' for 2, etc. That way, you can see that a single plot position may represent more than one data point. If there are more than 26 points at a given plot position, PROC PLOT will use the letter 'Z' and indicate on the output that there were *n* hidden observations, where *n* is the number of data points in excess of 26.

A PLOT statement like the one shown here, produces a single Y by X graph:

```
PLOT y_variable*x_variable;
```

If you want to produce multiple plots, you can use one of the following forms:

```
PLOT A*B C*D;
PLOT (A B C)*X;
PLOT (A B C)*(D E F);
```

The first PLOT request generates two graphs: one of A by B, the other of C by D. The second request generates three plots: A by X; B by X; and C by X. Finally, the third PLOT request produces graphs of all the variables in the first list by every variable in the second list:

A by D	B by D	C by D
A by E	B by E	C by E
A by F	B by F	C by F

Another way to specify plots (new with Release 6.07) is a plot request of the form:

```
PLOT (A B C) : (D E F);
```

The colon placed between the two lists, specifies that you want a plot of each variable in the first list (on the Y axis) paired with the corresponding positional variable in the second list (on the X axis). In the code immediately above, three plots (A by D, B by E, and C by F) are produced.

The Interactive Nature of PROC PLOT

PROC PLOT is one of the SAS System's interactive procedures. When you are running SAS software interactively using display manager, you can submit a PLOT statement, then return to the Program Editor window and submit another PLOT statement, without another PROC PLOT statement (even after a RUN statement is executed). When you need to produce multiple plots on the same data set, it is much more efficient to simply submit additional PLOT statements than to continually start the procedure over again with additional PROC PLOT statements. Restart PROC PLOT only if you want new options to be in effect or to plot data from a different data set.

Because of this interactive feature of PROC PLOT, display manager indicates that your procedure is still running, even though the current output is completely displayed. This message tells you that you are free to submit another request. To turn off this procedure, you must do one of the following: run another procedure; run a DATA step; submit a QUIT statement (enter the single statement QUIT; in your Program Editor window and submit it.)

Example 2

Placing Multiple Plots on One Set of Axes

FEATURES: PROC PLOT, PLOT Statement, OVERLAY Option

To plot DBP versus SBP, and HR (heart rate) versus SBP, on one set of axes, you use the OVERLAY option on the PLOT statement like this:

Example 2

```
PROC PLOT DATA=CLIN_2;
   TITLE 'Multiple Plots on One Set of Axes';
   PLOT (DBP HR)*SBP/OVERLAY;
RUN;
```

Note this is equivalent to:

```
PLOT DBP*SBP HR*SBP/OVERLAY;
```

This produces a plot like the one following:

Output from Example 2 - Placing Multiple Plots on One Set of Axes

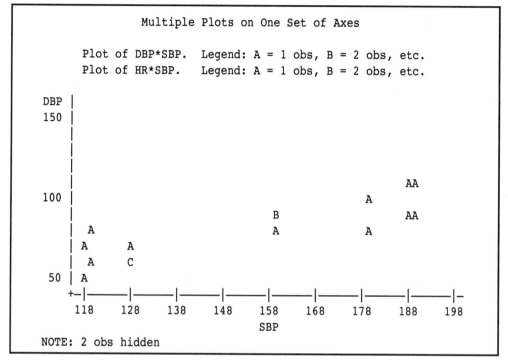

```
                      Multiple Plots on One Set of Axes

             Plot of DBP*SBP.  Legend: A = 1 obs, B = 2 obs, etc.
             Plot of HR*SBP.   Legend: A = 1 obs, B = 2 obs, etc.

   DBP |
   150 |
       |
       |
       |
       |                                                      AA
   100 |                                              A
       |                             B                        AA
       |  A                          A                A
       |  A        A
       |  A        C
    50 |  A
       +-|——————|——————|——————|——————|——————|——————|——————|——————|-
        118    128    138    148    158    168    178    188    198
                                    SBP
   NOTE: 2 obs hidden
```

Not too useful! You can't tell which points represent DBP and which points represent HR. Also, when you overlay plots, you only get one set of axes, the set for the first plot mentioned in the PLOT statement. Well, you cannot do anything about the second of these situations other than being prudent with plots you choose to produce, but you can do something to identify which points belong to which plots. See the next example.

Example 3

Placing Multiple Plots on One Set of Axes with Different Plotting Symbols

FEATURES: **PROC PLOT, PLOT Statement, OVERLAY Option, Plotting Symbols**

To help identify which points belong to which plots on a multi-plot output, use the following form of the PLOT statement:

```
PLOT y_variable*x_variable='plotting_symbol';
```

where *plotting_symbol* is any single character you choose. To use this technique with the previous graph, you write:

Example 3

```
PROC PLOT DATA=CLIN_2;
    TITLE  'Multiple Plots on One Set of Axes';
    TITLE2 'with Different Plotting Symbols';
    PLOT DBP*SBP='D'
         HR *SBP='H'/OVERLAY;
RUN;
```

This PLOT request, with a different symbol chosen to represent each of the relationships, gives you the following result:

Output from Example 3 - Placing Multiple Plots on One Set of Axes with Different Plotting Symbols

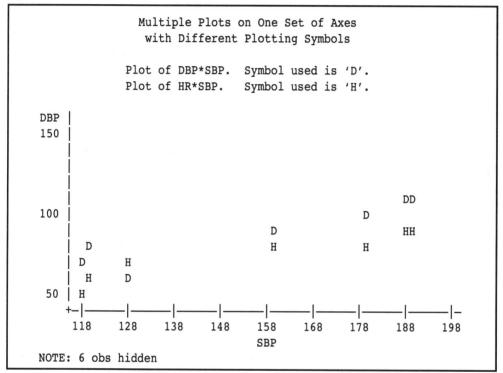

Now, you don't have the A, B, C, etc. convention to show you the location of multiple observations, but you can distinguish which points come from DBP by SBP and which come from HR by SBP. The message `Note: 6 obs hidden` tells you that some of the plotting symbols represent more than a single data point (but you don't know which ones). Sometimes you just can't have it all!

Example 4

> ## Using the Value of a Third Variable as the Plotting Symbol
>
> *FEATURES:* **PROC PLOT, Plotting Variable**

Another form of the PLOT statement is:

```
PLOT y_variable*x_variable=plotting_variable;
```

Using this form of the PLOT statement permits you to use the value of the plotting variable for each observation as the plotting symbol. This variable can be either a character or numeric variable in your data set. The procedure uses the first character of a character variable, or the first digit of a numeric variable, as the plotting symbol. To demonstrate this, plot DBP by SBP with the values of DRUGGRP (drug group) as the plotting symbol:

Example 4

```
PROC PLOT DATA=CLIN_2;
   TITLE 'Scatter Plot of SBP by DBP with';
   TITLE2 'Drug Group as the Plotting Symbol';
   PLOT DBP*SBP=DRUGGRP;
RUN;
```

This produces:

Output from Example 4 - Using the Value of a Third Variable as the Plotting Symbol

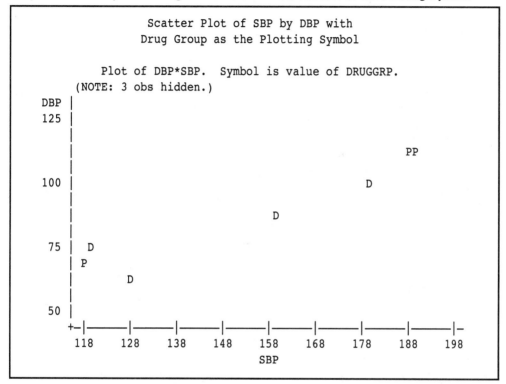

```
                       Scatter Plot of SBP by DBP with
                       Drug Group as the Plotting Symbol

                  Plot of DBP*SBP.  Symbol is value of DRUGGRP.
                 (NOTE: 3 obs hidden.)
      DBP |
      125 |
          |
          |
          |                                                      PP
          |
      100 |                                                D
          |
          |                                       D
          |
       75 |   D
          |   P
          |       D
          |
       50 |
          +-|———|———|———|———|———|———|———|———|-
           118   128   138   148   158   168   178   188   198
                                   SBP
```

Again, as with the case where you supplied the plotting symbol, the location of multiple observations is lost, but you do know how many observations are not displayed.

Note the difference between the two forms of the PLOT statement:

1.   PLOT *y_variable* * *x_variable* = '*plotting symbol*';

and

2.   *PLOT y_variable* * *x_variable* = *plotting_variable*;

In the latter case there are no quotation marks around the plotting variable. It is this distinction by which the procedure knows whether you are specifying a plotting symbol or a variable whose value is to be used as the plotting symbol.

Example 5

Labeling Individual Points

FEATURES: **PROC PLOT, Point-Labeling Feature**

In this example, you use the point-labeling feature added in Release 6.07. Because the placing of labels can become very complicated, we refer you to SAS Technical Report P-222, *Changes and Enhancements to Base SAS Software, Release 6.07* for the details and show you a labeled plot request where all the defaults have been chosen.

Suppose you want to see a plot of SBP (systolic blood pressure) versus HR (heart rate), and you would like to have each data point labeled so that you can see which person generated that data point. The following program accomplishes just that:

Example 5

```
PROC PLOT DATA=CLIN_2;
    TITLE 'Plot of SBP versus HR with';
    TITLE2 'NAME as the Labeling Variable';
    PLOT SBP*HR $ NAME='o';
RUN;
```

The values of the variable NAME are used to label the individual data points in this example. To specify a label variable, you follow the plot request by a dollar sign ($) and the name of the label variable. You may also specify a plotting symbol in quotation marks (as in Example 3) or a variable whose value will be used as a plotting symbol (as in Example 4).

Here is the output from the previous code:

Output from Example 5 - Labeling Individual Points

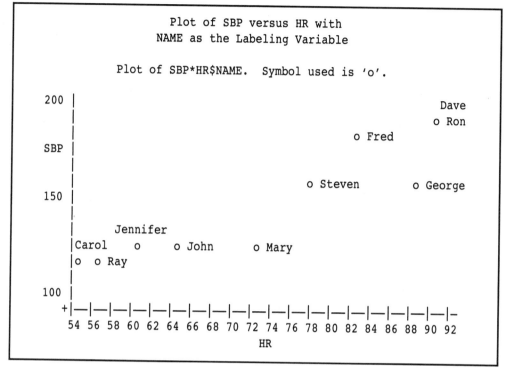

```
                        Plot of SBP versus HR with
                      NAME as the Labeling Variable

                 Plot of SBP*HR$NAME.   Symbol used is 'o'.

   200 |                                                      Dave
       |                                                    o Ron
       |                                        o Fred
   SBP |
       |
       |                                o Steven        o George
   150 |
       |
       |         Jennifer
       |Carol    o       o John      o Mary
       |o  o Ray
       |
   100 |
       +|—|—|—|—|—|—|—|—|—|—|—|—|—|—|—|—|—|—|—|—|-
        54 56 58 60 62 64 66 68 70 72 74 76 78 80 82 84 86 88 90 92
                                   HR
```

This is a really powerful feature that allows you to identify individual data points on a scatter plot. Obviously, this has limited application with large data sets because there is not enough room to fit all the labels on the plot.

Conclusion

You have now seen how easy it is to produce scatter plots with the PLOT procedure. Even with sophisticated statistical methods for investigating the relationship between variables, a simple scatter plot can still be very worthwhile. Here are some problems for you to sharpen your plotting skills:

Problems

The problems in this chapter all use SAS data set CHAP13 as shown here:

```
        Data Set CHAP13

    X    Y    Z    CODE    NAME

    1    2    1    Y       Mary
    2    3    3    N       Joe
    3    5    9    N       George
    4    7    6    Y       Henry
    7    8    4    Y       Bill
    9   11    5    N       Clifton
   12   15    2    N       Philip
   15   19    4    Y       John
```

13-1. Write the SAS statements to generate a plot of Y by X.

13-2. Write the SAS statements to generate a plot of Y by X with a lowercase letter O ('o') as the plotting symbol ('o' is RC's favorite plotting symbol).

13-3. Write the SAS statements to generate plots of Y by X, and Z by X, both on the same set of axes.

13-4. Redo Problem 12-3 using a separate plotting symbol for each of the two plots, e.g., 'Y' for the Y by X plot and 'Z' for the Z by X plot.

13-5. Write the SAS code to produce a single plot of Y by X with values of CODE as the plotting symbol.

13-6. Write the SAS code to produce a plot of Y versus X with each of the data points labeled by value of NAME.

A Collection of Efficiency Tips

CHAPTER

14   Efficiency
        Making Your Programs More Efficient

Chapter 14   Efficiency

Making Your Programs More Efficient

EXAMPLES

Introduction

How could we write a SAS book without touching on efficiency? We couldn't! We discuss efficient techniques for two reasons: First, you may have compelling reasons for wanting your programs to run more efficiently (time, money, etc.). Second, many of the examples we show in this chapter use programming tools we have discussed earlier, such as RETAIN and trailing @, and are definitely worth repeating, over and over and over.

We could expound at great length on just what efficiency is—but we won't. Let's just say that efficiency is not just saving CPU cycles, but optimally balancing your programming time, CPU time, and I/O time, depending on the particular application. There are some good programming practices that you should develop that will almost always make your programs run faster and are just as easy to write as inefficient ones. An important point to remember is that the SAS System is continually evolving and improving. What may be an inefficient strategy with one version of SAS software may no longer be inefficient with a future release.

One last note before we get started. We have dispensed with the FEATURES part of the Example boxes in this chapter. The material here is, for the most part, based upon features covered in earlier chapters. We feel that this chapter should be read as a whole and not used to look up specific efficiency issues. They are all important. Now, let's get started.

Example 1

> ### Avoiding Unnecessary DATA Steps — I

The lesson in this first example is a simple one. Do not read data (either raw or SAS system files) more than is necessary, and do not create SAS data sets more than is necessary. Here is an example where one data set is read and another one is created for absolutely no reason other than to be able to run a procedure without a DATA= option. Remember, without this option, the procedure will operate on the most recently created data set.

Example 1 - INEFFICIENT

```
DATA NEW;
    SET OLD;
RUN;

PROC MEANS N MEAN MIN MAX;
    VAR X Y Z;
RUN;
```

Creating the NEW data set is totally unnecessary.

Example 1 - EFFICIENT

```
PROC MEANS DATA=OLD N MEAN MIN MAX;
    VAR X Y Z;
RUN;
```

Using the DATA= option for any SAS procedure allows you to use a previously stored SAS data set. You should use the DATA= option for all SAS procedures that operate on data sets (there are some that don't, like PROC OPTIONS), even when it is not necessary. This is good programming style and an easy habit to make.

If you choose to ignore this recommendation, you can still avoid an unnecessary DATA step by using the _LAST_= option on an OPTIONS statement. In the previous example, using the following OPTIONS statement allows you to omit the DATA= option and still run PROC MEANS on data set OLD:

```
OPTIONS _LAST_ = OLD;
```

The reason this works is that _LAST_ represents the most recently created data set, which is the default argument for the DATA= option. If you change the value of _LAST_, you change the default value of DATA=. Seems like a roundabout, cumbersome way to avoid an easy productive habit.

Example 2

> ## Avoiding Unnecessary DATA Steps — II

In the last program, it was very obvious that the DATA step was unnecessary. Sometimes, it is a bit more subtle. Examine this example:

Example 2 - INEFFICIENT

```
DATA ONE;
   INPUT ID AGE HEIGHT WEIGHT;
DATALINES;
1 23 68 155
2 45 77 200
      .
      .
      .
;

PROC MEANS N MEAN STD DATA=ONE;
   VAR AGE HEIGHT WEIGHT;
RUN;

DATA EXTRA;
   SET ONE;
   LENGTH AGEGRP $ 8;
   IF         0 LE AGE LE 20 THEN AGEGRP='0 TO 20';
   ELSE IF   21 LE AGE LE 40 THEN AGEGRP='21 TO 40';
   ELSE IF         AGE GT 40 THEN AGEGRP='>40';
RUN;

PROC FREQ DATA=EXTRA;
   TABLES AGEGRP;
RUN;
```

Now examine the following program which eliminates the entire EXTRA data set and creates the variable AGEGRP at the same time the original data set is constructed.

Example 2 - EFFICIENT

```
DATA ONE;
   INPUT ID AGE HEIGHT WEIGHT;
   LENGTH AGEGRP $ 8;
   IF        0 LE AGE LE 20 THEN AGEGRP='0 TO 20';
   ELSE IF  21 LE AGE LE 40 THEN AGEGRP='21 TO 40';
   ELSE IF      AGE GT 40 THEN AGEGRP='>40';
DATALINES;
1 23 68 155
2 45 77 200
   .
   .
   .
;

PROC MEANS N MEAN STD DATA=ONE;
   VAR AGE HEIGHT WEIGHT;
RUN;

PROC FREQ;
   TABLES AGEGRP;
RUN;
```

Even though our conceptions of the processes that need to be performed are often like the inefficient example (that is step-wise), if you plan ahead, you can usually avoid unnecessary and inefficient operations. In this case, you realized that the variable AGEGRP should be created at the same time the original data set is built.

Example 3

Processing Selected Raw Data Records Using IF Statements

In cases where you only want to process selected records from a raw data file, you can make your programs more efficient by first reading only the variable(s) necessary to make the decision about whether or not you want to include the current record. The following example illustrates this concept:

Example 3 - INEFFICIENT

```
DATA SUBSET;
   INFILE 'input_file_spec';
   INPUT @1   ID        3.
         @5   GENDER    $1.
         @6   (Q1-Q10) ($1.);
   IF GENDER='M';
RUN;
```

A better approach is to avoid reading all the variables into the PDV unless you plan to output that observation to the data set being created. The following program does just that.

Example 3 - EFFICIENT

```
DATA SUBSET;
   INFILE 'input_file_spec';
   INPUT   @5   GENDER   $1. @;
   IF GENDER='M';
      INPUT @1 ID    3.
            @6 (Q1-Q10) ($1.);
RUN;
```

Use the trailing @ (see Chapter 1, "INPUT and INFILE," Example 10) to "hold the line" so that you can test the value of GENDER with a subsetting IF statement. If the value is not 'M' you can avoid the unnecessary I/O involved in reading all the other variables when gender is not an 'M'.

Example 4

> ## Processing Selected SAS Data Set Observations Using WHERE Statements in Procedures

When you only need to process a subset of an existing SAS data set, use a WHERE statement in the procedure to subset your data set rather than creating a new reduced data set and then running the procedure. For example:

Example 4 - INEFFICIENT

```
DATA SUBSET;
   SET OLD;
   WHERE GROUP='A';   /* WHERE statement in the DATA step */
RUN;


PROC UNIVARIATE DATA=SUBSET;
   VAR X Y Z;
RUN;
```

Why create that extra SAS data set SUBSET? It is much more efficient to instruct the procedure to operate on only the observations in the original data set OLD that meet the selection criteria, as follows:

Example 4 - EFFICIENT

```
PROC UNIVARIATE DATA=OLD;
   WHERE GROUP='A';   /* WHERE statement in the PROC step */
   VAR X Y Z;
RUN;
```

Of course, if you want to run PROC UNIVARIATE for each value of GROUP, it is better to pre-sort data set OLD by GROUP (using PROC SORT), and then use GROUP as a BY variable in the procedure. Also, if you plan to run several procedures on the same subset, you are probably better off storing the subset as a SAS data set and then running the procedures (see Example 12 later in this chapter).

Example 5

Dropping Unnecessary Variables When Building a SAS Data Set from Raw Data

Many programmers neglect dropping unnecessary variables. Carrying these along places a double burden on resources. First, the data sets are larger and more storage space is needed to hold them temporarily or permanently. Second, since the data sets and accompanying PDVs are larger, more CPU time is needed to process them.

In this example you read in student answers to a test (a multiple-choice test on SAS programming, perhaps) and compute a raw and percentage score for each student. You want a data set containing only raw and percentage scores for further analysis. The method you use, however, requires other intermediate variables to be created along the way. Compare the two following sets of code very closely. The second program has one very small addition which makes one very large difference.

Example 5 - INEFFICIENT

```
DATA SCORE;
   ARRAY KEY[5] $ 1;
   ARRAY Q[5] $ 1;
   RETAIN KEY1 'A' KEY2 'B' KEY3 'C' KEY4 'D' KEY5 'E';
   INPUT (Q1-Q5)($1.);
   DO I=1 TO 5;
      RAW+(Q[I]=KEY[I]);
   END;
   PERCENT=100*RAW/5;
DATALINES;
ABCDA
BBCAC
EBCAD
 ...
;
```

The variables KEY1-KEY5, Q1-Q5, and the DO loop counter I are key to the method used to derive the final scores, but they are extra baggage after they have served their purpose. Why keep them around?

Example 5 - EFFICIENT

```
DATA SCORE;
   ARRAY KEY[5] $ 1;
   ARRAY Q[5] $ 1;
   RETAIN KEY1 'A' KEY2 'B' KEY3 'C' KEY4 'D' KEY5 'E';
   INPUT (Q1-Q5)($1.);
   DO I=1 TO 5;
      RAW+(Q[I]=KEY[I]);
   END;
   PERCENT=100*RAW/5;
   KEEP RAW PERCENT;
   *or DROP KEY1-KEY5 Q1-Q5 I;
DATALINES;
ABCDA
BBCAC
EBCAD
 ...
;
```

That little KEEP (or DROP) statement makes the difference. The efficient program in this example uses only 16 bytes of storage for each observation, while the inefficient program wastes 5 bytes for each of the KEY1-KEY5 and Q1-Q5 variables, plus an extra 8 bytes for the DO loop counter. You should (almost) always remember to drop DO loop counters (I in this example) since they will (almost) never be of use. You may want to refer to Chapter 8, "RETAIN," Example 4, for an explanation of a similar program. The point here is merely to remember to drop unnecessary variables.

Example 6

> **Dropping Unnecessary Variables When Building a SAS Data Set by Setting an Existing One**

In the last example you built a new SAS data set from raw data and used intermediate variables along the way which were subsequently dropped before writing out the observations. It is also often the case where you need to create a new SAS data set from an existing one by manipulating a subset of existing variables, but you do not need all the variables in the existing data set. Here is one way to drop those unneeded variables from the new data set:

Example 6 - INEFFICIENT

```
DATA NEW;
   SET OLD;
   (programming statements)
   DROP X1-X20;  /* DROP statement */
RUN;
```

This certainly looks good at first glance. After all, you are not keeping those extra X1-X20 variables. You can do better.

Example 6 - EFFICIENT

```
DATA NEW;
   SET OLD (DROP=X1-X20);   /* DROP data set option */
   (programming statements)
RUN;
```

No, the difference is not saving the one line of code! The inefficient program uses a DROP statement while the efficient program uses a DROP= data set option. DROP (or KEEP) statements are independent stand-alone statements and do not take an equal sign before their variable lists. DROP= (or KEEP=) data set options are placed in parentheses following the data set names to which they refer, and they take the equal sign.

In the inefficient example, all the variables from the data set OLD are brought into memory (into the PDV) for each observation being built, and then the variables X1-X20 are dropped before the observation is written to the new data set. In the efficient program, variables X1 to X20 are never read in to memory, and subsequently are not written to the new data set. I/O processing is reduced, and the smaller PDV requires fewer CPU resources as well. These savings can be substantial.

Example 7

Using a LENGTH Statement

Even if you have a large amount of storage space, it is prudent to keep your SAS data sets as small as possible. This minimizes your storage needs, makes your backups (you DO back up your files, don't you?) run faster, and finally, reduces the execution time of your programs.

In a SAS system file, character and numeric variables are stored quite differently. It's not necessary to go into too many technical details (well, maybe a few) to make some strong recommendations. The length of a character variable should always be set to the maximum number of characters you need to store all values of the variable. For example, if you store GENDER as 'M' or 'F', you only need one byte of storage. If you input this variable with a column or pointer-format combination, and read from only one column, the length is automatically set to 1. However, if you use list-directed input like this:

```
INPUT ID GENDER $ HEIGHT WEIGHT ... ;
```

then the length of GENDER is set, by default, to 8 bytes. When you do this, you are using eight times as much storage as you need for this variable. If you are not careful, your SAS data set may be many times larger than necessary. To solve this problem, use a LENGTH statement to set the length of the variable before you write your INPUT statement. You cannot change the lengths of variables that already exist in data sets. The efficient code is:

```
LENGTH GENDER $ 1;
INPUT ID GENDER $ HEIGHT WEIGHT ... ;
```

A $ (dollar sign) after a variable name (e.g., GENDER $), indicates that the variable is a character variable. The 1 indicates the length for this variable. If you have several variables, all with the same length, you can list them together like this:

```
LENGTH GENDER RACE INSURED $ 1;
```

It's a good idea to specify the length of all character variables in a SAS program as they are created. This can be done using various statements: LENGTH, INPUT, RETAIN, ARRAY.

Numeric variables are more complicated. The default length for a SAS numeric variable is 8 bytes. This does *not* mean 8 significant figures; it means that 8 times 8, or 64 bits (8 bits per byte) are used to store the number. Numbers in a SAS program are stored the same way as in many other programming languages such as FORTRAN (remember that?), PL/1, BASIC, or C. The number is made up of a sign bit, a base (also called a mantissa), and an exponent, all of which are stored.

Eight bytes is equivalent to what used to be called "double-precision" in other languages. This will vary not only by which computer language you are using, but on which computer and under which operating system you are running. There is considerable controversy concerning the appropriate length of SAS numeric variables. All numeric variables are expanded to 8 bytes in memory and in all DATA and PROC steps. If you store a SAS numeric variable in less than 8 bytes, you lose precision. Be especially careful of statements such as:

```
IF X=1/3 THEN ...;
```

when you have stored X in less than full precision (8 bytes). Also, be aware that certain statistical procedures (such as multiple regression) may be sensitive to loss of precision. For many purposes, reducing the length of numeric variables to 4 should not cause you any trouble or concern. Suffice it to say that reducing any numeric variable to less than 8 bytes requires a bit of care and knowledge. There is a DEFAULT=*n* option available for the LENGTH statement which sets the length for all subsequent numeric variables being created.

If you are using codes to store information, use character variables rather than numerics. The numbers 0 and 1 take 8 bytes by default; the characters "0" and "1" can easily be read in to use only 1 byte. Use character variables when arithmetic will not be performed on the values.

Here is an example incorporating some of these concepts. First the inefficient:

Example 7 - INEFFICIENT

```
DATA LONG;
   INPUT ID 1-3
       @4 (Q1-Q10) (1.)
       @15 HEIGHT   2.
       @17 WEIGHT   3.;
DATALINES;
   . . .
;
```

Data set LONG is storing all the variables as numerics at 8 bytes apiece. The total storage length is 13*8 = 104 bytes. By using a LENGTH statement to reduce the precision for HEIGHT and WEIGHT (probably OK to do), and storing variables ID and Q1-Q10 as character, you can reduce the storage to 21 bytes, almost a five-fold reduction.

Example 7 - EFFICIENT

```
DATA SHORT;
   LENGTH HEIGHT WEIGHT 4;
   INPUT ID $ 1-3
       @4 (Q1-Q10) ($1.)
       @15 HEIGHT   2.
       @17 WEIGHT   3.;
DATALINES;
   . . .
;
```

Note that you do not need a LENGTH statement for variables ID and Q1-Q10 since their length is defined in the INPUT statement. However, without a LENGTH statement to specify a length of 4 bytes for HEIGHT and WEIGHT, the default length of 8 would be assigned. Remember that the number of columns from which you read a numeric variable *has nothing to do with the internal length* or number of bytes used to store it.

Example 8

> ## Using IF-THEN/ELSE Statements Instead of Multiple IF Statements

When you are testing for mutually exclusive conditions, use IF-THEN/ELSE statements rather than a series of IF statements.

Example 8 - INEFFICIENT

```
DATA ONE;
   SET TWO;
   IF   0 LE AGE LE 10 THEN AGEGRP=1;
   IF 10 LT AGE LE 20 THEN AGEGRP=2;
   IF 20 LT AGE LE 30 THEN AGEGRP=3;
   IF 30 LT AGE LE 40 THEN AGEGRP=4;
   IF       AGE GT 40 THEN AGEGRP=5;
RUN;
```

This code looks straightforward and will get the job done, but there is a large amount of totally unnecessary work being done. The next method shown is definitely the preferred method hands-down — no debating.

Example 8 - EFFICIENT

```
DATA ONE;
   SET TWO;
   IF         0 LE AGE LE 10 THEN AGEGRP=1;
   ELSE IF 10 LT AGE LE 20 THEN AGEGRP=2;
   ELSE IF 20 LT AGE LE 30 THEN AGEGRP=3;
   ELSE IF 30 LT AGE LE 40 THEN AGEGRP=4;
   ELSE IF       AGE GT 40 THEN AGEGRP=5;
RUN;
```

In the inefficient example, all the IF statements have to be executed, even if a previous IF statement was true. In the efficient example, as soon as an IF statement is true, no subsequent ELSE statements are executed.

Example 9

Arranging the Order of Your IF Statements

This hint is a bit subtle and is important only when you want to squeeze the last ounce of efficiency out of your system. This example uses the logic of the previous efficient example. As a matter of fact, the following inefficient code is exactly the same as the previous efficient code. Read on.

Example 9 - INEFFICIENT

```
DATA ONE;
   SET TWO;
   IF        0 LE AGE LE 10 THEN AGEGRP=1;
   ELSE IF 10 LT AGE LE 20 THEN AGEGRP=2;
   ELSE IF 20 LT AGE LE 30 THEN AGEGRP=3;
   ELSE IF 30 LT AGE LE 40 THEN AGEGRP=4;
   ELSE IF        AGE GT 40 THEN AGEGRP=5;
RUN;
```

If you know something about the contents of your data set, place the IF statements in decreasing order of probability of being true. Thus, if most of your subjects are in the 30-to-40 age group, followed by the greater-than-40 group, you should rearrange the IF-THEN/ELSE statements as follows:

Example 9 - EFFICIENT

```
DATA ONE;
   SET TWO;
   IF      30 LT AGE LE 40 THEN AGEGRP=4;
   ELSE IF        AGE GT 40 THEN AGEGRP=5;
   ELSE IF  0 LE AGE LE 10 THEN AGEGRP=1;
   ELSE IF 10 LT AGE LE 20 THEN AGEGRP=2;
   ELSE IF 20 LT AGE LE 30 THEN AGEGRP=3;
RUN;
```

The result here is that for most of the observations read in, the DATA step would stop processing after the first IF statement. The next largest group of observations would only need to process two IF statements, and so on. Only the smallest group of observations would have to process the entire set of IF statements.

Example 10

Using Multiple OR Operators instead of the IN Operator

This is an interesting example that demonstrates a point that was made in the introduction to this chapter, namely that the SAS System is continually changing and improving. When this example was first written, the title was reversed, with the IN operator being the recommended efficiency method! The way the system processes Boolean expressions was then improved to the point where the use of multiple OR operators is now very efficient, often more so than using an IN operator. When an IF statement contains a series of comparisons separated by OR operators, as soon as a hit is made, no further tests are done. This example also demonstrates that you may very well want to use an inefficient coding method when you are not in a limited resource production environment and where the relative importance of ease of coding (the IN operator) outweighs efficiency considerations.

Example 10 - INEFFICIENT

```
DATA NEW;
   SET OLD;
   IF GROUP IN ('A','C','E','Z');
RUN;
```

Just as you arranged the order of IF-THEN/ELSE statements in the previous example, you can also arrange the order of the IN list in decreasing probability of inclusion. So, if groups Z and C are the most common, you would put them at the front of the list:

```
IF GROUP IN ('Z','C','A','E');
```

The IN operator can also be used with numeric variables. For example, to print only observations corresponding to ID's 1, 5, and 13, you write:

```
PROC PRINT DATA=OLD;
   WHERE ID IN (1,5,13);
RUN;
```

Even though the IN operator is a very useful SAS feature, the following code may be more efficient than the preceding.

Example 10 - EFFICIENT

```
DATA NEW;
   SET OLD;
   IF GROUP='A' OR GROUP='C' OR GROUP='E' OR GROUP='Z';
RUN;
```

Although this program requires more effort to write, it runs faster than the less efficient example. Once again, you should order the OR list in order of decreasing probability of occurrence for absolute maximum efficiency.

Example 11

Using DATA _NULL_ When Creating Reports

If you only need to create a SAS data set to produce a report using PUT statements, use DATA _NULL_ instead of creating a real SAS data set. (See Chapter 5, "SAS Functions," Example 11, for a discussion of _NULL_.) When you use DATA_NULL_, the SAS System processes the observations but does not invoke the overhead of actually creating a new data set.

Example 11 - INEFFICIENT

```
DATA UNNECESS;
   FILE PRINT;
   SET OLD;
   IF AGE GT 50 THEN PUT ID= AGE=;
RUN;
```

Here you use a DATA step to put the data out without the need for a PROC PRINT. You only need to see those observations where age is greater than 50, so you use an IF statement to create a subset of data to process. You can achieve the same results without creating the unnecessary data set UNNECESS as follows:

Example 11 - EFFICIENT

```
DATA _NULL_;
   FILE PRINT;
   SET OLD;
   IF AGE GT 50 THEN PUT ID= AGE=;
RUN;
```

Example 12

Saving Data in SAS System Files

If you plan to run many analyses on a particular collection of data, make sure to save the data as a permanent SAS data set. This way you can avoid recreating it from raw data each time you do a run.

Example 12 - INEFFICIENT

```
DATA TEMP;
   INFILE 'input_file_spec';
   INPUT . . .;
RUN;

PROC anyproc DATA=TEMP;
   (SAS Statements)
RUN;

(at a future time)
DATA TEMP;
   INFILE 'input_file_spec';     * SAME AS BEFORE ;
   INPUT . . .;
RUN;

PROC anotherproc DATA=TEMP;
   (SAS Statements)
RUN;
```

Here the SAS data set TEMP is created from the same set of raw data each time a new procedure is run. This DATA step creation work only needs to be done once.

Example 12 - EFFICIENT

```
LIBNAME libref 'SAS_data_library';
DATA libref.PERMAN;
   INFILE 'input_file_spec';
      INPUT . . .;

PROC anyproc DATA=libref.PERMAN;
   (SAS Statements)
RUN;

(At a future time)
PROC anotherproc DATA=libref.PERMAN;
   (SAS Statements)
RUN;
```

Permanent SAS data sets and how to use a LIBNAME statement to create a libref are covered in Chapter 3, "SET, MERGE, and UPDATE," Example 1.

Example 13

Using PROC DATASETS to Modify Variables

PROC DATASETS is a procedure that you definitely should become acquainted with. It can accomplish a number of "housekeeping" chores very efficiently. Without it, you would need additional DATA steps and considerable programming. Some of the PROC DATASETS tasks include: copying, deleting, and renaming SAS data sets, renaming variables, changing or adding formats and labels, and appending data sets to other data sets. Here is an example in which you modify descriptive information on some variables in a SAS data set.

Suppose you want to rename variables X and Y, add a label to variable HT, and assign a format to variable DOB . First, here is the inefficient way to do it.

Example 13 - INEFFICIENT

```
LIBNAME libref 'SAS_data_library';
DATA NEW;
   SET libref.OLD (RENAME=(X=NEWX  Y=NEWY));
   LABEL HT='Height of Subject';
   FORMAT DOB MMDDYY8.;
RUN;
```

This does the trick, but you have to create a new data set to get it done. Not necessary. You can affect all the changes you need, and save considerable time too, by using PROC DATASETS to work directly on the existing data set as follows:

Example 13 - EFFICIENT

```
LIBNAME libref 'SAS_data_library';
PROC DATASETS LIBRARY=libref;
   MODIFY OLD;
      RENAME X=NEWX Y=NEWY;
      LABEL HT='Height of Subject';
      FORMAT DOB MMDDYY8.;
RUN;
```

For large data sets, this can be a tremendous savings. The time used for PROC DATASETS is independent of the number of observations in the data set because you are working on the information describing the data set overall, and not on individual observations in the data set.

Example 14

Using PROC DATASETS to Modify SAS Data Sets

PROC DATASETS can also perform a number of housekeeping operations on a data set itself, as opposed to the variables that make up the data set. In this example, you use PROC DATASETS to rename a SAS data set. First, here is the inefficient way to do it:

Example 14 - INEFFICIENT

```
DATA NEWNAME;
   SET OLDNAME;
RUN;
```

Here, a new data set is created for the sole purpose of renaming an existing one. Wasteful. Here is the better way:

Example 14 - EFFICIENT

```
PROC DATASETS;
   CHANGE OLDNAME=NEWNAME;
RUN;
```

In the efficient program, you avoid having to make a pass through the entire data set.

Example 15

> ## Using PROC APPEND to Join Similar Data Sets

Depending on the circumstances, this method can give you a tremendous increase in efficiency. Your goal is to join two (or more) similar data sets. When we say "similar," we mean that the data sets have the same variables and variable attributes. If you are adding records to a large master file from a small update file, the savings can be even greater. Compare the following two programs:

Example 15 - INEFFICIENT

```
DATA UPDATE;
   SET MASTER NEW;
RUN;
```

Here you create data set UPDATE by processing data sets MASTER and NEW sequentially. You go through all of the overhead of processing both data sets. This is unnecessary if the goal is simply to append one data set to another.

Example 15 - EFFICIENT

```
PROC APPEND BASE=MASTER DATA=NEW;
RUN;
```

In the efficient method, you merely add the observations of NEW to those of MASTER without processing either data set. Before running this procedure, you should run PROC CONTENTS on both data sets to be sure that they contain the same variables with the same attributes. If this is not true, you can use the FORCE option which will usually accomplish this, but be careful. You should fully understand this option before using it. Consult the SAS documentation for your operating system.

You can also restrict which observations from the DATA= data set are appended to the BASE= data set by using a WHERE= data set option. For example:

```
PROC APPEND
    BASE=MASTER
    DATA=NEW(WHERE=(AGE GE 40));
RUN;
```

You can also accomplish the exact same goal by using PROC DATASETS:

```
LIBNAME libref 'SAS_data_library';
PROC DATASETS LIBRARY=libref;
    APPEND BASE=MASTER DATA=NEW;
RUN;
```

or

```
LIBNAME libref 'SAS_data_library';
PROC DATASETS LIBRARY=libref;
    APPEND BASE=MASTER DATA=NEW(WHERE=(AGE GE 40));
RUN;
```

Example 16

Using a RETAIN Statement to Initialize Constants

If you write a DATA step in which you assign values to certain constants, you can either do the assignment work for each and every observation, or you can do it just once by using a RETAIN statement. Which do you suppose we recommend? Here is the inefficient method:

Example 16 - INEFFICIENT

```
DATA TEST;
INFILE 'file_specification';
    A = .10;
    B =1.57;
    PI=3.14159;
    INPUT X @@;
    Y=A*X+B*PI*X;
    DROP A B PI;
RUN;
```

In this code, the values for A, B, and PI are assigned at every iteration of the data set. You really only have to do it once and then merely RETAIN the values for all succeeding observations. It looks like this:

Example 16 - EFFICIENT

```
DATA TEST;
    INFILE 'file_specification';
    RETAIN A    .10
           B   1.57
           PI 3.14159;
    INPUT X @@;
    Y=A*X+B*PI*X;
    DROP A B PI;
RUN;
```

Example 17

Avoiding Unnecessary Sorts: Performing a Two-level Sort instead of a One-level and a Two-level Sort

Sorting data sets is resource intensive and should be avoided whenever possible, especially when you are dealing with large data sets. Beginning with Release 6.07, the SAS System is clever enough to keep track of the sort order of a SAS data set and will not perform a requested sort if it is not necessary (i.e., if the data set is already properly sorted). This last set of examples provides several hints that can reduce or eliminate the need to sort your data sets.

Suppose you need your data set sorted by YEAR for some procedures, and by YEAR and MONTH for others. Here is the inefficient code to do exactly that:

Example 17 - INEFFICIENT

```
PROC SORT DATA=TEST;
   BY YEAR;
RUN;

PROC anyprocs;
   BY YEAR;
   (SAS Statements)
RUN;

PROC SORT DATA=TEST;
   BY YEAR MONTH;
RUN;

PROC otherprocs;
   BY YEAR MONTH;
   (SAS Statements)
RUN;
```

Since you know that you need the data set TEST in YEAR order for some procedures and in YEAR MONTH order for others, you should run PROC SORT only once with YEAR and MONTH as the BY variables. Get it all done at once and avoid the unnecessary second sort. Here is the code:

Example 17 - EFFICIENT

```
PROC SORT DATA=TEST;
   BY YEAR MONTH;
RUN;

PROC anyprocs;
   BY YEAR;
   (SAS Statements)
RUN;

PROC otherprocs;
   BY YEAR MONTH;
   (SAS Statements)
RUN;
```

Example 18

> ## Avoiding Unnecessary Sorts: Using a CLASS Statement When Possible

It is usually preferable to use a CLASS statement when running PROC MEANS (or PROC SUMMARY) instead of pre-sorting your data set with a SORT procedure and then using a BY statement. However, if your data set is already sorted in the proper order, and you only need to examine those statistics that you would get when using a CLASS statement and the NWAY option (highest level _TYPE_ groups), a BY statement without a SORT procedure is preferable to CLASS. A CLASS statement uses more memory than a BY statement, with the amount of memory dependent on the number of CLASS variables as well as the number of levels for each CLASS variable. Running out of memory when using a CLASS statement may necessitate the use of the PROC SORT-BY statement combination.

Assume you have a data set TEST that is not sorted by the variable you wish to use for subgroup analyses, YEAR. Here is the inefficient method of deriving mean values for COST by YEAR.

Example 18 - INEFFICIENT

```
PROC SORT DATA=TEST;
   BY YEAR;
RUN;

PROC MEANS NOPRINT DATA=TEST;
   BY YEAR;
   VAR COST;
   OUTPUT OUT=MEANS MEAN=;
RUN;
```

Now here is the preferred method:

Example 18 - EFFICIENT

```
PROC MEANS NOPRINT NWAY DATA=TEST;
   CLASS YEAR;
   VAR COST;
   OUTPUT OUT=MEANS MEAN=;
RUN;
```

Example 19

> ## Making Your Sorts More Efficient: Sort Only What You Have to Sort

Drop variables and subset observations as part of your PROC SORT code rather than sorting first and then dropping and subsetting. In this example you want to create data set NEW as a sorted subset of data set OLD. You only want to keep selected observations and variables. Here is the inefficient method:

Example 19 - INEFFICIENT

```
PROC SORT DATA=OLD;
   BY ID DATE;
RUN;

DATA NEW;
   SET OLD(DROP=X1-X10);
   WHERE YEAR BETWEEN '01JAN90'D AND '31DEC93'D;
RUN;
```

Here you sort the entire data set OLD, then create data set NEW by setting a selected part of OLD. There is no need to sort all of OLD. Here is the better way:

Example 19 - EFFICIENT

```
PROC SORT DATA=OLD(DROP=X1-X10) OUT=NEW;
   BY ID DATE;
   WHERE YEAR BETWEEN '01JAN90'D AND '31DEC93'D;
RUN;
```

In the efficient example, you only sort those observations which meet the WHERE condition. In addition, you do not carry along any extra "baggage" by including the variables X1-X10, only to drop them later. The difference between these two programs, depending on how large a subset you are extracting and how many variables you are dropping, can be ENORMOUS!

Example 20

> ## Making Your Sorts More Efficient: Using the NOEQUALS Option

If you do not need to maintain the original order of observations within each BY group, you can specify the NOEQUALS option of PROC SORT to reduce machine time. The following program uses the default EQUALS option which does maintain the original order:

Example 20 - INEFFICIENT

```
PROC SORT DATA=TEST;
   BY YEAR;
RUN;
```

Use the NOEQUALS option to specify that the order of observations within the levels of the BY variables in the sorted data set does not have to be the same as that of the data set before sorting.

Example 20 - EFFICIENT

```
PROC SORT DATA=TEST NOEQUALS;
   BY YEAR;
RUN;
```

A Word on Indexing

It would be a serious omission if we did not mention indexing before leaving this chapter, so we mention it briefly. Do not take that as meaning that it is unimportant. It's just another topic that is beyond the scope of this book.

For the programmer working with large data sets, indexing is a method that trades disk storage for efficiency. The decreases in search time may be offset by the increased space needed to store the indices. The main advantage of indexing is that you can directly access an observation of an indexed variable. When you are considering a small subset of a large file, indexing can be significantly more efficient than processing without indices. Data can also be retrieved for BY-group processing without sorting when indexing is used.

Conclusion

You have now seen just a few methods that can make your programs more efficient. Some of them are really quite subtle, such as arranging the order of IF statements (Example 9), and some can make tremendous differences, such as avoiding multiple passes through a data set or unnecessary sorts.

You can also get carried away with efficient programming. If it takes you an hour longer to write an efficient program that runs 5 seconds faster, you are not necessarily being an "efficient programmer." You are perhaps being a *compulsive* programmer!"

Whether the program is to be run once or three times a day for the next ten years also is an important factor in deciding whether to go "all out" for efficiency.

Learning the techniques in this chapter, and using them or not as the need arises, will make you a better programmer and provide you with a better understanding of the SAS System. Now, for some practice.

Problems

Rewrite each of the following programs to make them more efficient:

14- 1.
```
DATA ONE;
    INPUT GROUP $ X Y Z;
DATALINES;
A 1 2 3
B 2 3 4
B 6 5 4
A 4 5 6
RUN;

PROC SORT DATA=ONE;
   BY GROUP;
RUN;

PROC MEANS N MEAN STD DATA=ONE;
   BY GROUP;
   VAR X Y Z;
RUN;

DATA TWO;
   SET ONE;
   IF 0 LE X LE 2 THEN XGROUP=1;
   IF 2 LT X LE 4 THEN XGROUP=2;
   IF 4 LT X LE 6 THEN XGROUP=3;
RUN;

PROC FREQ DATA=TWO;
   TABLES XGROUP;
RUN;
```

14-2. Data set OLD contains variables SCORE1-SCORE100, X1-X100, ID, and GENDER.

```
DATA NEW;
   SET OLD;
   RAWSCORE=SUM (OF SCORE1-SCORE100);
RUN;

PROC SORT DATA=NEW;
   BY GENDER;`
RUN;

PROC MEANS N MEAN STD MAXDEC=3;
   BY GENDER;
   VAR RAWSCORE;
RUN;
```

14-3. The raw data file BIGFILE contains one or more blanks between all data values. SAS data set variables ITEM1-ITEM5 are 1 byte in length.

```
DATA ONE;
   INFILE 'BIGFILE';
   INPUT GENDER $ ITEM1-ITEM5 X Y Z;
   IF GENDER = 'M' THEN COMPUTE = 2 * X + Y;
   IF GENDER = 'F' THEN COMPUTE = 2 * X;
RUN;

PROC FREQ DATA=ONE;
   TABLES ITEM1-ITEM5;
RUN;

PROC PLOT DATA=ONE;
   PLOT Z * COMPUTE;
RUN;
```

Note: Variables ITEM1-ITEM5 are used for frequencies only. No arithmetic operations are performed on these variables.

14-4. SAS data set ONE contains variables GROUP, GENDER, RACE, and X1-X100.

```
DATA TWO;
   SET ONE;
   IF GROUP=1 OR GROUP=3 OR GROUP=5;
RUN;

PROC FREQ DATA=TWO;
   TABLES GENDER * RACE;
RUN;
```

14-5. SAS data set LARGE contains the variables ID, DATE, YEAR, SCORE1- SCORE5, X1-X100. You want to create two new SAS data sets. The first one should contain the first observation for each date (the one with the lowest ID number on each date.) The other one should contain the last observation for each date (the one with the highest ID number on each date.) The new data sets are to contain only ID, DATE, and SCORE1-SCORE5. You also want to restrict the data to the years 1990 through 1993, inclusive.

```
PROC SORT DATA=LARGE;
   BY DATE;
RUN;

DATA FIRST;
   SET LARGE;
   BY DATE;
   WHERE YEAR BETWEEN 1990 AND 1993;
   DROP X1-X100;
   IF FIRST.DATE;
RUN;

DATA LAST;
   SET LARGE;
   BY DATE;
   WHERE YEAR BETWEEN 1990 AND 1993;
   DROP X1-X100;
   IF LAST.DATE;
RUN;
```

Appendix

Problem Solutions

Problem Solutions

Here are our solutions to the end-of-chapter problems. *Please* make an attempt to solve these problems yourself before looking at our solutions. You will learn much more that way.

Chapter 1 - INPUT and INFILE

Solution 1-1
```
DATA VSIGNS;
  INFILE  'VITAL';
  INPUT  ID $ HR SBP DBP;
RUN;
```

Did you remember to code ID as character because it contains letters and numbers?

Solution 1-2
```
DATA VSIGNS;
   INFILE  'VITALC' DLM=',';
   INPUT  ID $ HR SBP DBP;
RUN;
```

Solution 1-3
```
DATA COLLEGE;
   INPUT NAME : $9. TITLE $ TENURE $ NUMBER;
DATALINES;
Stevenson Ph.D. Y 2
Smith Ph.D.   N   3
Goldstein  M.D.  Y  1
RUN;
```

Solution 1-4
```
DATA COLLEGE;
   INPUT NAME & $16. TITLE $ TENURE $ NUMBER;
DATALINES;
George Stevenson   Ph.D. Y 2
Fred Smith    Ph.D.   N   3
Alissa Goldstein  M.D.  Y  1
RUN;
```

Solution 1-5
```
DATA RESPOND;
   INFILE 'FIRE';
   INFORMAT DATE MMDDYY8.;
   INPUT   CALL_NO   1-3
           DATE      5-12
           TRUCKS    14-15
           ALARM     17;
RUN;
```

Solution 1-6
```
DATA RESPOND;
   INFILE 'FIRE';
   INPUT @1   CALL_NO   3.
         @5   DATE      MMDDYY8.
         @14  TRUCKS    2.
         @17  ALARM     1.;
RUN;
```

Solution 1-7
```
DATA FACTORY;
   INPUT   @1   ID        $7.
           @1   F_NUM     2.
           @6   STATE     $2.
           @8   QUANTITY  2.
           @10  PRICE     DOLLAR7.;
DATALINES;
13AB2NY44   $123
22XXXCT88 $1,033
37123TX11$22,999
RUN;
```

Solution 1-8
```
DATA SCORES;
   INPUT @1  SS   $11.
         @13 (SCORE1 - SCORE10) (3.);
DATALINES;
123-45-6789 100 98 96 95 92 88 95 98100 90
344-56-7234  69 79 82 65 88 78 78 92 66 77
898-23-1234  80 80 82 86 92 78 88 84 85 83
RUN;
```

Solution 1-9

```
DATA PRESSURE;
   INPUT  @1 (SBP1 - SBP4) (3. + 3)
          @4 (DBP1 - DBP4) (3. + 3);
DATALINES;
120 80122 84128 90130 92
140102138 96136 92128 84
122 80122 80124 82122 78
RUN;
```

Solution 1-10

```
DATA HTWT;
   INFILE 'MIXED_UP';
   INPUT @12 TEST @;
      IF TEST = 1 THEN
         INPUT EMP_ID 1-3
               HEIGHT 4-5
               WEIGHT 6-8;
      ELSE IF TEST = 2 THEN
         INPUT EMP_ID 1-3
               HEIGHT 5-6
               WEIGHT 8-10;
RUN;
```

Solution 1-11

```
DATA CARS;
   INPUT MAKE : $10. MPG @@;
DATALINES;
Ford 20 Honda 29 Oldsmobile 20 Cadillac 17
Toyota 24 Chevrolet 17
RUN;
```

Solution 1-12

```
DATA SCORES;
   IF EOF1 = 0 THEN INFILE 'FILE_ONE' END = EOF1;
   ELSE INFILE 'FILE_TWO';
   INPUT NAME $ 1-10 SCORE 11-13;
RUN;
```

Chapter 2 - Data Recoding

Solution 2-1
Method 1 - IF/THEN-ELSE

```
DATA HTWT_2;
   SET HTWT;
   IF        0 LE HEIGHT LE 36 THEN HT_GROUP = 1;
   ELSE IF 37 LE HEIGHT LE 48 THEN HT_GROUP = 2;
   ELSE IF 49 LE HEIGHT LE 60 THEN HT_GROUP = 3;
   ELSE IF       HEIGHT GT 60 THEN HT_GROUP = 4;

   IF        0 LE WEIGHT LE 100 THEN WT_GROUP = 1;
   ELSE IF 101 LE WEIGHT LE 200 THEN WT_GROUP = 2;
   ELSE IF        WEIGHT GT 200 THEN WT_GROUP = 3;
RUN;

PROC FREQ DATA=HTWT_2;
   TABLES HT_GROUP * WT_GROUP;
RUN;
```

Method 2 - SELECT

```
DATA HTWT_2;
   SET HTWT;
      SELECT;
         WHEN ( 0 LE HEIGHT LE 36) HT_GROUP = 1;
         WHEN (37 LE HEIGHT LE 48) HT_GROUP = 2;
         WHEN (49 LE HEIGHT LE 60) HT_GROUP = 3;
         WHEN (      HEIGHT GT 60) HT_GROUP = 4;
      END;

      SELECT;
         WHEN (  0 LE WEIGHT LE 100) WT_GROUP = 1;
         WHEN (101 LE WEIGHT LE 200) WT_GROUP = 2;
         WHEN (      WEIGHT GT 200) WT_GROUP = 3;
      END;
RUN;

PROC FREQ DATA=HTWT_2;
   TABLES HT_GROUP * WT_GROUP;
RUN;
```

Method 3 - Using PROC FORMAT to Recode Values

```
PROC FORMAT;
   VALUE HTFMT     0-36   = '1'
                   37-48  = '2'
                   49-60  = '3'
                   61-HIGH = '4';

   VALUE WTFMT    0-100   = '1'
                  101-200 = '2'
                  201-HIGH = '3';
RUN;

PROC FREQ DATA=HTWT;
   TABLES HEIGHT * WEIGHT;
   FORMAT HEIGHT HTFMT.
          WEIGHT WTFMT.;
RUN;
```

Method 4 - Using a User-Defined FORMAT and a PUT Function

```
PROC FORMAT;
   VALUE HTFMT     0-36 = '1'
                   37-48 = '2'
                   49-60 = '3'
                   61-HIGH = '4';

   VALUE WTFMT    0-100   = '1'
                  101-200 = '2'
                  201-HIGH = '3';
RUN;

DATA HTWT_2;
   SET HTWT;
   HT_GROUP = PUT(HEIGHT,HTFMT.);
   WT_GROUP = PUT(WEIGHT,WTFMT.);
RUN;

PROC FREQ DATA=HTWT_2;
   TABLES HT_GROUP * WT_GROUP;
RUN;
```

Chapter 3 - Set, Merge, and Update

Solution 3-1
```
DATA ALL;
   SET ONE   (DROP=SEX)
       TWO   (KEEP=ID DOB SALARY)
       THREE (KEEP=ID DOB SALARY);
   RUN;
```

Solution 3-2
```
DATA ALL;
   SET ONE   (DROP=SEX)
       TWO   (KEEP=IDNUM DOB SALARY
              RENAME=(IDNUM=ID))
       THREE (KEEP=ID DOB SALARY);

       WHERE DOB LE '01JAN60'D AND DOB IS NOT MISSING
                            AND SALARY GE 50000;
   FORMAT DOB MMDDYY8.;
   RUN;
```

Following is an alternative solution that uses a WHERE data set option on the SET statement
instead of a WHERE statement. Although we didn't discuss a WHERE data set option in the
chapter, we thought you might like to see an example of how it can be used.

```
DATA ALL;
   SET ONE   (DROP=SEX
              WHERE=(DOB LE '01JAN60'D
                     AND DOB IS NOT MISSING
                     AND SALARY GE 50000))
       TWO   (KEEP=IDNUM DOB SALARY
              WHERE=(DOB LE '01JAN60'D
              AND DOB IS NOT MISSING
              AND SALARY GE 50000)
              RENAME=(IDNUM=ID))
       THREE (KEEP=ID DOB SALARY
              WHERE=(DOB LE '01JAN60'D
              AND DOB IS NOT MISSING
              AND SALARY GE 50000));
   FORMAT DOB MMDDYY8.;
   RUN;
```

Solution 3-3

a)
```
PROC PRINT DATA=MASTER;
   WHERE LASTNAME LIKE '%fly' AND
         AGE GE 40 AND
         GENDER EQ 'M';
      TITLE 'Possible Employee Names';
      ID FIRSTNAM;
      VAR LASTNAME;
   RUN;
```

b)
```
PROC PRINT DATA=MASTER;
   WHERE LASTNAME =* 'Klein' AND
         FIRSTNAM LIKE 'G____';
      TITLE 'Possible Employee Names';
      ID FIRSTNAM;
      VAR LASTNAME;
   RUN;
```

Solution 3-4

```
PROC SORT DATA=DEMOG;
   BY ID;
RUN;

PROC SORT DATA=SCORES;
   BY SSN;
RUN;

DATA BOTH;
   MERGE DEMOG  (IN=IN_DEMOG)
         SCORES (IN=IN_SCR
                   RENAME=(SSN=ID));
   BY ID;
   IF IN_DEMOG AND IN_SCR;
RUN;

PROC MEANS N MEAN MAXDEC=2 DATA=BOTH;
   CLASS GENDER;
   VAR IQ GPA;
RUN;

PROC MEANS N MEAN MAXDEC=2 DATA=BOTH;
   WHERE DOB LT '01JAN72'D and DOB IS NOT MISSING;
   CLASS GENDER;
   VAR IQ GPA;
RUN;
```

Solution 3-5

```
DATA NEWDATA;
   INPUT PART NUMBER PRICE;
DATALINES;
222 15 .
123 . 1500
333 20 2000
RUN;

PROC SORT DATA=NEWDATA;
   BY PART;
*As an alternative, you could have entered the part
 numbers in order;
RUN;

DATA MASTER;
   UPDATE MASTER NEWDATA;
   BY PART;
RUN;
```

Chapter 4 - Table Lookup

Solution 4-1

```
PROC SORT DATA=SALES;
   BY PART_NO;
RUN;

DATA NEWSALES;
   MERGE PARTS
         SALES (IN=INSALES);
   BY PART_NO;
   IF INSALES;
    TOTAL = QUANTITY * PRICE;
   KEEP ID TRANS TOTAL;
RUN;

PROC SORT DATA=NEWSALES;
   BY ID;
RUN;
```

```
PROC PRINT LABEL;
   TITLE 'Sales totals for each Salesperson and Transaction';
   LABEL ID = 'Employee ID'
         TRANS = 'Transaction Number'
         TOTAL = 'Sales per Transaction';
   ID ID;
   VAR TRANS TOTAL;
   FORMAT TOTAL DOLLAR4.;
RUN;

DATA ALLTHREE;
   MERGE EMPLOY (DROP=DOB) NEWSALES (IN=INNEW);
   BY ID;
   IF INNEW;
RUN;

PROC MEANS SUM DATA=ALLTHREE MAXDEC=0;
   TITLE 'Sales Totals for each Employee';
   CLASS ID;
   VAR TOTAL;
RUN;

PROC MEANS SUM DATA=ALLTHREE MAXDEC=0;
   TITLE 'Sales Summary by Gender';
   CLASS GENDER;
   VAR TOTAL;
RUN;


************************************************************
* You can replace the two previous PROC MEANS with this *
* alternate code if you want a formatted report        *
***********************************************************;
PROC MEANS DATA=ALLTHREE NOPRINT;
   CLASS GENDER ID;
   VAR TOTAL;
   OUTPUT OUT=TOTALS SUM=;
RUN;
```

```
PROC PRINT LABEL DATA=TOTALS;
   TITLE 'Sales Totals for each Employee';
   WHERE _TYPE_ = 1;
   * _TYPE_ = 1 will select the sums for each
     ID.  See Chapter 10 for details;
   LABEL ID    = 'Employee ID'
         TOTAL = 'Sales per Sales Person';
   ID ID;
   VAR TOTAL;
   FORMAT TOTAL DOLLAR4.;
RUN;


PROC PRINT LABEL DATA=TOTALS;
   TITLE 'Sales Totals for Gender';
   WHERE _TYPE_ = 2;
   * _TYPE_ = 2 will select the sums for each
     GENDER.  See Chapter 10 for details;
   LABEL ID    = 'Employee ID'
         TOTAL = 'Total Sales';
   ID GENDER;
   VAR TOTAL;
   FORMAT TOTAL DOLLAR4.;
RUN;
```

Solution 4-2

```
PROC FORMAT;
   VALUE DXCODE
        1 = 'Cold'
        2 = 'Flu'
        3 = 'Asthma'
        4 = 'Chest Pain'
        5 = 'Maternity'
        6 = 'Diabetes';
RUN;


DATA CLINICAL;
   INFILE 'CLINICAL';
   INPUT ID  DATE : MMDDYY8. BILLING DX;
RUN;


DATA NEW;
   SET CLINICAL;
   DESCRIP = PUT (DX,DXCODE.);
RUN;
```

Chapter 5 - SAS Functions

Solution 5-1
```
DATA FUNCT1;
   SET ORIG;
   LENGTH CHAR_ID $ 4;
   LOGSCORE = LOG (SCORE);
   PROPX = ARSIN (SQRT(PROP));
   RND_IQ = ROUND (IQ,10);
   TEMP = PUT (ID,5.);
   CHAR_ID = SUBSTR (TEMP,1,2) || SUBSTR (TEMP,4,2);
   DROP TEMP;
RUN;
```

Solution 5-2
```
DATA SUMMARY;
   SET SCORES;
   SUM_X = SUM (OF X1-X20);
   IF NMISS (OF Y1-Y20) LT 5 THEN
      MEAN_Y = MEAN (OF Y1-Y20); *ELSE MEAN_Y=. BY DEFAULT;
   X_MIN = MIN (OF X1-X20);
   X_MAX = MAX (OF X1-X20);
RUN;
```

Solution 5-3
```
DATA TEMP;
   INFILE 'TEMPER';
   INPUT HOUR DUMMY $ @@;
    IF DUMMY = 'N' THEN TEMP_F = .;
      ELSE IF INDEX(DUMMY,'C') NE 0 THEN
      TEMP_F = 9*INPUT (SUBSTR(DUMMY,1,LENGTH(DUMMY)-1),5.)/5 + 32;
      ELSE TEMP_F = INPUT (DUMMY,5.);
   DROP DUMMY;
RUN;
```

Solution 5-4
```
DATA VALID INVALID;
   RETAIN DIGITS '0123456789';
   INPUT  @1 STRING $15.;

   *Remove blanks;

   STRING = COMPRESS (STRING);
   *Take out the parentheses and dash(-) from the number;
```

```
        NUMBERS = COMPRESS (STRING,'()-');
        IF INDEX (STRING,'(') NE 1 OR
           INDEX (STRING,')') NE 5 OR
           INDEX (STRING,'-') NE 9 OR
           VERIFY (NUMBERS,DIGITS) NE 0 THEN OUTPUT INVALID;
        ELSE OUTPUT VALID;
        DROP NUMBERS DIGITS;
     DATALINES;
     (988)463-4490
     (241) 343-2233
     456-5034
     (123)456-7890
     (271)SH4-1234
     (592)2578362
     RUN;
```

Solution 5-5

```
     a) DATA TWO_B;
           SET TWO;
           DATE1 = PUT (INPUT(DATE2,DATE7.),MMDDYY8.);
        RUN;

        PROC SORT DATA=ONE;
           BY DATE1;
        RUN;

        PROC SORT DATA=TWO_B;
           BY DATE1;
        RUN;

        DATA BOTH;
           MERGE ONE TWO_B;
           BY DATE1;
        RUN;

     b) DATA ONE_B;
           SET ONE;
           DATE = INPUT (DATE1,MMDDYY8.);
        RUN;

        DATA TWO_B;
           SET TWO;
           DATE = INPUT (DATE2,DATE7.);
        RUN;
```

```
PROC SORT DATA=ONE_B;
   BY DATE;
RUN;

PROC SORT DATA=TWO_B;
   BY DATE;
RUN;

DATA BOTH;
   MERGE ONE_B TWO_B;
   BY DATE;
   FORMAT DATE MMDDYY8.;
RUN;
```

Solution 5-6

```
DATA TIMEAVE;
   SET STOCKS;
   XXX1 = LAG (XXX);
   YYY1 = LAG (YYY);
   XXX2 = LAG2 (XXX);
   YYY2 = LAG2 (YYY);
   XXX3 = LAG3 (XXX);
   YYY3 = LAG3 (YYY);
   AVE_XXX = MEAN (OF XXX XXX1 XXX2 XXX3);
   AVE_YYY = MEAN (OF YYY YYY1 YYY2 YYY3);
   KEEP DAY AVE_XXX AVE_YYY;
RUN;
```

Solution 5-7

Solution without arrays:

```
DATA NEW;
   SET SCORES;
   X1 = INPUT (SUBSTR(STRING,1,1),1.);
   X2 = INPUT (SUBSTR(STRING,2,1),1.);
   X3 = INPUT (SUBSTR(STRING,3,1),1.);
   X4 = INPUT (SUBSTR(STRING,4,1),1.);
   X5 = INPUT (SUBSTR(STRING,5,1),1.);
   KEEP ID X1-X5;
RUN;
```

Solution using arrays:

```
DATA NEW;
   SET SCORES;
   ARRAY X[5] X1-X5;
   DO POINTER = 1 TO 5;
      X[POINTER] = INPUT (SUBSTR(STRING,POINTER,1),1.);
   END;
   KEEP ID X1-X5;
RUN;
```

Chapter 6 - SAS Dates

Solution 6-1

```
DATA DATES1;
   INPUT @1  ID     $3.
         @4  ADMIT  MMDDYY6.
         @10 DISCH  MMDDYY6.
         @16 DOB    MMDDYY8.;
   AGE   = INT((ADMIT-DOB)/365.25);
   DAY   = WEEKDAY (ADMIT);
   MONTH = MONTH (ADMIT);
   FORMAT ADMIT DISCH MMDDYY8.
          DOB DATE9.
          DAY DOWNAME3.;

DATALINES;
00101059201079210211946
00211129211159209011955
00305129206099212251899
00401019301079304051952
;

PROC PRINT DATA=DATES1;
RUN;

PROC MEANS DATA=DATES1 N MEAN MAXDEC=1;
   VAR AGE;
RUN;

PROC CHART DATA=DATES1;
   VBAR DAY / DISCRETE;
RUN;
```

```
PROC FREQ DATA=DATES1;
   TABLES MONTH;
RUN;
```

Solution 6-2

```
DATA AGECOMP;
   SET DATES2;
   DOB = MDY (MONTH,15,YEAR);
   AGE = ROUND ((TODAY()-DOB)/365.25,1);
   FORMAT DOB MMDDYY8.;
RUN;
```

Solution 6-3

```
DATA VISIT;
   SET DATES3;
   AGE = ROUND((MDY(VISIT_D,VISIT_M,VISIT_Y)-DOB)/365.25,1);
RUN;
```

Solution 6-4

```
DATA DATES4;
   INPUT @1  DATE     MMDDYY8.
         @11 CRAYONS  COMMA6.;
   QUARTER = INTCK ('QTR','01JAN90'D,DATE);
DATALINES;
02/01/90  12,500
02/08/90  12,600
04/01/90  13,000
05/05/90  12,800
08/05/90  14,000
12/12/90  14,200
02/18/91  14,400
02/22/91  14,100
05/01/91  15,000
;

PROC MEANS DATA=DATES4 N MEAN MAXDEC=0;
   CLASS QUARTER;
   VAR CRAYONS;
RUN;
```

Solution 6-5

```
DATA GOODATES;
   SET CLIENTS;
   DAY   = WEEKDAY (DOB);
   MONTH = MONTH (DOB);
   IF GENDER = 'M' AND DAY IN (4,5) AND MONTH IN (1,3) OR
      GENDER = 'F' AND DAY = 6 AND MONTH IN (8,9);
RUN;

PROC SORT DATA=GOODATES;
   BY GENDER;
RUN;

PROC PRINT DATA=GOODATES;
   TITLE "Clients Meeting the Astrologer's Criteria";
   ID ID;
   BY GENDER;
   VAR DOB DAY MONTH;
   FORMAT DOB MMDDYY8.;
RUN;

*** Alternate solution ***;

DATA GOODATES;
   SET CLIENTS;
   LENGTH DAY MONTH $ 3;
   DAY   = PUT(DOB,DOWNAME3.);
   MONTH = PUT(DOB,MONNAME3.);
   IF (GENDER = 'M' AND UPCASE(DAY)   IN ('WED','THU')
                    AND UPCASE(MONTH) IN ('JAN','MAR'))
   OR (GENDER = 'F' AND UPCASE(DAY)   =  'Fri'
                    AND UPCASE(MONTH) IN ('AUG','SEP'));
RUN;

PROC SORT DATA=GOODATES;
   BY GENDER;
RUN;

PROC PRINT DATA=GOODATES;
   TITLE "Clients Meeting the Astrologer's Criteria";
   ID ID;
   BY GENDER;
   VAR DOB DAY MONTH;
   FORMAT DOB MMDDYY8.;
RUN;
```

This alternate program makes good use of SAS system formats and functions. The two system date formats DOWNAME*n*. and MONNAME*n*. translate SAS date values into the day of the week and the month of the year, respectively, using various formats depending on the *n* numeric width specification you add to the end of the format name. A '3' following the format specification yields three-character day names and three-character month names. The PUT function creates the character variables DAY and MONTH by applying the formats to the date variable DOB. The results are the three-character day and month names. The UPCASE function ensures that the program always works consistently without having to ever worry about case settings. You can find out more about using PUT functions in Chapter 2, "Data Recoding," and about formats in Chapter 11, "PROC FORMAT."

Chapter 7 - SAS Arrays

Solution 7-1

```
DATA NEW;
    SET OLD;
    ARRAY HTIN[10];
    ARRAY WTLB[10];
    ARRAY HTCM[10];
    ARRAY WTKG[10];
    DO I = 1 TO 10;
        HTCM[I] = 2.54 * HTIN[I];
        WTKG[I] = WTLB[I] / 2.2;
    END;
RUN;
```

Note that we omitted the element lists from our array definitions. When you do this, the SAS System automatically suffixes the series of numbers from the index (1 to 10 from index [10] in this example) to the array bases (HTIN, WTLB, HTCN and WTKG) to make up the elements. The array HTIN, for example, is automatically constructed with the elements HTIN1-HTIN10.

Solution 7-2

```
DATA NEW;
    SET SURVEY;
    ARRAY MINUS_1[100] X1-X100;
    ARRAY NUM99[50] Y1-Y50;
    ARRAY NODATA[5] $ A B C D E;
    DO I = 1 TO 100;
        IF MINUS_1[I] = -1 THEN MINUS_1[I] = .;
    END;
    DO I = 1 TO 50;
        IF NUM99[I] = 99 THEN NUM99[I] = .;
    END;
```

```
        DO I = 1 TO 5;
            IF NODATA[I] = 'NO DATA' THEN NODATA[I] = ' ';
        END;
        DROP I;
    RUN;
```

The first two DO loops can be coded alternatively as one DO loop as follows:

```
    DO I = 1 TO 100;
        IF MINUS_1[I] = -1 THEN MINUS_1[I] = .;
        IF I LE 50 AND NUM99[I] = 99 THEN NUM99[I] = .;
    END;
```

Solution 7-3

```
    DATA FOURPER;
        SET ONEPER;
        ARRAY XHR[4] HR1-HR4;
        DO TREAT = 1 TO 4;
            HR = XHR[TREAT];
            OUTPUT;
        END;
        KEEP ID TREAT HR;
    RUN;
```

Solution 7-4

```
    DATA FOURPER;
        SET ONEPER;
        ARRAY XHR[4] HR1-HR4;
        DO I = 1 TO 4;
            IF      I = 1 THEN TREAT = 'A';
            ELSE IF I = 2 THEN TREAT = 'B';
            ELSE IF I = 3 THEN TREAT = 'C';
            ELSE IF I = 4 THEN TREAT = 'D';
            HR = XHR[I];
            OUTPUT;
        END;
        KEEP ID TREAT HR;
    RUN;
```

Here is an interesting alternative to the previous code using some of the functions discussed in Chapter 5, "SAS Functions."

```
DATA FOURPER;
   SET ONEPER;
   ARRAY XHR[4] HR1-HR4;
   DO I = 1 TO 4;
   TREAT = TRANSLATE (PUT(I,1.),'ABCD','1234');
   HR = XHR[I];
      OUTPUT;
   END;
   KEEP ID TREAT HR;
RUN;
```

Solution 7-5
```
DATA ONEPER;
   SET THREEPER;
   BY ID;
   RETAIN SBP1-SBP3 DBP1-DBP3;
   ARRAY XSBP[3] SBP1-SBP3;
   ARRAY XDBP[3] DBP1-DBP3;
   XSBP[TIME] = SBP;
   XDBP[TIME] = DBP;
   IF LAST.ID THEN OUTPUT;
   KEEP ID SBP1-SBP3 DBP1-DBP3;
RUN;
```

Chapter 8 - RETAIN

Solution 8-1
```
DATA DIET2;
   SET DIET;
   BY ID;
   RETAIN WEIGHT;
   IF FIRST.ID THEN MEAN_WT = WEIGHT;
   ELSE MEAN_WT = MEAN_WT + WEIGHT;
   IF LAST.ID  THEN DO;
      MEAN_WT = MEAN_WT / 4;
      OUTPUT;
   END;
RUN;
```

The solution using a sum statement looks like this:

```
DATA DIET2;
   SET DIET;
   BY ID;
   IF FIRST.ID THEN MEAN_WT = WEIGHT;
   ELSE MEAN_WT + WEIGHT;
   IF LAST.ID  THEN DO;
      MEAN_WT = MEAN_WT / 4;
      OUTPUT;
   END;
RUN;
```

Solution 8-2

```
DATA READING;
   INFILE 'TESTSCOR';
   RETAIN GROUP;
   INPUT DUMMY $ @@;
   IF (DUMMY='A' OR DUMMY='B' OR DUMMY='C') THEN DO;
      GROUP=DUMMY;
      DELETE;
   END;
   ELSE SCORE=INPUT (DUMMY,5.);
   DROP DUMMY;
RUN;
```

What about that DELETE statement? Aren't we deleting each initial occurrence of a new group? Yes, we are, but don't worry. We retain it as GROUP in each subsequent observation until we get to a new group.

Two alternatives to the line, IF (DUMMY='A' ...) THEN DO; are:

```
IF DUMMY IN ('A', 'B', 'C') THEN DO;
IF VERIFY (DUMMY,'CAB') EQ 0 THEN DO;
```

These are explained in Chapter 5. You choose.

Chapter 9 - PROC PRINT

Solution 9-1

```
PROC PRINT DATA=DONOR;
   VAR F_NAME L_NAME AMOUNT DATE;
   FORMAT AMOUNT DOLLAR8. DATE MMDDYY8.;
RUN;
```

Solution 9-2

```
OPTIONS NOCENTER NODATE NONUMBER;

PROC PRINT DATA=DONOR N LABEL UNIFORM;
    TITLE 'Report on the Donor Data Base';
    TITLE2 '-----------------------------';
    ID F_NAME;
    VAR L_NAME AMOUNT DATE;

    SUM AMOUNT;

    LABEL F_NAME = 'First Name'
          L_NAME = 'Last Name'
          AMOUNT = 'Amount of Donation'
          DATE   = 'Donation Date';

    FORMAT AMOUNT DOLLAR8. DATE DATE7.;
RUN;
```

Note: The UNIFORM option forces the listings on multiple pages to be spaced identically.

Solution 9-3

```
a) PROC PRINT DATA=DONOR HEADING=VERTICAL WIDTH=MINIMUM;
    VAR F_NAME L_NAME AMOUNT DATE;
    FORMAT AMOUNT DOLLAR8. DATE MMDDYY8.;
  RUN;

b) PROC PRINT DATA=DONOR HEADING=HORIZONTAL WIDTH=UNIFORM;
    VAR F_NAME L_NAME AMOUNT DATE;
    FORMAT AMOUNT DOLLAR8. DATE MMDDYY8.;
  RUN;
```

Chapter 10 - PROC MEANS and PROC UNIVARIATE

Solution 10-1

```
PROC MEANS DATA=GRADES;
    CLASS GENDER;
    VAR SCORE;
    OUTPUT OUT=MEAN_GRD MEAN=;
RUN;
```

Solution 10-2

```
PROC MEANS DATA=GRADES NOPRINT NWAY;
   CLASS GENDER WEIGHT;
   VAR SCORE;
   OUTPUT OUT=PROB2 MEAN=MEAN_SCOR;
RUN;

PROC PRINT DATA = PROB2;
RUN;
```

Solution 10-3

```
PROC MEANS DATA=GRADES NOPRINT;
   CLASS GENDER WEIGHT;
    VAR SCORE;
   OUTPUT OUT=PROB3 MEAN=;
RUN;

DATA BYGENDER;
   SET PROB3;
   WHERE _TYPE_ = 2;
RUN;
```

Solution 10-4

```
PROC MEANS DATA=EXPER NOPRINT NWAY;
   CLASS GROUP TIME;
   VAR SCORE;
   OUTPUT OUT=MEANOUT MEAN=;
RUN;

PROC PLOT DATA=MEANOUT;
   PLOT SCORE * TIME = GROUP;
RUN;
```

Solution 10-5

```
PROC SORT DATA=CLINTEST;
   BY PATNUM DATE;
RUN;

DATA LAST (RENAME=(DATE=LASTDATE CHOL=LASTCHOL));
   SET CLINTEST (KEEP = PATNUM DATE CHOL);
   BY PATNUM;
   IF LAST.PATNUM;
RUN;
```

```
* Output means for each patient to a data set;
PROC MEANS DATA=CLINTEST NOPRINT NWAY;
   CLASS PATNUM;
   VAR CHOL SBP DBP HR;
   OUTPUT OUT=STATS
          MEAN=MEANCHOL MEANSBP MEANDBP MEANHR;

RUN;

* Combine the LAST data set with the STATS data set;
DATA FINAL;
   MERGE STATS LAST;
   BY PATNUM;
RUN;

* Print a final report;
PROC PRINT DATA=FINAL LABEL DOUBLE;
   TITLE 'Listing of data set FINAL in Problem 10-5';
   ID PATNUM;
    VAR LASTDATE LASTCHOL MEANCHOL MEANSBP MEANDBP
       MEANHR;

   LABEL LASTDATE = 'Date of Last Visit'
         MEANCHOL = 'Mean Chol'
         MEANSBP  = 'Mean SBP'
         MEANDBP  = 'Mean DBP'
         MEANHR   = 'Mean HR'
         LASTCHOL = 'Last Chol';

   FORMAT MEANCHOL MEANSBP MEANDBP MEANHR LASTCHOL 5.0;
RUN;
```

Chapter 11 - PROC FORMAT

Solution 11-1

```
PROC FORMAT;
   VALUE $GENDER 'M'='Male'
                 'F'='Female';

   VALUE $RACE   'W'='White'
                 'A'='African American'
                 'H'='Hispanic'
                 OTHER ='Other';
```

```
VALUE ISSUE    1='Str Disagree'
               2='Disagree'
               3='No opinion'
               4='Agree'
               5='Str Agree';

VALUE YESNO    0='No'
               1='Yes';
RUN;
```

The following DATA step statement will assign the above formats to the variables listed:

```
FORMAT GENDER        $GENDER.
       RACE          $RACE.
       ISSUE1-ISSUE5 ISSUE.
       QUES1-QUES10  YESNO.;
```

Solution 11-2
The solution to this problem requires you to create a control data set from the raw data file ZIP and then to use the new data set as input to PROC FORMAT.

```
DATA ZIPCODES;
   RETAIN FMTNAME '$ZIPCODE'  TYPE 'C';
   INFILE 'ZIP';
   INPUT START $ 1-5
         LABEL $ 6-20;
RUN;

PROC FORMAT CNTLIN=ZIPCODES;
RUN;
```

Solution 11-3
```
DATA CONTROL;
   RETAIN FMTNAME 'PARTS'  TYPE 'N';
   SET INVENTRY (RENAME=(PART_NO = START
                         DESCRIPT = LABEL));
RUN;

PROC FORMAT CNTLIN=CONTROL;
RUN;
```

Solution 11-4
```
PROC FORMAT;
   INVALUE $GENDER 'F','M'=_SAME_
                   OTHER = ' ';
   INVALUE $RACE   'W','B','I','H' = _SAME_
                   OTHER = ' ';
RUN;
```

One final point (a reward for those of you making it this far): You can add an UPCASE option to the INVALUE statement to convert all input data values to uppercase before they are tested. This saves you the task of having to use the UPCASE function in the DATA step to accomplish this very frequently needed task. INVALUE options are placed in parentheses directly after the name of the INFORMAT you are creating. The modified code reads:

```
PROC FORMAT;
   INVALUE $GENDER (UPCASE) 'F','M' = _SAME_
                            OTHER = ' ';

   INVALUE $RACE   (UPCASE) 'W','A','N','H' = _SAME_
                            OTHER = ' ';
RUN;
```

Chapter 12 - PROC CHART

Solution 12-1
```
PROC CHART DATA=SALES;
   VBAR ITEM;
RUN;
```

Solution 12-2
```
PROC CHART DATA=SALES;
   HBAR ITEM / NOSTAT;
RUN;
```

Solution 12-3
```
PROC CHART DATA=SALES;
   VBAR ITEM / TYPE=PERCENT;
RUN;
```

Solution 12-4
```
a) PROC CHART DATA=SALES;
      VBAR QUANTITY;
   RUN;
```

b)
```
PROC CHART DATA=SALES;
    VBAR QUANTITY / MIDPOINTS = 0 TO 40 BY 10;
  RUN;
```

Solution 12-5
```
PROC CHART DATA=SALES;
  VBAR PRICE / DISCRETE GROUP=ITEM;
RUN;
```

Solution 12-6
```
PROC CHART DATA=CLINICAL;
  VBAR DRUGGRP / SUMVAR=SBP TYPE=MEAN;
RUN;
```

Solution 12-7
```
PROC CHART DATA=CLINICAL;
  VBAR CHOL / GROUP=DRUGGRP SUBGROUP=ROUTINE;
RUN;
```

Solution 12-8
```
PROC CHART DATA=CLINICAL;
  BLOCK DRUGGRP / SUMVAR=DBP TYPE=MEAN GROUP=ROUTINE;
  FORMAT DBP 4.;
RUN;
```

Chapter 13 - PROC PLOT

Solution 13-1
```
PROC PLOT DATA = CHAP13;
  PLOT Y * X;
RUN;
```

Solution 13-2
```
PROC PLOT DATA = CHAP13;
  PLOT Y * X = 'o';
RUN;
```

Solution 13-3
```
PROC PLOT DATA = CHAP13;
  PLOT (Y Z) * X / OVERLAY;
 *ALTERNATIVE CODE = PLOT Y * X   Z *  X / OVERLAY;
RUN;
```

Solution 13-4
```
PROC PLOT DATA = CHAP13;
   PLOT Y * X = 'Y'
        Z * X = 'Z'/ OVERLAY;
RUN;
```

Solution 13-5
```
PROC PLOT DATA = CHAP13;
   PLOT Y * X = CODE;
RUN;
```

Solution 13-6
```
PROC PLOT DATA = CHAP13;
   PLOT Y * X $ NAME = 'o';
RUN;
```

Chapter 14 - Efficiency

Solution 14-1
```
DATA ONE;
   INPUT @1 GROUP $1.
         @3 (X Y Z )(1. + 1);
   IF      0 LE X LE 2 THEN XGROUP=1;
   ELSE IF 2 LT X LE 4 THEN XGROUP=2;
   ELSE IF 4 LT X LE 6 THEN XGROUP=3;
DATALINES;
A 1 2 3
B 2 3 4
B 6 5 4
A 4 5 6

PROC MEANS N MEAN STD DATA=ONE;
   CLASS GROUP;
   VAR X Y Z;
RUN;

PROC FREQ DATA=ONE;
   TABLES XGROUP;
RUN;
```

Main Points:
1. We eliminated an unnecessary DATA step (DATA TWO) by creating variable XGROUP in the first DATA step (DATA ONE.)
2. We used formatted input instead of list-directed input in the DATA step.

3. We used IF/THEN-ELSE structures to create XGROUP.
4. We eliminated the unnecessary SORT procedure and used a CLASS statement instead of a BY statement in the FREQ procedure.

An alternative is to use PROC FORMAT to create a grouping format for X and then place a FORMAT statement in the PROC FREQ code to process X in the formatted subgroups.

Solution 14-2

```
DATA NEW;
    SET OLD (KEEP=SCORE1-SCORE100 GENDER);
    RAWSCORE = SUM (OF SCORE1-SCORE100);
    DROP SCORE1-SCORE100;
RUN;
PROC MEANS N MEAN STD MAXDEC=3;
    CLASS GENDER;
    VAR RAWSCORE;
RUN;
```

Main Points:

1. We used a KEEP option on the SET statement to bring only those variables into the PDV that were necessary for the tasks at hand.
2. We used a DROP statement to drop SCORE1-SCORE100; we only needed these variables to calculate RAWSCORE.
3. We eliminated the SORT procedure and used a CLASS statement in the MEANS procedure instead of a BY statement.

Solution 14-3

```
DATA ONE;
    INFILE 'BIGFILE';
    LENGTH GENDER ITEM1-ITEM5 $ 1;
    INPUT GENDER ITEM1-ITEM5 X Y Z;
    COMPUTE = 2 * X + Y * (GENDER = 'M');
RUN;

PROC FREQ DATA=ONE;
    TABLES ITEM1-ITEM5;
RUN;

PROC PLOT DATA=ONE;
    PLOT Z * COMPUTE;
RUN;
```

Main Points:

1. We used a LENGTH statement to declare ITEM1-ITEM5 (and GENDER) as character variables with a length of 1 byte each.

2. We condensed the two IF statements into one statement. COMPUTE is equal to the sum of (2 * X) and (Y * *another value*). The other value is either 1 (when GENDER = 'M') or 0 (when GENDER NE 'M'.)

We could have also used an IF/THEN-ELSE construction as follows:

```
IF      GENDER = 'M' THEN COMPUTE = 2 * X + Y;
ELSE IF GENDER = 'F' THEN COMPUTE = 2 * X;
```

Solution 14-4

There are two main areas of attack in this problem to make the code more efficient. We could either eliminate the DATA step entirely by using a WHERE statement in the PROC FREQ code, or make the DATA step more efficient (if we knew we would be doing more analyses on the subset.)

```
* Eliminate the DATA step and use a WHERE statement to
* directly process a subset of the original data set;
PROC FREQ DATA=ONE;
  WHERE GROUP IN (1,3,5);
    TABLES GENDER * RACE;
RUN;


* Make the DATA step more efficient by using
* KEEP and WHERE data set options;
DATA TWO;
    SET ONE (KEEP=GENDER RACE GROUP
             WHERE=(GROUP IN (1,3,5)));
RUN;
PROC FREQ DATA=TWO;
    TABLES GENDER * RACE;
RUN;
```

Solution 14-5

Sometimes it is actually more efficient to create what may seem like an unnecessary intermediate data set. The approach we took here was to do all the selection work in the SORT procedure and output a small, sorted temporary data set. This was then further processed with FIRST. and LAST. variables to create the final two data sets we needed.

```
PROC SORT DATA=LARGE (DROP=X1-X100)
          OUT=TEMP;
  WHERE YEAR BETWEEN 1990 AND 1993;
  BY DATE ID;
RUN;
```

```
DATA FIRST LAST;
   SET TEMP;
   BY DATE ID;
   IF FIRST.DATE THEN OUTPUT FIRST;
   ELSE IF LAST.DATE THEN OUTPUT LAST;
   * only the first and last records
   * for each date are output;
RUN;
```

This program and the inefficient program in Problem 14-5 were run on a UNIX-based minicomputer against a SAS data set containing approximately 9000 observations. There was a greater than 50% reduction in CPU time in the improved program.

Index

Call your local SAS® office to order these other books and tapes available through the Books by Users℠ program:

An Array of Challenges — Test Your SAS® Skills
by **Robert Virgile** . . . . .Order No. A55625

Applied Multivariate Statistics with SAS® Software, Second Edition
by **Ravindra Khattree**
and **Dayanand N. Naik** . . . . .Order No. A56903

Applied Statistics and the SAS® Programming Language, Fourth Edition
by **Ronald P. Cody**
and **Jeffrey K. Smith** . . . . .Order No. A55984

Beyond the Obvious with SAS® Screen Control Language
by **Don Stanley** . . . . .Order No. A55073

Carpenter's Complete Guide to the SAS® Macro Language
by **Art Carpenter** . . . . .Order No. A56100

The Cartoon Guide to Statistics
by **Larry Gonick**
and **Woollcott Smith** . . . . .Order No. A55153

Categorical Data Analysis Using the SAS® System
by **Maura E. Stokes, Charles S. Davis,**
and **Gary G. Koch** . . . . .Order No. A55320

Common Statistical Methods for Clinical Research with SAS® Examples
by **Glenn A. Walker** . . . . .Order No. A55991

Concepts and Case Studies in Data Management
by **William S. Calvert**
and **J. Meimei Ma** . . . . .Order No. A55220

Efficiency: Improving the Performance of Your SAS® Applications
by **Robert Virgile** . . . . .Order No. A55960

Essential Client/Server Survival Guide, Second Edition
by **Robert Orfali, Dan Harkey,**
and **Jeri Edwards** . . . . .Order No. A56285

Extending SAS® Survival Analysis Techniques for Medical Research
by **Alan Cantor** . . . . .Order No. A55504

A Handbook of Statistical Analyses Using SAS®
by **B.S. Everitt**
and **G. Der** . . . . .Order No. A56378

The How-To Book for SAS/GRAPH® Software
by **Thomas Miron** . . . . .Order No. A55203

In the Know ... SAS® Tips and Techniques From Around the Globe
by **Phil Mason** . . . . .Order No. A55513

Integrating Results through Meta-Analytic Review Using SAS® Software
by **Morgan C. Wang** and
Brad J. Bushman . . . . .Order No. A55810

Learning SAS® in the Computer Lab
by **Rebecca J. Elliott** . . . . .Order No. A55273

The Little SAS® Book: A Primer
by **Lora D. Delwiche** and
Susan J. Slaughter . . . . .Order No. A55200

The Little SAS® Book: A Primer, Second Edition
by **Lora D. Delwiche** and
Susan J. Slaughter . . . . .Order No. A56649
(updated to include Version 7 features)

Logistic Regression Using the SAS System: Theory and Application
by **Paul D. Allison** . . . . .Order No. A55770

Mastering the SAS® System, Second Edition
by **Jay A. Jaffe** . . . . .Order No. A55123

Multiple Comparisons and Multiple Tests Using the SAS® System
by **Peter H. Westfall, Randall D. Tobias, Dror Rom, Russell D. Wolfinger,**
and **Yosef Hochberg** . . . . .Order No. A56648